The Inquisitors and the Jews in the New World

The Inquisitors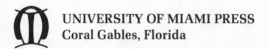

and the Jews

in the New World

SUMMARIES OF PROCESOS, 1500-1810,
AND BIBLIOGRAPHICAL GUIDE

by Seymour B. Liebman

UNIVERSITY OF MIAMI PRESS
Coral Gables, Florida

Manufactured in the United States of America

Library of Congress Cataloging in Publication Data
Liebman, Seymour B   1907-
    The inquisitors and the Jews in the New World.
    Bibliography: p.
    1. Maranos in Latin America.   2. Inquisition.
Latin America.   3. Latin America—Religion. I. Title.
F1419.J4L52   272'.2'098   72-85110
ISBN 0-87024-245-8

Frontispiece: Various forms of the sanbenito, according to an old Italian engraving.

To Clara Auerbach and Herman Wiener,
honored matriarch and patriarch

Contents

o

Illustrations

An effigy used at autos-da-fé for those who had escaped or died before an auto. The sanbenito with the name of the penitent, date, and appropriate cross was placed on the figure prior to its being carried on a pole to the tableau of the auto.

Preface

The publication of two of my books, *Guide to Jewish References in the Mexican Colonial Era* and *The Jews in New Spain,* brought many inquiries from students, researchers, and faculty members in the United States as well as from several foreign countries for leads to additional material and information about the interrelationships between the secret Jewish communities of New Spain and other parts of the New World during the colonial period. It is most gratifying to know that paths which were broadened by my previous writings have stimulated scholarly interest.

Although engaged in work on the history of the Jews in South America and the Caribbean and on a translation of the *Relación* by Mathias de Bocanegra of the 1649 auto-da-fé in Mexico, the steady stream of inquiries caused me to halt my research and translation in order to compile the material for this volume. It is my hope that the digests of the many procesos, together with the other data appended to each, will be of assistance to those who are interested in the fields of Latin American colonial history and the history of the Jews in the New World.

Acknowledgments

I wish to extend my thanks to the University of Pennsylvania Press for permission to use data included in my book, *A Guide to Jewish References in the Mexican Colonial Era, 1521-1821*.

Part of the research for this book was funded by the American Philosophical Society (1967), part by the Memorial Foundation for Jewish Culture (1968),and part by the National Foundation for Jewish Culture (1971). During the time that I worked in the Archivo Histórico Nacional de Madrid in 1972, Dr. Gustav Henningsen of Denmark directed my attention to certain Inquisition libros and legajos that pertain to Jewish history in Spain and the New World and to Jewish religion. His kindnesses facilitated my labors. Some of these documents have gone unnoticed for centuries.

Alfredo Castillero C.,Panamanian historian and professor, in a letter to me dated May 11, 1970, wrote that his research over a period of years in the Archivo de las Indias had revealed many references to the presence in Panama of merchants of Jewish origin during the years 1550 to 1570. He wrote that they controlled "the transshipment of merchandise across the Isthmus." He graciously supplied the names of people accused of being Jews or Judaizantes by Bishop Pablo de Torres as well as by other officials of the Royal Treasury and by governors. Castillero's information was amplified at our personal meeting in his office in Panama City in 1971, and these data have been included herein.

The Dory Auerbach family and the A. B. Wiener family, in honor of Clara Auerbach and Herman Wiener, have generously supported the publication of the present study.

The beginning and end of all my efforts are due to the encouragement of my beloved wife Malvina.

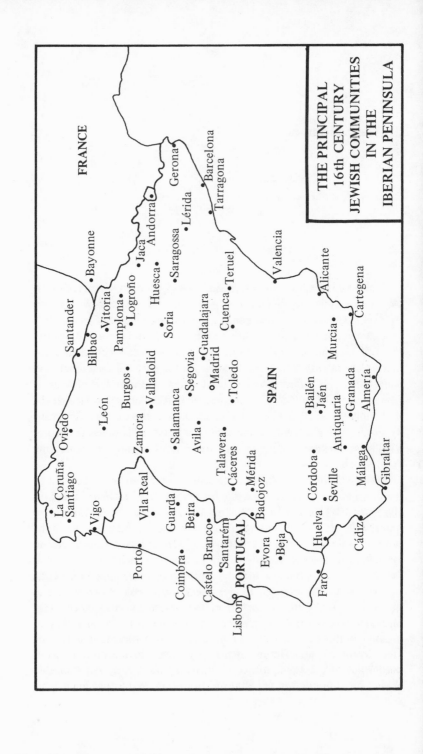

THE PRINCIPAL
16th CENTURY
JEWISH COMMUNITIES
IN THE
IBERIAN PENINSULA

FRANCE

SPAIN

PORTUGAL

Bayonne
Santander
Bilbao
Vitoria
Pamplona
Logroño
Jaca
Andorra
Huesca
Saragossa
Lérida
Gerona
Barcelona
Tarragona
Valencia
Alicante
Cartegena
Murcia
Teruel
Cuenca
Guadalajara
Soria
Madrid
Toledo
Segovia
Avila
Salamanca
Valladolid
Burgos
León
Zamora
Oviedo
La Coruña
Santiago
Vigo
Porto
Vila Real
Guarda
Beira
Castelo Branco
Santarém
Coimbra
Lisbon
Evora
Beja
Faro
Badojoz
Mérida
Cáceres
Talavera
Huelva
Córdoba
Seville
Cádiz
Gibraltar
Málaga
Antiquaria
Granada
Almería
Jaén
Bailén

Introduction

With the exception of Brazil and the northeast coastal region of South America, all of that continent as well as Central America, Mexico, and some of the Caribbean islands formed a part of the Spanish colonial empire from 1492 to the 1820s. Early in the sixteenth century, the first division of the region into viceroyalties occurred. The first two were New Spain, with Mexico, now Mexico City, as its capital, and Peru, with Lima as the seat of that viceroyalty. Peru encompassed almost all of Spanish South America. In 1610, what is now Venezuela, Colombia, Panama, and part of Ecuador became the viceroyalty of New Granada, with Cartagena as the capital. Rio de la Plata was formed of territories presently occupied by Argentina, Uruguay, and Paraguay, with Buenos Aires as the capital.

Each bishop of the Roman Catholic Church possesses the right of inquisition (the right to inquire) within his diocese on matters of faith and morals. This is part of his episcopal powers. When the bishop presides at hearing on matters of faith or morals at Inquisition trials, he sits and signs documents as ecclesiastical judge ordinary. He can excommunicate and conduct an auto-da-fé.

An apostolic inquisitor may be a bishop or other appointee of the pope. The title is intended to give strength and greater importance to the holder of the title than that of the bishop as ecclesiastical judge ordinary. The apostolic inquisitor may supercede the local bishop or bishops in the area assigned to him as the papal representative. Alexander Herculano discusses the rights and powers of apostolic or papal inquisitors at great length in his *History of the Origin and Establishment of the Inquisition in Portugal.*[1] Apostolic inquisitors could come from any rank or any monastic orders, but usually Franciscans or Dominicans served as apostolic inquisitors.

Shortly prior to the Albigensian Crusades (1212-1220), Pope Innocent III delegated three Cistercian monks to go to Toulouse and to take action against the heretics in Aix, Arles, and Narbonne as well as in the neighboring dioceses. Their actions and subsequent disputes led to the creation of the title "Inquisitors of the Faith."

Although Pope Gregory IX (1227-1242) is generally credited with the organization of the Inquisition as an instrument to investigate heresies and to protect the faith, it had existed for a considerable time prior to Gregory, who only formalized it. Pope Paul III in 1549 instituted the Supreme Tribunal, which was composed of six cardinals called "Inquisitors General" who were to direct the institution from its headquarters in Rome. Prior to this, the popes themselves presided over the tribunal of the Holy Office of the Inquisition, which became known as the Suprema. This Suprema is not to be confused with the Suprema in Spain, which was the court of last resort for the branches of the Holy Office established there. Technically one could appeal from the Suprema in Spain to that at Rome. Unless otherwise indicated Suprema used herein will be that of Spain.

An apostolic Inquisition existed in parts of the Iberian peninsula prior to the ascendancy of Ferdinand and Isabella to their respective thrones. Pope Gregory XI had sent Dominicans and a Franciscan to Aragon with the title "Inquisitors." One of the Dominicans was the famous Eymericus (1320-1399). These inquisitors did not operate in the kingdoms of Castile and León until their Catholic majesties asked for them.

In November 1478, at the request and insistence of the King and Queen, Pope Sixtus IV issued a bull authorizing the establishment of the Holy Office in Castile, Aragon, and León, but it did not begin to operate until 1480, and its first auto-da-fé took place on February 6, 1481. In 1484 Torquemada became the first to hold the title of "Inquisitor General" in Spain (used here as a geographical term since the nation as we know it did not come into being until 1516). He prepared "Instructions" to insure uniformity of procedure for all tribunals under his jurisdiction. His successor, Cardinal Jiménez de Cisneros, completed the organization in 1498.

José Toribio Medina uses the full title, "El Tribunal del Santo Oficio de la Inquisición . . . " for four of his classics on the history of the institution in the New World. Richard E. Greenleaf uses "The Holy Office of the Inquisition" for episcopal and apostolic inquisitors even prior to the establishment of the first two formal tribunals in the New World in 1569.[2] Greenleaf does indicate that the words "The Tribunal" distinguish between episcopal and apostolic on the one hand and the awesome Dominican institution on the other. "Monastic inquisitions" are not discussed as they are not germane to this book.

The Holy Office of the Inquisition was established in Portugal in 1536. It did not come into complete control of the Jews in Lusitania until 1547. Alexandre Herculano's classic work (now in two English translations, my preference being the edition of Yosef Hayim Yerushalmi of Harvard University) relates the tawdry history of the decades prior to 1547 during which Jews and conversos and "New Christians" (those who professed Catholicism but practiced Judaism to a greater or lesser degree) fought for their lives and the privilege of leaving Portugal at first with and ultimately without their possessions. *"Sem victimas, sem carceres atulhados, sem autos da fé, a Inquisiçao era uma puerilidade. A phrase energica dos cardeaes ácerca dos desojos dos inquisidores portugueses eram uma terrivel verdade: queriam carne."* (Without victims, without full jails, without autos-da-fé, the inquisition was child's play. The lively expression of the cardinals regarding the wishes of the Portuguese inquisitors was a frightening truth: they wanted flesh.) Rome called them "devourers of human flesh."[3]

Under the Bull Omnimoda of 1522, the pope had granted special permission to the prelates of the monastic orders in the New World to perform all episcopal functions except ordination when there were no bishops in the vicinity or when the diocesan site was two days or more distant. This bull was issued because of the shortage of secular clergy to carry on the spirit and conquest of the new lands. Torquemada's organizational and administrative ability and his zeal for the preservation of the Faith set the course of the Spanish Inquisition for the 341 years of its existence. As the activities of the Holy Office expanded, it became necessary to establish branches with the Suprema as the head office. The Suprema was also the court of last resort for hearing appeals from the various branch Tribunals throughout Spain and the New World.

In order to achieve homogeneity, Ferdinand and Isabella felt that they had to eradicate two groups from their lands: *Judaizantes* and *Moriscos.* The Moors were not banished until 1609. Although members of both of these groups had been converted to Catholicism, many of them secretly practiced the rites of their original faith or the faith of their ancestors, Judaism and Islam. Such Judaizantes and Moriscos were considered heretics. The Church had taken the position that "once a Catholic, always a Catholic." One could convert to Catholicism, but once a member of the Faith it was forbidden to leave the fold. Some of these "heretics" and other unbaptized Jews often attempted to wean other converts or children of converts away from Christianity. These would-be proselytizers were called *dogmatizadoras.* The Inquisition used a pungent phrase to describe those who returned or "relapsed" to their original faith: "As a dog returning to its vomit."

As early as 1508, bishops in Havana and Puerto Rico were informing Madrid that the New World was being filled with *hebreo cristianos* (Hebrew Christians), *nuevo cristianos* (New Christians), *conversos* (converts), *Moriscos,* and other heretics in spite of several decrees barring their entry. The first of such decrees had been issued as early as 1493. Only those who could prove that they were descendants of *católicos viejos* (old Catholics) for at least four generations were entitled to certificates of *limpieza de sangre* (purity of the blood) and licenses to migrate to the New World. The first decree that barred those who had been reconciled or whose ancestors had worn sanbenitos from going to Mexico was issued in 1523. Silvio Zavala wrote: "The Holy Office in Spanish America persecuted the apostates, Moriscos, Jews, Protestants and, in general, heretics. It manifested in America the same intransigency that had characterized the religious life of the Peninsula since the beginning of the modern period."[4]

The need for a tribunal of the Holy Office in Mexico was expressed as early as 1532. The Franciscans repeated the request a few years later. Francisco Tello de Sandoval, Visitor and Apostolic Inquisitor, wrote to Prince Philip on September 19, 1545, that the Holy Office was needed in the New World.[5] Hubert Herring stated that ". . . there was a complete unanimity among the great-spirited clerics . . . in welcoming the stern discipline of the Holy Office. It was just and good in their eyes that punishment be meted out . . . to Jews, who, because of Portuguese laxity, were slipping into Brazil and from there into Spanish America."[6]

On January 25, 1569, Philip II issued a royal cedula creating two tribunals, one for New Spain and one for Peru. On August 16, 1570, he delineated the territory of the Mexican branch. It was to include all of the audiencias of Mexico, Guatemala, New Galicia, and the Philippines.

The entire political organization of each viceroyalty was directed to give the tribunals of the Holy Office complete cooperation. The tribunals were to be autonomous institutions whose decrees were unassailable by any secular authority. Even the king could only fume and rage: the Holy Office was free of his control.

In 1580 Philip II of Spain took over the Portuguese throne. Spain ruled Portugal until 1640 when Portugal regained its sovereignty. In 1580 and 1581, many Jews residing in Portugal accurately anticipated the arrival of Spanish inquisitors to man the Holy Offices in Coimbra, Lisbon, and Evora because the Spaniards regarded the Portuguese as too lenient in their treatment of Jews, Moors, and other heretics. Many of the Jews in Portugal crossed the border into Spain. Many others, by one means or another, wended their way to the New World.

A license from the *Casa de la Contratación* was necessary in order to go to the New World, and immigration was limited to Spaniards with certificates of *limpieza de sangre,* attesting that the holder was an "old Catholic" as distinguished from a New Christian. Licenses were required to travel from one viceroyalty to another. Clarence Haring in *The Spanish Empire in America* wrote:[7]

> As far back as 1501 Governor Ovando when preparing to go to Hispaniola had been instructed that no Jews, Moors, reconciled heretics . . . be allowed in the colony. And later decrees had excluded their sons and grandsons, . . . But these laws were difficult or impossible to enforce, especially as the *conversos* or New Christians comprised the class most likely to possess the aptitude and capital, to develop colonial trade and industry. Moreover there were always ways of reaching America, clandestinely or for a price. . . . In spite of prohibitive laws, therefore, Jews and New Christians, both Spanish and Portuguese, were found in the Indies in increasing numbers.

Since no licenses were required for members of a ship's crew and Jews were shipowners as well as ship captains, many Jews came as members of the crew and then "jumped ship" in Veracruz (where a Jewish community was established soon after the conquest of Mexico), in Cartagena, or in secret ports that were used for smuggling, for example, Campeche or Santa Marta. No licenses were required for servants of legitimate passengers. Consequently a Jew who secured a license by one means or another, such as the use of a name taken from the tombstone of an old Christian, was able to take with him his family and three or four coreligionists as "servants."

Brazil had a large Jewish population because the Portuguese Inquisition had deported many Jews there. Some went to Rio Hacha and Cartagena (Colombia) and then to Lima. Some of those in Brazil went to Buenos Aires, crossed the pampas and the Cordilleras, and settled in what are now Chile, Bolivia, and Peru. In South America they were scattered over the territory in numerous, sparsely settled, rural areas except for colonies established in Lima, Potosí, Tucumán, and Santiago. The Jews in Medellín and surrounding towns, like the Jews in the state of Nuevo León, Mexico, found refuge from the Holy Office. It should be noted that groups of Jews were established in places in the New World other than those mentioned in this book. In 1514 King Ferdinand, after the death of Isabella, had granted permission for conversos and their descendants to emigrate to the New World. This permission was revoked in 1518 by his son, Charles I of Spain, Charles V of the Holy Roman Empire. A somewhat similar relaxation of the laws barring migration of New Christians to the New World was made in the early seventeenth century. This leave was also withdrawn after a decade.

As a formal institution, the Holy Office and each of its tribunals had a staff ranging from *comisarios,* secretaries, *fiscales,* attorneys to represent minors (anyone under the age of twenty-five who was apprehended), *alguaciles,* surgeons, and other ministering officials. One cannot overlook the harsh rules of the Holy Office. The burden of proof of innocence was on the defendant; the defendant had no right of confrontation with the witnesses against him or of cross-examination; the defendant was denied the privilege of choosing his own legal counsel; and he was not apprised of the charges against him at the time of arrest or even at the first or second hearing. It is necessary to distinguish between the institution and those who administered it. When rules were abrogated or violated, it was the individual Dominican monks and officials who were the perpetrators of the abuses. When prisoners were tortured or condemned to be "relaxed" (a euphemism for burning at the stake), it was the monastic inquisitors who meted out these sentences. The venality of some inquisitors is almost beyond description. Juan Sáenz de Mañozca, who served in New Granada, Peru, and New Spain, possibly epitomizes the worst. Sentences of life imprisonment were rarely enforced beyond a few years, and sometimes confinement was in a convent or monastery or even a private home. A sentence to serve in the slave galleys of oceangoing vessels was tantamount to a death sentence; there is no record of the release of any galley prisoner.

We must also distinguish between the inquisitors, the general populace, and the secular clergy. Richard E. Greenleaf wrote, "Anti-Semitism and prejudice against the foreigner on the part of some colonists are evident from the earliest years of the conquest. But since a sizable number of the settlers came from questionable backgrounds [many secret Jews being among them], the total picture probably was one of tolerance—at least until the Counter Reformation reached Mexico."[8] Greenleaf also indicates that the failure of the bishops in Mexico to initiate more proceedings against Jews or Judaizantes from 1543 to 1571 in spite of the public knowledge of their presence may have been due to the suspicion that "the colonists of Mexico often denounced their economic competitors as Jews."[9] We add as another reason for this leniency or tolerance the fact that many of the clergy, both secular and monastic, were of Jewish ancestry.

The tolerance mentioned by Greenleaf was also practiced by many of the secular clergy as well as monks of almost all monastic orders. Of course, there were some secret Jews in the contemplative orders, as described by Haim Beinart in "The Judaizing Movement in the Order of San Jeronimo in Castille."[10] An illustration not only of tolerance but of aid and succor extended to Portuguese Jews is cited by José Toribio Medina in *La Inquisición en el Rio de la Plata.*[11]

When the Spanish governors of Buenos Aires in 1619 and subsequent years arrested some Jews who had arrived from Brazil and sought to apprehend others, friars came to the rescue of both groups. The group found asylum and sanctuary in monasteries. Some monks even deposited bail for those incarcerated. When the Jews were freed but ordered to await trial, they fled from Buenos Aires to Asunción, Corrientes, or Santiago del Estero where they found safety among their coreligionists. Because there was a forfeiture of the bail deposited by the friars, the Jewish communities reimbursed the friars for all losses sustained. Other members of the clergy would go into the jails and declare that the prisoners were not "prohibited persons." In other cases they would perform marriages between Jewish immigrants and girls of the town who were secret Jewesses, thereby securing the right of residence for the immigrants.

The question of the amount of credibility to be accorded to the Inquisition testimony was discussed by Vicente Riva Palacio:[12]

... but in these cases, it is clearly evident that the accused observed the Law of Moses; the declarations of the prisoners, their accomplices ..., the written documents and the books they read ... demonstrate that these people knew and observed the laws and ceremonies of the Jews. In no other manner can one understand how they were able to give such detailed and exact explanations of the fasts, the ablutions, the observance of the Sabbath, and of the Psalms, and of the prayers that they recited, because regardless of the torture to which you can subject a man or woman, he or she could not supply information of rites and ceremonies of a faith of which he has no knowledge.

Some general observations should be borne in mind. The Edicts of Faith or Edicts of Grace were uniform for all tribunals, and the rules of the Suprema were applicable to all. The personalities of the inquisitors produced variations in the observation of the canons of the Holy Office. The application of torture in the tribunals of Lima and Cartagena was more common than in New Spain or Rio de la Plata, while sentences to serve in the galleys that plied the waters between the Philippines and Acapulco were more common in Mexico.

The auto-da-fé was a religious performance depicting The Last Judgment. On the day that an auto-da-fé was to be celebrated publicly, the prisoners had to walk from the secret cells in the House of the Inquisition to the central plaza where a large platform had been erected. The place for the fires or the stake was called the *quemadero*.

In the procession, the prisoners were accompanied by friars exhorting them to have faith in Jesus. Each prisoner held a green candle in his hand, wore a sanbenito, and, depending on the nature of the crime, wore a head covering, a *coraza*. At the head of the procession, an official or friar carried an emblem or flag on which was a green cross on a dark background having an olive branch on the right and a sword on the left. The olive branch indicated clemency for those who sought forgiveness and the sword for those who persisted in their errors. José del Olma provides a graphic description of the entire affair.[13]

The sanbenito had a yellow cross on the back and front of the garment and was made of a rough material like burlap. Other symbols, including figures of devils, were included. One could tell the nature of the individual's wrongdoing by the representations on the garment. The auto-da-fé was conducted with great solemnity and fanfare. It was intended to strike terror in the onlookers as well as the prisoners since it symbolized the ultimate judgment day.

When the time came to doff the sanbenito, it was hung on the cathedral walls with the name of the former wearer and the nature of his crime. When the space on the walls was insufficient to bear further garments, a *tabilla,* a small rectangular piece of cloth, was submitted and the name of the individual, his crime, and the date thereof were imprinted on it. *México Viejo,* by Luis González Obregón, has an Appendix of forty pages, which is a copy of a list made by P. Pichardo of the sanbenitos and tabillas hanging in the Mexican Cathedral. Many new names and pertinent data appear that have been added in this compilation.

In the March of the Green Cross to the quemadero, there were effigies representing those who had fled as well as the bones of those who had been sentenced to the pyre but who had died previously. These bones had been disinterred and they were paraded along with the living. In addition to the public autos, there were nonpublic autos, and private reading of sentences in the hearing room of the tribunal.

In *A Connecticut Yankee in King Arthur's Court,* Mark Twain advanced the theory that the sounds of human voices never disappear but remain in the air around us. He suggested that with the proper machine we could "tune in" on conversations of hundreds, if not thousands, of years ago and thereby facilitate the study of history.

Archaeologists reconstruct ancient civilizations from shards, potsherds, and ruins. Linguists decipher and reconstruct dead tongues from ancient tablets. Historians avail themselves of old documents. Archives are veritable mines of treasured history, the primary sources for the stories of our ancestors. Some historical writers and students, however, fail to go to the primary sources. This failure may be attributed to the high regard in which some earlier historians are held. Many persons consider the works of some of these early historians to be definitive and assume that they are the result of research of all pertinent material from all available sources.

In his paper for the 1970 annual meeting of the American Historical Association titled "The Social History of Colonial Latin America," James Lockhart noted that while historians are at liberty to study whatever they choose, they "usually take the easiest (*most synthetic*) sources first. When the easiest source is exhausted, . . . a new generation of historians takes the next easiest, and so on" (emphasis mine). We are thus led to the cliché that history does not repeat itself, but historians repeat each other's errors.

Lockhart listed a cycle of sources for Latin American colonial history. He stated that two sources, trial records and testimonials and notarial records, were not only readily accessible but required more special skills to use them. He also noted that they are "more primary, raw, minute, local, fresh."

In reference to Latin America, Charles Gibson stated that "Students have tended to rely excessively on the writings of José Toribio Medina and Henry C. Lea."[14] Professor Gibson's comment was brought home forcefully to me in June 1972 when I was working in the Archivo Histórico Nacional de Madrid. I perceived that Medina had relied very heavily on relaciones of autos-da-fé and that he had overlooked several cases of importance as well as repeating the occasional errors in the relaciones. Woodrow Borah in his review of Greenleaf's *Zumárraga and the Mexican Inquisition* commented that the book "demonstrates how great is the need and how rich the possibilities for considerably more research." Borah added that "further exploration of the history of the early Inquisition in Mexico demands a knowledge of intellectual and religious history, ethnology, and social and abnormal psychology."[15] The observations of Gibson and Borah may well be extended to the entire Spanish colonial period and should emphasize all the branches of the institution throughout the New World.

Diligent research is required not only in the obvious sources but also in many collateral fields since contemporary references are to be found in other quarters. Greenleaf writes, "This description of the controversial auto-de-fé of 1528 was not unearthed until 1945, and until that time the actual date of the burnings was not known."[16] The date was discovered in the notarial records of the municipality of Mexico City.

Julio Jiménez Rueda wrote in his foreword to the updated, 1952 edition of Medina's *Historía del Tribunal del Santa Oficio de la Inquisición en México* that in the Inquisition section of the Mexican National Archives:[17]

> We find in those venerable folios not only the history of our religious heretics but also of great importance, data concerning the history of ideas, morals, and of the economy of our country during the three centuries of the viceroyalty. Each trial proceeding recorded meticulously, with a care which makes each an inexhaustible fount of political and social life, not only of Spain and Mexico, but also of many of the nations with whom they were in conflict. . . .

The original *procesos* (records of the trial) in Peru were reported to have been burned.[18] Despite the fires, destruction was not total. I examined a few documents in the Biblioteca Nacional in Lima in 1965. Furthermore, copies or duplicate originals of some procesos may be found in the Archivo Histórico Nacional de Madrid. The existence in this archive of *relaciones* of pending cases and of many original procesos or copies that emanated from Peru and New Granada should facilitate research and open new fields. The Archivo de las Indias in Seville offers similar research opportunities.

There are two basic difficulties that confront the dedicated researcher of Spanish colonial history who elects to work in primary sources: the sources are scattered as seeds on the wind, and the researcher must master paleography of medieval Spanish. In my *Guide to Jewish References in the Mexican Colonial Era, 1521-1821,* there is a listing of places where original procesos are to be found and of others where there are typescripts.[19] The Spanish literary giant Dr. Américo Castro called my attention to a denunciation and testimony taken by the Mexican Inquisition which is in the D.R.T. (Daughters of Revolution of Texas) Library, the Alamo, San Antonio, Texas. In late 1970, as a result of a bequest by Hans Krause to the Library of Congress, Manuscript Division, historians learned of the existence of several important Inquisition documents that Krause owned. Many other documents are still in private possession, and others are scattered over the world in university libraries, museums, and institutions, some uncatalogued.

Few people were aware that Walter Douglas had bequeathed his art collection and manuscripts to the Henry E. Huntington Library in San Marino, California before my article provided the first published list of these treasures as well as statistical data gleaned from the contents of the volumes.[20] The collection includes forty-seven volumes of original Inquisition papers. Publication of the *Research Studies of the State College of Washington* journal in 1946 and 1947 informed some historians for the first time of the location of certain Inquisition documents and the Regla papers.[21]

Alfonso Toro, a Mexican historian and paleographer, wrote in the introduction to *Los Judios en la Nueva España* that there are many more cases concerning Jews before the inquisitors than may be indicated by the Index of the Mexican National Archives or even the flyleaves of the various procesos. While the flyleaves and the Index to the

New World Inquisition volumes may state an accusation to be blasphemy or heresy, a reading of each proceso may indicate that in many cases the final sentence was predicated upon the finding that the prisoner was a Jew. Toro added that many of the people accused of blasphemy had ideas "de judíos o judaizantes."[22] Part 2 of Toro's book contains a list of Jews before the Inquisition in the sixteenth century. A comparison of the cases set forth by Toro with his citations in the Volume of Documents and the case number in the Index, which Toro did not cite, is given in Appendix A of my *Guide to Jewish References.*

The discrepancies and the omissions in every source, primary and secondary, create the necessity of checking and cross-checking the correctness and completeness of all material. My article on the "Abecedario" illustrates many inconsistencies, omissions, and differences among the numerous sources upon which many authors have relied. Because of these discrepancies and omissions, I have listed after most names in this work the primary source and one or more secondary sources. I do not profess to have exhausted all sources. Other problems involved in research, especially concerning the Jews in the New World during the colonial period, are treated in my article "Research Problems in Mexican Jewish History."[23]

In *Historia del Tribunal del Santo Oficio de la Inquisición en México,* with additions by Julio Jiménez Rueda, there is an alphabetical list of those who appeared before the Holy Office. Jiménez Rueda made his additions from AGN records. Luis González Obregón utilized the same sources as Medina when he did research for Henry C. Lea. Genaro García has no names that do not appear in either the books of Medina or González, but these two writers have names that do not appear in either volume 5 or 28 of Genaro García's *Documentos Ineditos para la historia de México.*

The fact that Medina and Toro agree should not be accepted as proof positive of what they wrote. The case of Blas Mosquera appears in Toro, p. 9, under date October 1556. After the name *"judío, por golpes que dió a un sacerdote"* (for blows which he gave to a priest) appears. AGN volume 30, No. 1, fol. 28, has a proceso against a Nicolas Mosquera who was the bomber of the ship *The Good Angel,* and the charge was that of striking a priest. While the error in the Christian name is not of great significance, the absence of the charge of *por judío* as stated by Medina and Toro does matter.

William Harris Rule wrote in his *History of the Inquisition* that "the Holy Office took for granted that every Jew was an enemy of all

Christians, and an obstructor of the Inquisition."[24] Rule also supplied the canons of the Inquisition that justified the arrest of Jews: "The Jews, if they were to impiously say that our Saviour Jesus Christ were a mere man . . . or that His most Holy Mother was not a virgin . . . or if they were to prevent any Hebrew or any other infidel who wished to become a Christian, or were to advise or induce him not to do so. . . ."[25] There were several other acts and statements or the possession of certain books that justified the arrest of Jews whose rights to live as Jews were either proscribed completely or severely limited. Lack of baptism was no bar to the assumption of jurisdiction by the Inquisition.

Those Jews who converted to Catholicism voluntarily were known as *meshumadim* (Hebrew). The involuntary converts or forced ones were the *anusim*. Most Portuguese Jews are classified as anusim during the colonial period.

It is difficult to distinguish between Portuguese and Spanish Jews after 1500 without a study of the genealogies of the individuals who appeared before the different tribunals. With the expulsion from Castile and Aragon in 1492, some 100,000 Spanish Jews secured licenses to immigrate and reside for a limited period in Portugal. During the period between 1497 and 1553, many young Jews in Portugal were forcibly baptized, and their parents then "voluntarily" converted in order to retain their children. Jewish writers and rabbis are concerned with the difference between voluntary and forced apostasy.

The word *marrano* (pig) was not used in the New World tribunals— neither in the procesos nor in any of the documents or correspondence that I have read. Lea uses the word only four times in his four-volume *History of the Inquisition in Spain*. None of the four references were attributed to the Inquisition. Lea wrote that the word was used as an epithet by Christians for "Judaizing Christians" and that it means "both hog and accursed."[26] Yakov Malkiel's learned treatise on the word should terminate any discussion on any variations of the word's meaning or attempts to trace the word to Hebrew sources.[27] In *La familia Carvajal* Toro wrote that the Jews in Spain first applied the term to Jews who had voluntarily converted to Christianity. Antonio Domín- guez Ortiz in *The Golden Age of Spain* uses the word three times and always with respect to "forced converts" to Christianity. This noted Spanish historian uses "crypto-Jews" only twice, and on one occasion he uses the term crypto-Jews as a synonym for judaizantes.[28]

Only an insignificant number of revisionists bar the term "Jew" to

Marranos or crypto-Jews. These same few overlook that they have cited
with approval such books as *The History of the Marranos* by Cecil Roth;
La Inquisición en Hispanoamerica: Judíos, Protestantes y Patriotas by
Boleslao Lewin; and the numerous works of José Toribio Medina. Roth
(p. xiii) refers to "a history of the Marranos or secret Jews," as do others.
Günther Friedlander in his *Los Héroes Olvidados* wrote *"de la historia
judía en América Latina . . . "* (p. 7), which is an account of those arrested
by the inquisitors in the New World. Günter Böhm wrote *Los Judíos en
Chile colonial.* C. R. Boxer, in his *Salvador de Sá,* wrote that in the
seventeenth century, "The provinces of Rio de La Plata, Paraguay and
Tucumán were frequented by wealthy Portuguese Jewish refugees from
the Inquisition . . . " (p. 78). Most Hispano-Americanists who, as have
some of the aforementioned writers, worked in primary sources in the
archives, note that in the seventeenth century in the New World, "Portuguese" and "Jew" were synonyms. More authorities are listed in note 13,
p. 179, of my article "The Great Conspiracy in Peru."

Yosef H. Yerushalmi has, we hope, permanently stilled the voices that
"have been raised to deny radically the very notion of the Jewish
character of the Marranos" in his book *From Spanish Court to Italian
Ghetto.*[29] The author "firmly disagrees with those who consider Mar-
ranism" a fiction deliberately created and retained as a weapon by the
enemies of the New Christians" and that "the Spanish Inquisition was
only the instrument employed in an attempt to destroy the Converso
Class, and it fabricated the charge of crypto-Judaism."[30] If Professor
Yerushalmi's documentation is insufficient to convince the unbelievers
and revisionists, then a study of the trials of the Jews referred to in this
book should be persuasive. My translation of the *Relación* of the 1649
auto-da-fé (Coronado Press) facilitates the task of finding the proof that
the Jews in the New World in the seventeenth century knew some
Hebrew prayers, that rabbis ordained in Italy, Holland, and elsewhere
were present, that circumcision was practiced, and that rites and ceremonies of Judaism were observed. This book should be studied in depth
for those interested in persons involved in that auto.

The statement has been frequently made that in the seventeenth
century, especially in the New World, the word "Portuguese"was synonymous with "Jew."[31] This does not mean there were no Portuguese
Christians in the Indies. There were many, especially in Brazil, but their
numbers in the Spanish colonial empire were minimal in comparison to

the number of Portuguese Jews. Many of these Jews were of Spanish descent. Lea makes the point: "Intermarriage had been frequent and so large a portion of the population of Portugal was thus contaminated that foreigners generally regarded the Portuguese as all Jews."[32]

The term Judaizante was applied to Jewish apostates to Catholicism who practiced Judaism secretly. In some instances the term was synonymous with Jew. Since the Church neither permitted nor recognized apostasy to other faiths, since this would be a desecration of the sacrament of baptism, which made one a Catholic for life, New Christians who followed Jewish rites or who reverted to Judaism were usually called judaizantes. Many of the procesos reveal that the prisoners confessed *ser judío* (to being a Jew). The charge against some was *judío judaizante,* meaning that the prisoner was a Jew who practiced Judaism.

The words *crypto-judío, nuevo christiano* (also spelled without the "h"), judaizante, and Marrano have been used interchangeably by many authors. Domínguez Ortiz defines Marrano as a synonym for a Jew who is an insincere convert to Christianity; he also uses conversos, Marranos, and cristianos nuevos as antonyms for christianos viejos, old Catholics.[33] He uses the word "judaizante" twice in his book and we may presume that he employs judaizante as a synonym for converso because he notes that of the 123 "judaizantes" condemned to death at Lérida, 1487-88, 118 had fled and of the five remaining for the auto, four were priests. Domínguez Ortiz also comments that the majority of the Portuguese Marranos remained devoted to their faith and that they are to be differentiated from their Spanish coreligionists if there is to be a comparison of conversions of both groups.[34]

Lewin writes in his *Cómo Fue la Inmigración Judía a la Argentina* "Es de imaginarse, pues, que tambien los marranos, tanto aquellos que fueron criptojudíos como los que eran cristianos nuevos, alli asentaron sus reales." Then he writes, "La inmigración criptojudía a Hispano-américo tiene, asimismo, idéntico origen. No fueron marranos españoles los que constituyeron sino *cristaos novos* portugueses, por las tres razones siguientes; 1°, porque en España la conversion fue, mas o menos, voluntaria a deferencia de Portugal donde fue llevada a cabo con medidas violentas y contra un numeroso grupo no dispuesto a transigir con su conciencia y que por ello había abandonado su pais de origen; 2°, por la discriminación racial que practicaban las autoridades españoles en relación con los que querían establecerse en las Indias; y 3°, porque los criptojudíos portugueses, como los primeros colonizadores del Brasil, estaban en las mejores, a veces apremiantes, condiciones de establecerse en las colonias españolas."[35]

John A. O'Brien in his book, *The Inquisition* writes, "*conversos* (Jewish converts), Christians in name but frequently still Jews at heart."[36]

Gerson D. Cohen, Chancellor of the Jewish Theological Seminary and former professor of history at Columbia University, wrote in his essay-review of *The Marranos of Spain* by B. Netanyahu:[37] "The historian is not at liberty to restrict his definition of Jewishness to one laid down by rabbis or their adherents. . . . no matter how christianized the Marrano way of life may have become they need not—and apparently did not—cease to be a Jewish group historically, sociologically, or · even religiously."

A clarification of the scope and nature of the material contained in this book is in order. I have provided, where possible, summaries of inquisitorial proceedings against Jews in the Spanish colonial empire in the New World from the time of discovery until the Latin American nations attained their independence and the harrassment of Jews ceased. Genealogical and bibliographical data also appear.

I have divided the data according to the viceroyalties—New Spain, Cartagena or New Granada, Peru or New Castile, and Rio de la Plata. The tribunal at Cartagena was not established until 1610. Prior to that all prisoners south of New Spain were sent to Lima, Peru, for trial. The primary sources are in the archives indicated. The genealogies, which include places of birth, marriages, and residences, open new avenues for researchers, scholars, and students and offer new statistics on crypto-Jews in the Iberian Peninsula. Information on the Caribbean area is omitted because of the destruction by fire, hurricane, and flood of most of the episcopal and apostolic Inquisition records.

The number of names in the present text could be easily tripled and yet not exhaust the total population of Jews in the Spanish colonial empire. Many of the procesos list names of other Jews who had fled or died, and they are not included herein. Despite the valiant efforts of the inquisitors, many did escape; and despite the dedication to their task, the inquisitors were unable to commence every proceeding or even complete those that they initiated. This is a partial explanation of the presence of only fragmentary material for some of the cases.

I have not read all, not even a major portion, of the procesos. Those read were those of leading Jews and some of their close associates. I have glanced at many others in order to gain insight into the lives and activities of the times. Where inquisitors were zealous and of a curious bent, much information on the daily rounds and holy day acts were placed into the record. The tribunal secretaries faithfully recorded all the testimony. Errors in spelling do abound, and transliterations of Hebrew and some Portuguese sometimes makes difficult recognition of the original words.

A few non-Jews charged with practicing Jewish rites are included in the present work to illustrate that some inquisitors decreed acquittals or suspended cases; others presumed that all apprehended were guilty regardless of proof or lack thereof. For example, Padre Hidalgo of Mexico (1810), the George Washington of his country, was accused of apostasy, Lutheranism, and Judaism, among several other charges. I have excluded most cases similar to Hidalgo's. Those charged with judaizante are included.

Much confusion exists among the names because of the poor orthography of the secretaries of the Holy Office. Some examples follow. A study of the names Leonor Vaez, Leonor Vaz, and Leonor Baez shows that in the 1640s there were at least three women known by one or more of the aforementioned spellings. In some instances they can be identified, separated, or distinguished because of their marital status or other genealogical data. With respect to one of them, I cannot be certain whether she was actually in New Spain. The patronymic Enriquez is also spelled Henriquez. The letters "v" and "b" were used interchangeably, as were "x" and "j." Juarez often appears also as Suarez or Xuarez. Accent marks rarely appear in the original sources.

Since the Inquisition secretaries were Spanish and not generally familiar with the place-names of Portugal, there is a multiplicity of place spellings. San Vicente Davera appears as "beira," "da Vera," and in other forms. Transliterations of Portuguese and Hebrew words make them almost unrecognizable at first glance. In this text Casteloblanco has been adopted even though the Portuguese city is now spelled Castelo Branco. The spelling of some of the place-names follows the original; certain others follow *The Columbia Lippincott Gazetteer.*

The archives are replete with data that are of particular historical concern. While much of this material was not appropriate for inclusion here, I have listed in Appendix B documents with special Jewish interest. For example, there is a decree by Bishop Juan de Palafox Mendoza in July 1642 that prohibited any Portuguese from embarking any ship leaving Veracruz.[38] Some historians believe that this was the beginning of the roundup of Jews in Mexico that resulted in a series of autos-da-fé in the years 1646 to 1648 and finally culminated in the great auto of April 11, 1649.

Some of the information in this volume may appear to be patently erroneous, but I must point out that some of these "errors" are those of the Inquisition. The AGN index states that in tomo 389, expediente 9, "testimony about the criminals who went to Spain" appears and that the year is "1640." Actually, all of the people listed in the document appeared in autos in Mexico subsequent to 1640. They are all Jews. Dr. Pilar León-Tello, Senior Archivist at the AHN and a noted Spanish historian, researched these records in Spain at my request. She advised me by letter that only two of the more than 100 prisoners sentenced to serve prison terms in Spain ever arrived, and these two never served jail terms.[39]

In AGN 416, expediente 42, there is a notation "Memorandum of prisoners who had given testimony and who were exiled to Spain with *Sign of Jews.*" Mathias de Bocanegra reported in the *Relación* of the 1649 auto that Maria Gomez and other members of her family desired to exchange "el osculo de paz al modo judaico," the kiss of peace in the Judaic manner, while they were on the platform waiting to be tied to the stake. I know of only one other instance where a reference to a "kiss of peace" appears in the Inquisition records—in Montesino's Relación of the auto-da-fé of 1639 in Lima.[40]

In legajo 1738, expediente 1 of the AHN, "Certificacion de la Visita de los procesos de fé" dated September 28, 1657, there is a listing of all of the cases from the Mexican tribunal examined by the Visitador Dr. Pedro de Medina Rico. Among the cases are several, if not many, pertaining to those charged with being observers of the Law of Moses, Judaizers, Jews, etc. Several of these names do not appear in the AGN Indice, and I have not found the procesos of any of these people, but their names are included in this compilation. Often the Indice is in error in giving the location of a proceso, and even the index page of many volumes is in error in referring to the foja (page number).

Ernesto Chinchilla Aguilar's *La Inquisición en Guatemala,* long out of print, lists a few names for Jews not encountered elsewhere. I have included these, though some may be questionable. For example, the only evidence against Juan Lopez as a Jew was that he had interred in his house a person who had been baptized and for Juan Pascal of San Salvador the charge "por decirse que tenía un becerro escondido."[41]

Attention is called to discrepancies in dates by various authors, including myself. Sometimes the dates used are dates of arrests and in other cases they are dates of autos-da-fé. Appendix A is, I believe, the most complete list of all autos-da-fé in the New World. I also believe that the dates in the section on Peru and Cartagena constitute the first complete listing of all autos-da-fé whether or not Jews were involved.

In many cases from Mexico, I have omitted the Archivo General de la Nación citation but have used specific references to my *Guide to Jewish References in the Colonial Era.* For the general reader, the AGN citations would be superfluous, but for the researcher and scholar, they should be employed. This has reduced the size of this book without burdening those who work in this field. The bibliography is selective. I have exercised the right to eliminate some works that others consider authoritative.

Appendix A reveals that the Mexican tribunal was the most active. It presided at 129 autos, autillos, and private reading of sentences in New Spain. I have been able to verify 1,744 individual trials between 1522 and 1709. During this same period, there were less than 100 acquittals, and while there were only forty-nine who went alive to the stake, it must not be overlooked that fifty persons died in the cells (some were suicides), four became insane, and 192 were consigned to the galleys for periods varying from three years to ten or more. I have also verified that there were 541 trials conducted by inquisitors between 1650 and 1800. In addition to the trials, the inquisitors were occupied by many other duties such as the search for prohibited books, studying *limpiezas de sangre,* and being subjected to *visitas.*

I close this introduction with a wish expressed in several of my articles and books: I hope that others will pursue the threads of the lives of the people named in the text as well as correct and amplify the text itself.

Of equal, if not greater, importance than the Jewish aspect of colonial history is the indication to the general historian of these virtually untapped sources for reconstructing details of colonial life in the New World.

Explanatory notes and abbreviations

Accents: In the biographical data, all Spanish accent marks except the tilde have been omitted.

Biographical information: first gives genealogical, occupational, and other data. Inquisition charge(s) and sentence, if known, follow. Comments by compiler appear in brackets. For information on terms, see Glossary; for specific dates of autos, see Appendix A.

Abbreviations: a. alias   m. married
        b. born   r. resided or residence
        ca. circa

Archival references (see Selected Bibliography for details)

Abec. Abecedario

AGN Ramo de la Inquisición del Archivo General de la Nación (Mexico City)

AGN (Riva Palacio) Archivo General de la Nación (Mexico City)

AHN Archivo Histórico Nacional de Madrid (Spain)

Conway Archives (Library of Congress Archives, Washington, D.C.)

Gilcrease Institute (Tulsa, Oklahoma)

Huntington Library (San Marino, California)

Lea Memorial Library (Philadelphia, Pennsylvania)

Washington State University Library (Pullman, Washington)

Other references (see Selected Bibliography for complete data)

Bibliographical citations have been shortened; when an author has more than one book cited, a short title is also given. Numerals following authors' names or short titles are page citations except for Liebman, *Guide,* for which numerals indicate entry numbers. Additional information on the persons in the auto-da-fé of April 11, 1649 is in Liebman, *Jews and the Inquisition of Mexico.*

The Inquisitors and the Jews
in the New World

Viceroyalty of
NEW SPAIN

Mexico

Viceroyalty of
NEW GRANADA

Cartagena
Bogotá

GUIANA

BRAZIL

Lima

Viceroyalty of
PERU

Rio de
Janeiro

Buenos Aires

Viceroyalty of
LA PLATA

**THE SPANISH
VICEROYALTIES
IN THE AMERICAS**

ONE

New Spain

Abeña, Manuel de. *See* Luis Nuñez Perez.

Acosta, Andres de: 1623 letter signed by the comisario of Chiapas states that Acosta, then dead, had been a Jew, as were all his family and children.

    AGN 345, No. 7; Chinchilla Aquillar 184.

Acosta, Antonio de. *See* Manuel de Acosta a. Francisco de Torres.

Acosta, Cristobal: formerly r. Maracaibo or Caracas: denounced in 1649. Judaizante.

    AGN 503, fol. 105.

Acosta, Enrique Jorge de. Judaizante; reconciled 1648 auto.

    Medina, *México* 195.

Acosta, Francisco de: age 28; Portuguese; r. Cartagena, Puebla, and Guatemala; son of Juan Baez a Juan Vaez Mesignana and Isabel de Acosta, both of Lisbon. Judaizante, observer of Mosaic laws; reconciled in 1647 auto, jail for 1 year, exile from the Indies, Seville, and Madrid.

    Abec.; AGN 366, No. 4; AGN 388, No. 7; AGN 417, No. 14; García 28:112; Liebman, *Jews* 323; Medina, *México* 116, 194; Medina, *Lima* 2:43.

Acosta, Gaspar de: named in the proceso of Diego Diaz Nieto.

    Abec.; AGN 159, No. 2.

Acosta, Isabel de (m. Juan Baez). *See* Francisco de Acosta.

Acosta, Isabel de (m. Manuel Mendez de Miranda). *See* Manuel Mendez de Miranda.

Acosta, Manuel de: arrested 1597. Suspicion of judío.

    AGN 238, No. 13.

Acosta, Manuel de a. Francisco de Torres: age 29; b. Lisbon; r. Mexico; son of Antonio de Acosta, b. Orense, Galicia, and Juana Lopez, Portuguese, both Hebrews; merchant; came to Mexico from Seville in 1638; m. Isabel Tinoco; father of 3-year-old daughter, Micaela. Judaizante, observer of Mosaic laws; reconciled in auto of 1648, confiscation of property, sanbenito, 200 lashes, 5 years in galleys, life imprisonment.

> Abec.; AGN 390, No. 11; AGN 405, No. 2; AGN 413, fol. 122; AGN 414, No. 8; AGN 415, No. 6; AGN 417, No. 16; AGN 418, No. 1; García 28:235.

Acosta, Melchor de: age 64; Portuguese; r. Veracruz; blacksmith; m. Maria de Bustos, "of noble descent"; tortured. Suspicion of judío; case suspended in 1646.

> Abec.; AHN 1738, No. 1.

Acuña, Alvaro de: Portuguese; merchant, circumcised; apparently circumcised other Jews in New Spain; described as "dogmatista, Rabino, primo de los Tristanes" in Bocanegra's *Relación;* termed "a great Jew" by Gabriel de Granada; died at sea en route to Spain. Judío.

> AGN 412, No. 3; AGN 415, fols. 99, 301, 389; AGN 418, No. 10; AGN 419, No. 4; AGN 453, fol. 409; "Trial of Gabriel de Granada."

Aeres (Arias), Maria. *See* Gonzalo Vaez and Simon Vaez Sevilla.

Aguado, Ignacio. *See* Pedro Fernandez de Castro.

Aguilar, Maria de: r. San Luis Potosi; 1646 proceso. Suspicion of judaizante.

> AGN 425, No. 5.

Aguirre y Roche, Teresa de. *See* Bernardo Lopez de Mendizabal.

Agurto, Gaspar de. *See* Leonor Nuñez (b. Seville).

Agurto, Leonor: testimony by Antonio Fernandez Chillon. Judaizante.

> AGN 421, No. 8.

Alarcon, Cristobal de: r. Xicayau; circumcised his son. Judaizante.

> AGN 343, No. 19.

Alba, Isabel de: r. Oaxtepec; denounced in 1650. Wearing silk and being the daughter and sister of penitents of the Holy Office.

> AGN 435, fol. 244.

Albalaez, Julian de: r. Chamacuero, Michoacan; 1642 testimony; escaped. Judaizante.

> AGN 415, No. 1; AHN 1738, No. 1.

ALBAREZ. *See* ALVAREZ.

Albor, Pedro de. Suspicion of judío, 1539.

Medina, *México* 96.

Albuquerque, Francisco: buyer and seller of Negro slaves; arrested 1629 after visiting Diego Perez de Albuquerque in prison. Judío; reconciled, confiscation of property, sanbenito, 100 lashes, six years in galleys.

AGN 823, fol. 21; Medina, *México* 176.

Alcazar, Maria Felipa de: b. Spain; r. Oaxaca. Accused in 1739 of "acts of Judaism, idolatry, witchcraft, and pacts with the devil." [Probably she was of the "alumbrado" sect.]

AGN 876, No. 41.

Alfar, Gaspar a. Gaspar de los Reyes: imprisoned in Havana; tried and sentenced in 1646 auto by the tribunal in New Spain. Saying mass several times without authorization; defrocked, 200 lashes, sent to the galleys for life.

García 28:137. [Not to be confused with Gaspar Rodriguez Alfaro a. Gaspar Alfar.]

Alfar, Gaspar de. *See* Gaspar Rodriguez Alfaro.

Alfaro, Bartolome: testified against several other Jews.

AGN 425, No. 12.

Aliaya Cardona, Francisco: r. Sinaloa; accused in 1627. Judío.

AGN 360, fol. 441.

Almeyda, Andres: 1641 and 1642 testimony by Gaspar de Robles and Luis Nuñez Perez.

AGN 390, No. 11; AGN 414, No. 1.

Almeyda, Jorge de: b. Portugal; m. Leonor de Andrade of Carvajal family; mine owner in Taxco; escaped first attempt by Inquisition to interrogate him; tried in absentia in 1607. Heresy, apostasy, judaizante; burned in effigy.

Abec.; AGN 126, No. 12; AGN 150, No. 1; AGN 251A, No. 5; AGN 254A; Adler, "Almeyda" 31-79 (entire trial); Liebman, *Jews* 167, 171, 174, 193, 194, 205; Medina; *México* 101, 107.

Almonacer, Miguel de: Notary of Secrets of the Holy Office; together with Diego de Almonacer, presumed to be his brother, and Juan Ramos tried to entrap Jews; engaged in conversation with Jews while in secret cells; discovered that Jewish prisoners were leaking secrets of the Holy Office to other Jews outside; testified against Isabel de Rivera.

AGN 393, No. 4; AGN 401, No. 4; AGN 413, fols. 5-50.

Alonso, Hernando: b. Condado de Niebla, Spain ca. 1460; blacksmith, ship's carpenter, and purveyor of meat in Mexico. Heresy, judaizante; relaxed alive in 1528 auto.

AGN 223, No. 33; Liebman, "Alonso," 291; Liebman, *Guide* 1039; Medina, *México* 95.

Alonso, Maria de. *See* Alvaro Diez de Lineo.

Altamirano, Fray Lorenzo a. Fray Angel: b. Alburquerque; son of Garcia Rol·and Lorenzo Angel, both convicted of judío in Llerena; brother of P. Camargo and P. Altamiro; r. Guatemala; denounced in 1582 by another monk as the brother of a Jew relaxed in Llerena. Suspicion of judío, descendant of Jews.

AGN 125, No. 54; AGN 126, No. 5; AGN 215, No. 2; Chinchilla Aquillar, 47, 182.

Altamiro, P: Portuguese; brother of P. Camargo and Lorenzo Altamirano. Descendant of Jews.

AGN 368, No. 112.

Alva, Beatriz de: 1642 testimony by Isabel Duarte. Judaizante.

AGN 415, fol. 368.

Alva, Manuel: 1642 testimony by Violante Suarez.

AGN 415, fol. 451.

Alvarado, Diego a. Muñoz: age 56; b. Popayan, Peru; r. Puebla; commercial dealer; died in secret cells. Suspicion of judaizante and observer of Mosaic laws, 1682; relaxed in effigy in 1688 auto.

Abec.; AGN 644, No. 3; AGN 673, No. 30; AHN 1731, No. 36; Medina, *México* 278.

Alvarado, Juana de. *See* Diego Mendez Marino.

Alvarez, Ambrocio: r. Veracruz; named in proceso of Catalina Enriquez. Judío.

Proceso of Catalina Enriquez at Huntington Library.

Alvarez, Francisco: m. Inez Hernandez; brother-in-law of Manuel de Morales; a fugitive. Observer of Mosaic laws, judío.

Abec.; Toro, *Judíos,* 62.

Alvarez, Gaspar. *See* Ana Gomez (b. Madrid).

Alvarez, Isabel. *See* Ana Lopez de Chavez.

Alvarez (Albarez), Jeronimo: r. Mexico; mulatto; circumcised; tortured. Judaizante; absolved.

AHN 1738, No. 1.

Alvarez, Jorge: b. Fondon; m. Ana Baez; merchant. Suspicion of judío;

reconciled in 1601 auto; 10 years service in galleys between Spain and New Spain, 200 lashes, exile from New Spain and the Indies.
> Abec.; AGN (Riva Palacio) 18, No. 1; AGN 152, No. 2; AGN 153, No. 1; AGN 252A, 18, No. 3; AGN 152, No. 2; AGN 153, No. 1; AGN 252A, No. 2A; AGN 254A, No. 10; García 5:102; Medina, *México* 112, 159.

Alvarez, Manuel: age 60; b. Fondon; merchant; m. Leonor Rodriguez. Observer of Mosaic laws and judaizante; reconciled in 1601 auto, sanbenito, confiscation of property, abjuration de vehementi, life imprisonment.
> Abec.; AGN 159, Nos. 3, 5; Medina, *México* 159.

Alvarez, Mayor: 1646 proceso. Judaizante.
> AGN 419, No. 28.

Alvarez, Nuño. *See* Diego Suarez de Figueroa.

Alvarez, Pedro: r. San Miguel; 1650 proceso. Judaizante.
> AGN 435, No. 30.

Alvarez, Pelayo: b. Freyre; r. Taxco; commercial dealer; died in secret cells at age 74. Judío and observer of Mosaic laws; reconciled in effigy in 1601 auto.
> Abec; Medina, *México* 162; Toro, *Judíos* 63.

Alvarez, Simon: testified against Blanca Enriquez, Rafaela Enriquez, and Francisco Diaz; implicated them as observers of Mosaic laws and judíos; said he had followed their practices. Judaizante.
> AGN 417, fols. 567-582.

Alvarez de Acosta, Luis: Portuguese; r. Jalapa; 1626 accusation from Los Reyes, Peru. Judaizante.
> AGN 362, fol. 106; AGN 366, No. 4.

Alvarez de Arellano, Manuel: age 43; b. Yelves; son of Luisa Mendez and Manuel Lopez; brother of Francisco Nuñez; circumcised; a mortician for the Jews; traveled a great deal between Spain and Mexico bringing merchandise such as linen for shrouds from Rouen and other things for Jewish burials, including earth purportedly from the Holy Land; alleged to have had an illicit affair with Rafaela Enriquez; had been arrested in 1642 in Havana, where he had been saved from a sinking ship. Judío and observer of Mosaic laws; reconciled in 1647 auto, confiscation of property, sanbenito, jail for one year, abjuration de vehementi, exile.
> Abec.; AGN 405, No. 1; AGN 417, fol. 549; AGN 453, fol. 612; AHN 1738, No. 1; Medina, *México* 117, 194.

Alvarez Pliego, Fernando: b. Oporto; aged and sickly; r. Tula; tortured. Observer of Mosaic laws; abjuration de vehementi, fined 500 pesos, jailed.

    AGN 59, No. 1; Medina, *México* 74, 75; Toro *Judíos* 10 lists as Hernando Pliego, Portugal, descendant of Jews, with same AGN citation.

AMESQUITA, AMEZQUITA. *See also* MESQUITA.

Amezquita, Fernando: former r. Caracas or Maracaibo; 1649 proceso. Judaizante.

    AGN 503, No. 7.

Amezquita, Francisco. *See* Francisco Mezquita a. Amezquita.

Amezquita Sarmiento, Luis. *See* Luis Mezquita Sarmiento.

Andrada, Diego de. *See* Manuel Tabares. *See also* Diego de Andrada under Peru.

Andrada, Diego Marcos de: 1589 proceso. Judaizante.

    AGN (Riva Palacio) 12, No. 4.

Andrada, Fernando: 1644 proceso. Judaizante.

    AGN 419, No. 23.

Andrada Pardo, Diego: r. Nicaragua; 1572 proceso. Judío.

    AGN 52, No. 2.

Andrade, Isabel de. *See* Isabel de Carvajal.

Andrade, Leonor de: b. Benavente; daughter of Francisca de Carvajal; m. Jorge de Almeyda; arrested in 1589. Judaizante; reconciled. Rearrested in 1595 as a relapsa; garroted in auto of 1596.

    Abec.; AGN (Riva Palacio) 12, No. 2; Medina, *México* 108, 174; *see also* references for Carvajal family.

Andres, Gaspar: formerly from Maracaibo; r. Veracruz; absolved ca. 1642 of judaizante; denounced in 1650. Saying that the leg of the animal had not been well roasted and that the landrecilla had not been removed.

    AGN 399, No. 2; AGN 435, No. 100; AHN 1738, No. 1.

Anfroy, Pierres: French. Heresy and judío.

    AGN 50; Toro, *Judíos* 9.

Angel, Fray. *See* Fray Lorenzo Altamirano.

Angel, Lorenzo. *See* Fray Lorenzo Altimirano.

Angeles, Juana de los. *See* Juana Rodriguez.

Angelini, Juan: Soldier in the Regiment of America; 1765 proceso; testimony from Saragossa and Barcelona. Judaizante and heresy.

    AGN 1038, No. 5.

Anonymous. A number of unnamed Jews were denounced in 1714 by two monks; four of the accused r. in Puebla.

AGN 551, No. 84.

Antonio, Diego: testimony by Isabel de Silva in 1642. Judaizante.

AGN 415, fol. 598.

Antonio, Marco: b. Casteloblanco; single; fencing master; r. Villa de la Trinidad, Guatemala. Heresy and judaizante; reconciled in 1596 auto, sanbenito, confiscation of property, life imprisonment.

Abec. cites r. as Casteloblanco; AGN (Riva Palacio) 16, No. 1 cites r. as Cubillana; García 5:99, Medina, *México* 124; Toro, *Judíos* 66, 76.

Antuñez, Clara a. Clara Enriquez (Henriquez) a. Clara Duarte: age 19; b. Mexico; daughter of Diego Antuñez and Isabel Duarte; sister of Manuel Antuñez. Judío, judaizante, and observer of Mosaic laws; reconciled in 1646 auto, sanbenito, confiscation of property, abjuration de vehementi, jail for one year, exile from the Indies, Seville, and Madrid.

Abec.; AGN 391, No. 10; AGN 392, No. 17; AGN 404, No. 1; AGN 408, No. 3; AGN 413, fols. 202-206, 247-249; AGN 414, fol. 247-249; AGN 415, fol. 514; AGN 419, No. 39; AGN 453, fol. 6; García 28:45; Medina, *México* 113, 193.

Antuñez, Diego a. Diego Antuñez de Torres: Portuguese; "a circumcised Jew"; merchant; m. Isabel Duarte; died in the secret cells. Observer of Mosaic laws; relaxed in effigy in 1649 auto.

AGN 392, No. 17; AGN 404, No. 4; AGN 413, fols. 202-206; AGN 453, fol. 6; AGN 414, No. 10.

Antuñez, Isabel la de. *See* Isabel Duarte.

Antuñez, Manuel: age 22; b. Mexico; son of Diego Antuñez and Isabel Duarte; no occupation; single. Judío and observer of Mosaic laws; reconciled in 1646 auto, sanbenito, confiscation of property, jail for one year, abjuration de vehementi.

Abec.; AGN 392, No. 17; García 28:71; Medina, *México* 193.

Arana, Martin de. *See* Martin de Asana.

Aranjo (Araujo), Juan de: Portuguese; studied in a Jewish school in Angola; broker of Negroes; died in Caracas when a church collapsed. Judaizante; relaxed in effigy in 1649 auto.

AGN 415, No. 1; Emmanuel 1:38; proceso at Gilcrease Institute.

Aranz, Francisco de: 1642 proceso. Judaizante.

AGN 453, fol. 477.

Araujo, Juan de. *See* Juan de Aranjo.

Arbolaez, Juan or Julian de: nephew of Alvaro de Acuña; r. Chamacuero; 1648 proceso; fugitive. Judaizante.
    AGN 431, No. 71; Medina, *México* 205.

Arellano, Gabriel de: r. Queretaro; 1681 proceso. Judío.
    AGN 450, No. 10; AGN 452, fol. 707.

Arevalo, Juan de: r. Mexico. Judaizante.
    AGN 1738, No. 1.

Arias, Gabriel: 1642 testimony. Judaizante.
    AGN 415, fols. 94, 487.

Arias, Gabriel: "gachupin," 1732 proceso. Suspicion of judío.
    AGN 841, No. 12.

Arias, Leonor: r. Campostela. Suspicion of judío.
    AGN 49, No. 5; Toro, *Judíos* 156 gives date as 1569 and charge as blasphemy.

Arias Maldonado, Pedro: r. Veracruz; merchant; m. Catalina Enriquez; 1649 proceso; deceased; testimony of Catalina Enriquez. Judaizante; relaxed in effigy in 1649 auto.
    AGN 433, fol. 492; proceso of Catalina Enriquez at Huntington Library.

Arizmendi, Pedro de: "Maestro"; 1626. Descendant of Jews.
    AGN 1552, fol. 299.

Arnao, Ventura: r. Ixmiquilpan; 1727 proceso. Judío.
    AGN 818, No. 3.

Arroja, Jorge de. *See* Juan de Roxas.

Asana (Arana), Martin de: r. Durango; accused in August 1570. Suspicion of judío, observer of Mosaic laws.
    AGN 44, No. 1 cites name as Arana; Liebman, *Guide* 1026; Medina, *México* 96; Rueda 85; Toro, *Judíos* 9 cites as Arana and Sañen and also errs in the date.

Astorga (Astoraga), Juan de: b. Seville; clogmaker; accused in 1554. Putting a cross inside a shoe.
    AGN 30, No. 11; Liebman, *Guide* 1023; Medina, *México* 96 gives date as 1539; Toro, *Judíos* 9, 119.

Ayllon (Allon), Juan de: Portuguese; circumcised; broker of *"jonga"* and Negroes; m. Catalina Pedorsa; reputed to be one of the outstanding Jews in the Mexico City Jewish community; died prior to his trial. Observer of Mosaic laws; relaxed in effigy in 1649 auto.

AGN 414, fol. 282; AGN 415, fols. 101, 380; Medina, *México* 408.

Azcazibar, Santiago a. Santiago Raymundi y Arengo: r. San Jose del Parral; self-denounced. Judío.

AGN 1145, No. 3

Azevedo, Leonor de. *See* Sebastian Vaez.

Baca, Jorge Jacinto. *See* Jorge Jacinto Bazan

BAEZ. *See also* VAEZ.

Baez (Vaez), Ana: b. Fondon; m. Jorge Alvarez. Judaizante; abjuration de vehementi, reconciled in 1596 auto.

AGN 152, No. 2; García 5:94; Toro, *Judíos* 11.

Baez (Vaez), Antonio a. Antonio Vaez Casteloblanco or Tirada a. Antonio Tirado a. Captain Casteloblanco: b. Portugal; brother of Simon Vaez Sevilla; was considered a learned Jew; circumcised Tomas Treviño de Sobremonte when they were cellmates 1624-1625. Observer of Mosaic laws and dogmatizer; two years in jail after 1625 auto. Rearrested; relaxed with garrote in 1649 auto. *See also* Antonio Baez Castillo.

Abec.; Bocanegra; Liebman, *Guide* 445, 492, 497, 499, 500, 524, 616.

Baez, Francisco: a friend of Manuel de Lucena and the Carvajal family; a Jew; fled or tried to flee to Peru in 1595.

Martínez del Rio 112.

Baez (Vaez), Jorge a. Jorge Baez Alcaiceria a. Jorge Lais: b. San Vicente Davera; r. Puebla de los Angeles; peddler. Observer of Mosaic laws; reconciled in 1596; confiscation of property, sanbenito, jail for four years.

Abec.; AGN 156, No. 2; García 5:99; Liebman, *Guide* 1124; Medina, *México* 124; Toro, *Judíos* 60.

Baez, Joseph a. Jose Baez y de la Torre; single; accused in 1635. Judaizante, observer of Mosaic laws; reconciled in 1635 auto.

Abec.; AGN 381, No. 5.

Baez, Juan a. Juan Vaez Mesignana. *See* Francisco de Acosta.

Baez, Luis. *See* Antonio de Caceres.

Baez de Acevedo, Antonio: r. Maracaibo. Judío.

AHN 1738, No. 1.

Baez Alcaiceria, Jorge. *See* Jorge Baez.

Baez Castillo, Antonio: possibly the same person as Antonio Baez a. Antonio Vaez Casteloblanco.

AGN 414, fol. 116.

Baez y de la Torre, Jose. *See* Joseph Baez.

Baeza, Juan de: b. Seville; accused of circumcising children with his fingernails ca. 1540. Suspicion of judío.
    AGN 125, Nos. 5, 7 (2 trials); Greenleaf, *Zumárraga* 98.

Bandejo, Diego. *See* Diego Rodriguez.

Baptista, Maria: 1642 proceso. Judaizante.
    AGN 453, fol. 126.

Baptista del Bosque, Juan. *See* Esperanza Rodriguez.

Barahona, Francisco Victoria: b. Pazos, Galicia; had been punished for judaizante in Peru; his testimony from Peru concerning observers of Mosaic laws was adduced against him and several others in New Spain; arrested in 1622. Bigamy.
    AGN 335, No. 41; AGN 366, No. 4; Medina, *Lima* 2:26.

Barbosa, Francisco de: Portuguese; r. San Luis Potosi; testimony of Antonio de Arismonde Gogorren. Suspicion of judío.
    AGN 425, fol. 464.

Barbosa, Manuel: denounced in 1650. Communicating with the descendants of Jews.
    AGN 435, fol. 388.

Barrassa, Gonzalo: Portuguese. Judaizante.
    AGN 383, No. 18.

Barrera, Felix: r. Real de los Alamos; married; 1718 proceso. Suspicion of judío.
    AGN 772, No. 8.

Barrientos, Diego: testimony. Jewish ancestry.
    AGN 373, No. 19.

Barrientos, "Fulano": b. Spain. Denounced himself 1714 as one penanced by the Holy Office.
    AGN 758, No. 11.

Barrientos, Pedro: testimony regarding his Jewish ancestry.
    AGN 373, No. 19.

Barrios, Manuel Francisco de: tortured. Judaizante; absolved.
    AHN 1738.

Bases, Manuel de: Portuguese. Judío, having Jewish parents, observer of Mosaic laws; reconciled, confiscation of property, sanbenito, 200 lashes, eight years in the galleys, life imprisonment.
    Abec.; Liebman, *Jews* 311.

Bautista, Juan: r. Puebla; former r. Tetuan, Morocco, where he said that he had been very happy with the Jews for four years; carpenter; 1607 proceso. Suspicion of judío.

>AGN 471, Nos. 11, 28.

Bazan, Jorge Jacinto a. Jorge Jacinto Baca: b. Malaga; son of Diego Nuñez Baca, b. Rambla, near Cordoba, and Elena (Helena) Rodriguez, b. Malaga; both parents died in Marseilles; cousin of Juan Pacheco de Leon; was in Salonica, Pisa, Leghorn, and Marseilles before coming to New Spain; came to Mexico in 1637 with a letter to Simon Vaez Sevilla, recommended by a "famous rabbi who lived in Simon Vaez's house" as a good match for Blanca Juarez; m. Blanca Juarez, a great beauty and related to Simon Vaez Sevilla; circumcised; merchant. Judío; reconciled in auto of 1648, sanbenito, confiscation of property, exile from the Indies, life imprisonment, 200 lashes.

>Abec.; fragments AGN 392, Nos. 3, 12, 13, 16; AGN 503, No. 70; Proceso at Huntington Library; García 28:228; Medina, *México* 118, 195; Nehama 5:15 says that Jorge Jacinto Bazan or Baca escaped from the Inquisition of "Brazil" and returned to Salonica; Roth 14.

Bello, Juan: r. Ecatepec; 1659 proceso. Judaizante.

>AGN 446, No. 7.

Belmonte, Manuel Francisco de: b. Cubillan; r. Sultepec; miner. Observer of Mosaic laws; reconciled, confiscation of property, sanbenito, 100 lashes, life imprisonment.

>Abec.; García 5:101; Medina, *México* 124; Toro, *Judíos* 60, 76.

Benites, Antonio: Portuguese. Denounced: Judío.

>AGN 356.

Benitez, Daniel: b. Borgoñon; r. Tachamachalco; tailor. Suspicion of judío and Lutheranism.

>AGN 151, No. 3; Medina, *México* 124; Toro *Judíos* 10 lists as Daniel Sastre.

Benitez, Diego: reconciliado; requested permission to open a stall in 1605.

>AGN 281, No. 25.

Benitez, Isabel: believed to be a sister of Diego Benitez; a former reconciliada; denounced in 1604. Wearing silk.

>AGN 368, fols. 20-25; Medina, *México* 124.

Bernal, Pedro: Observer of Mosaic laws; reconciled in 1648 auto.

>Medina, *México* 194.

Blandon, Francisco a. Francisco Lopez Blandon or Terrazas: b. Mexico;
son of Leonor Nuñez; brother-in-law of Tomas Treviño de Sobremonte; m. Mayor Lopez; accused in 1634. Judaizante; reconciled in
1635 auto. Rearrested in 1643. Relapso; relaxed alive age 41, in
1649 auto.
> Abec.; AGN 378, No. 2; AGN 381, No. 5; AGN 426, fol. 521;
> AGN 435, fols. 41-45; Liebman, *Guide* 1145, 1162; McClaskey,
> 25; Medina, *México* 119, 185, 204.

Bolta, Juan Tomas la: r. Oaxaca; army scout; 1721 proceso. Suspicion
of judaizante.
> AGN 789, No. 17.

Borullo, Manuel: Portuguese. Declaration: suspicion of judío.
> AGN 22, No. 9; Toro, *Judíos* 102.

Bosque, Isabel del: age 24; daughter of Esperanza Rodriguez; confessed
to judío and judaizante. Observer of Mosaic laws; reconciled in auto
of 1646, abjuration de vehementi, confiscation of property, sanbenito, exile.
> Abec.; AGN 427, No. 6; García 28:57; Medina, *México* 193.

Bosque, Juana del: age 29; b. Cartagena; r. Guadalajara; daughter of
Esperanza Rodriguez; mulatto; seamstress; m. Blas Lopez; confessed.
Observer of Mosaic laws; reconciled auto of 1646, confiscation of
property, sanbenito, exile.
> Abec.; AGN 427, No. 6; AGN 499, No. 9; Medina, *México* 115, 193.

Bosque, Juan Baptista del. *See* Esperanza Rodriguez.

Bosque, Maria de. *See* Maria Rodriguez del Bosque.

Botello, Andres: accusation from comisario in the Philippines. Judaizante.
> AGN 416, No. 34.

Botello, Francisco: b. Priego, Andalusia, ca. 1594; son of Diego Rodriguez Botello, b. either Sernacela or Viseo, Portugal, and Isabel Fernandez, b. Priego; both parents had been imprisoned by the Holy
Office in Cordoba and freed in 1605 under the Bull of Pardon;
nephew of Antonio Fernandez Cordado, his mother's brother, reconciled in 1635; brother [sic] of Ana Gomez Botello; r. Tacubaya;
innkeeper; m. Maria de Zarate. Suspicion of judío; reconciled in
1649 auto, confiscation of property, sanbenito, exile, abjuration de
vehementi, 200 lashes. Rearrested. Relapso; relaxed in 1659 auto.
> AGN 404, No. 4; AGN 412, No. 1; Liebman, *Guide* 1155;

McClaskey 4; Medina, *México* 203, 247, 248, 249, 266.

Brago, Baltazar del. *See* Baltazar de Ubago.

Bravo, Agustin: denounced in 1695. Stating he had stayed in the house of a Jew while in Jamaica.

AGN 530, No. 38.

Bravo, Antonio: Portuguese, brother of Agustin Bravo and of Duarte Lopez; r. San Salvador, Guatemala; 1663 proceso. Suspicion of judío.

AGN 594, No. 4.

Briceño, Maria: grandmother of Antonia Carbajal; died in 1609 in Guatemala.

AGN 285, No. 8; Chinchilla Aquillar 183.

Briones, Diego de: Suspicion of judío.

AGN 30, No. 13; Medina, *México* 96; Toro, *Judíos* 9 gives date as 1544.

Burgos, Antonio de: testimony in 1642 by Francisco Lopez de Fonseca, Rafaela Enriquez, and Thomas Nuñez de Peralta. Judaizante.

AGN 405, No. 8; AGN 415, fol. 307; AGN 419, No. 36; Medina *México* 194.

Burgos, Felipe de: testimony in 1642 by Francisco Lopez de Fonseca, Beatriz Enriquez, Rafaela Enriquez, and Thomas Nuñez de Peralta. Judaizante.

AGN 405, No. 8; AGN 415, fol. 303; AGN 419, No. 15.

Burgos, Juan Laureano de: mayor of Zacualpa; 1765-1782 proceso. Judaizante.

AGN 1002, No. 21.

Burgos, Luis de; age 66; b. Villanueva de los Infantes, bishopric of Toledo; son of Simon Rodriguez, breeder of suckling pigs, and Maria Diaz, both New Christians; circumcised; a merchant. Judaizante; reconciled in 1646 auto, sanbenito, exile, abjuration de vehementi, fined 3,000 pesos for extraordinary expenses of the Holy Office.

Abec.; AGN 413, fols. 157, 158; García 28:41.

Burgos, Simon: r. Pachuca; merchant; m. Ana Gomez Botello. Judaizante; reconciled in 1635 auto.

Abec.; Medina, *México* 185.

Bustos "Family:" denounced in 1694. Descendants of Jews.

AGN 695, No. 74.

Bustos, Maria de. *See* Melchor de Acosta.

Caceres, Antonio de: grandson of Luis Baez, relaxed in effigy; r. Puebla; 1707 proceso. Judaizante.

    AGN 731, No. 20.

Caceres, Leonor de: b. Mexico; daughter of Catalina de Leon de la Cueva. Judaizante; reconciled in 1601 auto. Rearrested 1652; released 1653.

    Abec.; AGN 560, No. 1; most of her proceso is at Huntington Library; Liebman, *Enlightened*, 141-147; Liebman, *Jews*, 171, 179, 186, 198, 201, 274, 293; Medina, *México* 160.

Calbo Diez, Antonio: pharmacist; 1731 proceso. Judío.

    AGN 834, No. 12.

Calvo, Diego: Portuguese; came from Lima; 1641 proceso. Observer of Mosaic laws.

    AGN 390, No. 18.

Calvo, Francisco: clergyman; two procesos. Suspicion of judío, judaizante.

    AGN 455, fol. 805.

Camargo, P.: Portuguese; son of Lorenzo Angel who was relaxed by the Inquisition of Llerena, while his wife was reconciled; brother of Fray Lorenzo Altamirano and P. Altamiro. Descendant of Jews.

    AGN 368, No. 112.

Campo, Alonso Romero del: b. Cuenca; reconciled at Cuenca after accusation of judío; proceso. Wearing silk, riding a horse, and carrying arms.

    AGN 274, No. 12.

Campo, Rodrigo del: b. Villa del Quintar, near Toledo; public scribe; arrested in 1593. Judaizante, observer of Mosaic laws; reconciled in 1603 auto.

    Abec.; AGN 223, No. 33; AGN 274, No. 18; AGN 277, No. 12; Medina, *México* 171.

Campos, Ana de: daughter of Manuel Diaz and Ines Gomez; m. Francisco de Campos Morales, the son of her father's brother. Testimony by Isabel de Silva and Maria de Rivera. Judío.

    AGN 383, No. 7; AGN 415, fol. 89.

Campos, Catalina de: age 85; b. Lisbon; daughter of Gaspar Diaz and Isabel Rodriguez; sister of Ana de Campos and of Francisco de Campos Morales; widow of Antonio de Gama; mother of Maria de Campos; needed medical attention in prison; died in the cell; had not been visited for so long that rats ate part of her body. Observer of Mosaic laws; relaxed in effigy in 1649 auto.

Abec.; AGN 429, No. 13; Medina, *México* 277.

Campos, Cridonia (Gridonia) de: Portuguese; m. Alvaro Nuñez de Segovia who died in Havana; mother of Francisco de Campos Segovia; died in cells. Observer of Mosaic laws; relaxed in effigy in 1649.

> Abec.; AGN 405, No. 9; AGN 415, fols. 385, 463; AGN 418, No. 10; AGN 453, fol. 1.

Campos, Domingo de: r. Campeche. Judaizante; reconciled.

> AHN leg. 1738, exp. 1, 99.

Campos, Francisco: 1642 testimony by Bartolome Alfaro. Judaizante.

> AGN 425, No. 12.

Campos, Guiomar. *See* Francisco de Campos Morales.

Campos, Isabel de a. Isabel de Segovia: b. Seville; had lived in Valladolid; testimony by Ursula Zib, Blanca de Rivera, Maria de Rivera, and Isabel Antuñez in 1649; deceased. Judaizante; relaxed in effigy in 1649 auto.

> Abec.; AGN 405, No. 1; AGN 415, Nos. 1, 4, 5, 7; AGN 431, fol. 510; AHN 1738, No. 1.

Campos, Jose de: b. Mexico; r. Veracruz; denounced in 1650. Saying that he could not believe that his uncle, Francisco de Campos Segovia, had been a Jew.

> AGN 435, fol. 388.

Campos, Juan: testimony by Blanca Rivera. Judaizante.

> AGN 404, fol. 174; AGN 404, No. 4.

Campos, Maria de: age 35; b. Montemayor; daughter of Catalina de Campos and Antonio Pinto de Gama; m. Francisco de Herrera; 1646 proceso. Suspicion of judío; acquitted in February 1649; her sequestered property was returned.

> AGN (Riva Palacio) 23, No. 2.

Campos, Pedro de: r. Campeche; 1648 proceso; tortured. Judío and judaizante.

> AGN 430, fols. 48-530.

Campos Morales, Francisca: 1642 proceso. Judío.

> A typescript of the proceso is at the American Jewish Historical Society.

Campos Morales, Francisco de: b. Montemayor ca. 1579; son of Gaspar Diaz and Isabel Rodriguez, both reconciled by the Holy Office of Evora as judaizantes; brother of Catalina de Campos, r. San Lucar de Barrameda, and of Guiomar de Campos of Carmona, Andalucia, the widow of Simon Gomez, a confectioner in Lisbon, and brother of Ana, the widow of Manuel de Silba; all these relatives had been reconciled by the Inquisition at Evora; circumcised; m. Ana de Campos; childless; a merchant and encomendero in China. Observer of Mosaic laws; reconciled in 1649 auto; exile, fined 1,000 Castilian ducats for extraordinary expenses of the Tribunal of the Holy Office.

    Abec.; Bocanegra, Medina, *México* 203.

Campos Segovia, Diego de: Portuguese; son of Alvaro Nuñez de Segovia and Cridonia de Campos; his parents were termed Hebrew New Christians in Bocanegra's *Relación;* brother of Francisco de Campos Segovia and Isabel de Campos Segovia, both convicted as judaizante and relaxed in the 1649 auto; r. Campeche; merchant; fugitive. Judaizante.

    Abec.; AHN 1738, No. 1; Medina, *México* 205.

Campos Segovia, Francisco de: b. Seville; son of Alvaro Nuñez de Segovia and Cridonia de Campos; according to Bocanegra's *Relación,* full brother of Isabel Segovia Campos [Isabel de Campos] and Diego de Campos Segovia, "menos la madre;" [sic]; r. Veracruz; merchant. Observer of Mosaic laws; relaxed in effigy in 1649.

    Abec.; AGN 407, No. 7; AGN 415, No. 1; AGN 503, No. 4; Bocanegra.

Candia, Francisco de: 1601. Suspicion of judaizante.

    AGN 256, No. 12.

Canizo Perez, Luis: testimony by Blanca de Rivera in 1642. Judaizante.

    AGN 407, fol. 380.

Caravallo (Carballo), Antonio: age 36; b. Badajoz, Castile; son of Antonio Rodriguez, b. Casteloblanco, a trader, and Leonor Nuñez, b. Guarda; both parents Hebrew New Christians "who went to lands to live freely in Judaism and where one could openly profess one's faith"; circumcised; m. Isabel de Silva a. Isabel Correa, daughter of Elena de Silva, sister of Simon Vaez Sevilla; a group, led by Antonio Baez Casteloblanco, met in his house on Fridays and Saturdays to observe Jewish rites and ceremonies; was called "Plato" while in the cells by the other incarcerated Jews; tried to commit suicide while in the cell. Judío and observer of Mosaic laws; reconciled in auto of 1649, abjuration de vehementi, confiscation of property, sanbenito, 200 lashes, life imprisonment.

    Abec.; AGN 409, No. 2; AGN 413, fols. 84-187, 239-246; AGN 414, fols. 465, 587; AGN 415, fol. 172; AGN 417, Nos. 14, 16; AGN 434, fol. 250; Medina, *México* 203.

Caravelle, Antonio. *See* Antonio Carrasco.

Caravelle, Francisco. *See* Francisco Carrasco.

Carbajal. *See also* Carvajal.

Carbajal, Antonia: r. Guatemala; grandaughter of Maria Briceño, who died in 1609 in Guatemala; accused 1609. Observer of Mosaic laws.
AGN 285, No. 8.

Carbajal, Gaspar de: son of Francisco Rodriguez de Matos and Francisca Carvajal; Dominican priest. Suspected observer of Mosaic laws; penanced in chapel February 24, 1590, suspended and ordered into reclusion.
Abec.; AGN 126, No. 12.

Carballo, Antonio. *See* Antonio Caravallo.

Cardenas, Jose de: mayor of Tecali, near Puebla; stated that he was circumcised; 1735 proceso. Judío.
AGN 1175, No. 1, 30.

Cardoso, Diego. *See* Sebastian Cardoso.

Cardoso, Francisco. *See* Juan Cardoso.

Cardoso, Juan a. Gabriel Peregrino: age 57; b. Semede; son of Francisco Cardoso and Maria Duarte, both New Christians, r. Semede; circumcised; merchant; single; had lived in Amsterdam; used tallit, Jewish prayer shawl, and knew Hebrew prayers; Observer of Mosaic laws; confessed. Reconciled in 1647, sanbenito, confiscation of property, abjuration de vehementi, jail for six months, exile.
Abec.; AGN 399, No. 12; AGN 421, No. 11; García 28:120.

Cardoso, Manuel: 1594 proceso. Judaizante.
AGN 223, fol. 457.

Cardoso, Sebastian: age 56; b. Seville; son of Diego Cardoso, dealer in oil, and Antonia Gomez, both b. in Villa de Marchena, Andalucia; circumcised; secretary to his brother-in-law Simon Vaez de Sevilla; m. Micaela Enriquez; known as "Tarima" (low bench) in the secret cells. Judío; reconciled together with his wife in 1648 auto; abjuration de vehementi, sanbenito, confiscation of property, life imprisonment.
Abec.; AGN 416, No. 41; AGN 426, fol. 418; García 28:258; Medina, *México* 195.

Cardoso, Sebastian. *See* Sebastian de la Peña.

Cardoso, Tomas: r. Taxco. Judaizante.
AGN 303, No. 67.

Carmona, Anton: denounced by sister-in-law. Judío.
AGN 1A, No. 10.

Carrasco, Antonio a. Antonio Caravelle: 1692 proceso. Judaizante.

AGN 527, fols. 287-431; Medina, *México* 278, 415.

Carrasco, Francisco a. Francisco Caravelle: 1694 proceso. Judaizante.
AGN 527, fols. 287-431; Medina, *México* 278, 415.

Carrasco, Manuel: b. Villaflor; son of Francisco Rodriguez Carrasco and
Felipa Lopez, both of Villaflor; owner or foreman of sugar mill in
the Valley of Amilpas; single although about to marry Clara Antuñez
when she was apprehended; confessed. Judío, observer of Mosaic
laws; reconciled in auto of 1646, abjuration de vehementi, confiscation of property, sanbenito, jail for six months, then exile.
Abec.; AGN 404, No. 4; AGN 405, No. 9; AGN 406, fol. 563;
AGN 407, No. 1; AGN 413, fols. 155, 156; AGN 414, fol. 221;
AGN 427, No. 2; García 28:72; Medina, *México* 193.

Carretero, Pedro a. Pedro de la Vega. r. Puebla; 1694 proceso against
him "and others." Judaizante.
Abec.; AGN 694, Nos. 2, 3; Medina, *México* 279.

Carrion, Alvaro de: b. Cerbera de Rio Pisuerga; r. Ticuatla, near Pachuca; married; arrested 1596; tortured. Observer of Mosaic laws;
reconciled in 1601 auto; sanbenito, confiscation of property, 100
lashes, life imprisonment.
Abec.; AGN (Riva Palacio) 55, No. 4; Medina, *México* 159.

Carrion, Isabel de: denounced in 1626. Judaizante and porging.
AGN 356, fol. 77 (second part of proceso only).

CARVAJAL. *See also* CARBAJAL.

Carvajal, Ana de a. Ana de Leon Carvajal a. Ana Rodriguez de Matos: b.
Mexico; daughter of Francisca de Carvajal; arrested 1589; died in cell
of cancer of the breast. Suspicion of judío and heresy; case suspended. Rearrested 1595; observer of Mosaic laws; reconciled in
auto of 1601. Relapsa; relaxed in effigy in 1649 auto.
Abec.; Liebman, *Jews,* 8; Medina, *México* 94, 160, 203.

Carvajal, Antonio de. *See* Francisca de Carvajal.

Carvajal, Baltasar. *See* Miguel de Carvajal.

Carvajal, Francisca de: b. Benavente, Castile; daughter of Gaspar de
Carvajal and Catalina de Leon, both b. Salamanca; sister of Luis de
Carvajal y de la Cueva and of Antonio de Carvajal of Guatemala, also
sister of Domingo de Carvajal, a deceased Jesuit; widow of Francisco
Rodriguez de Matos; mother of nine children; revealed under torture
that all of her family except her son Gaspar, a Dominican monk,
were Jews. Judaizante; reconciled, life imprisonment. Sentence commuted, rearrested in 1595. Relapsa; relaxed in 1596 auto along with
two daughters and a son.

Abec.; AGN (Riva Palacio) 12, No. 1; AGN 223, No. 2; García 5:106; Greenleaf, *Mexican Inquisition* 169-171; Liebman, *Enlightened* 23, 26, 30, 146; Liebman, *Jews* ch. 8; Medina, *México* 94, 125; Martínez del Rio.

Carvajal, Isabel de a. Isabel de Andrade a. Isabel Rodriguez de Andrade: b. Benavente; daughter of Francisca de Carvajal; widow of Gabriel de Herrera; arrested first in 1589; tortured; arrested a second time in 1595. Judaizante; relaxed after garrote in 1596 auto.

AGN 558; Liebman, *Enlightened* 23, 29, 31, 32, 33, 58; Liebman, *Jews* ch. 8.

Carvajal, Leonor. *See* Leonor de Andrade (Mexico).

Carvajal, Luis de a. Joseph Lumbroso a. El Mozo: b. Benavente, ca. 1567; son of Francisca de Carvajal; first arrested in 1589 as a result of the admissions of his sister Isabel, who was tortured. Judaizante; reconciled, prison in a Franciscan monastery. Rearrested in 1595. Relapso; relaxed in 1596 auto.

AGN 1487, No. 2; AGN (Riva Palacio) 14; Lea, *Spanish Dependencies* 208, where he is confused with his uncle; Liebman, *Enlightened;* Liebman, *Jews* 55, 63, 67, 70, 125, 141, 146, 152, 153, 158, ch. 8, 184, 193, 263, 270; Medina, *México* 127-132.

Carvajal, Mariana de a. Mariana Nuñez; b. Benavente 1574; single; daughter of Francisca de Carvajal and Francisco Rodriguez de Matos. Judaizante; arrested in 1589, reconciled, rearrested 1595; found insane 1596; secret cells until 1601, when she was found sane and relaxed on March 25.

Abec.; AGN 129, No. 13; AGN (Riva Palacio) 15, No. 3; Riva Palacio, *Libro Rojo;* Liebman, *Jews,* ch. 8 and 198, 199; Medina, *México* 160, 161.

Carvajal, Miguel de a. Miguel Rodriguez: b. Benavente; son of Francisca de Carvajal and Francisco Rodriguez de Matos. Judaizante; escaped with his brother Baltasar in 1589.

Abec.; AGN (Riva Palacio) 12, No. 1; AGN 223, No. 2; García 5: 106; Greenleaf, *Mexican Inquisition*, 169-171; Liebman, *Enlightened,* 23, 26, 30, 146; Liebman, *Jews;* Medina, *México*, 94, 125; Martínez del Rio.

Carvajal y de la Cueva, Luis de a. El Viejo; admiral and governor; not a Jew, though a descendant of Jews; brother of Francisca de Carvajal; one brother was a Jesuit. Concealer and helper of Jews; reconciled; abjuration de vehementi; one year jail, where he died.

Abec.; AGN 1487, No. 3; Lea, *Spanish Dependencies* 208; Liebman, *Enlightened* 10, 23, 26, 28, 30; Liebman, *Jews,* chs. 8-10; Medina, *México* 127, 132.

Castaño, Duarte de: age 40; b. Abrantes, Portugal; son of Francisco de Melo, b. Rodrigo, Spain, doctor, and Maria Castaño, b. Abrantes; r. Veracruz; former resident of Caracas; merchant; m. Antonia de Silba; b. Lisbon. Judaizante; reconciled in 1649 auto; sanbenito, confiscation of property, abjuration de vehementi, exile.

Abec.; AGN 497, No. 8; Medina, *México* 203.

Castaño, Isabel de: r. Zacatecas; daughter of Juana de Villegas and Hernan Rodriguez. Parents were New Christians and she was descendant of Jews.

AGN 356, fol. 156.

Castaño, Maria. *See* Duarte de Castaño.

Castaño de Sosa, Gaspar: Army captain under Luis de Carvajal y de la Cueva.

Bancroft, *North Mexican States,* vol. 1, 128; Bancroft, *Arizona,* vol. 17, 100; Don Cleofas Calleros of El Paso, Texas (personal communication, 1966), reported that his research indicated Castaño was of Jewish descent if not a judío himself; Castañeda, vol. 1, 181 [where no mention is made of his faith]; Hull.

Castellanos, Julian de: b. Xarandilla; brother of Tomas de Fonseca of Tapujagua; 1590 proceso. Judaizante.

AGN (Riva Palacio) 55, No. 11.

Castro, Antonio de: b. Casteloblanco; testimony of Isabel de Silva in 1642. Judaizante.

AGN 415, fol. 526.

Castro, Luisa de. *See* Juan Rodriguez Juarez.

Castro, Mariana de. *See* Pedro Fernandez de Castro.

Castro, Pedro de. *See* Margarita Morera.

Cercado, Juan: denounced in 1539. Suspicion of being a Jewish convert in Ocaña, Spain

AGN 40, No. 3D.

Cerda, Manuel de. *See* Manuel de la Zerda.

Chartre, Pedro: French. Heresy and suspicion of judío; January 1572.

AGN 51, No. 1; Toro, *Judíos* 9.

Cisneros, Mateo de: Vicar General of Michoacan. Information in 1679 that his parents and other ancestors were all Jews in Toledo and their sanbenitos were hanging in the church of San Vicente.

AGN 438, No. 41.

Clara, Isabel a. Isabel Clara Hernandez: Portuguese, m. Francisco Hernandez, brother of Manuel de Morales. Judío; escaped with brother, relaxed in effigy in 1601 auto.

> Abec., AGN 154, No. 3; Medina, *México* 62.

Cordova, Ruiz de. *See* Maria de Mercado.

Coronel, Francisco. *See* Manuel Coronel.

Coronel, Manuel a. Martin Manuel Coronel: b. Camiña, Portugal; son of Francisco Cronel, merchant, and Felipa Rodriguez, b. Camiña; first cousin of Thomas Mendez who was reconciled in Mexico in auto of 1647, the son of Francisco Rodriguez, reconciled as judaizante in Lisbon; first cousin of Pedro Mendez, also reconciled as judaizante in Lisbon; r. Veracruz; broker; m. Leonor Nuñez. Judaizante; escaped the Inquisition; relaxed in effigy in 1649 auto.

> AGN 398, No. 2; AGN 405, No. 7; Medina, *México* 205.

Correa, Alberto Marte: age 72; b. Veracruz; tortured in 1647; never confessed. Judaizante.

> Abec.

Correa, Ana: accused of judaizante in 1644.

> AGN 414, fol. 110; AGN 425, No. 46.

Correa, Diego a. Diego Correa Silva: b. Portugal; son of Sumen Correa and Francisca Correa, b. Lisbon; m. Catalina Rivera; had one son, Luis, b. Seville. Suspicion of judío; reconciled in auto of 1649, sanbenito, confiscation of property, abjuration de vehementi, life imprisonment in Spain.

> Abec.; AGN 390, No. 11; AGN 405, No. 1; AGN 467, No. 27; Medina, *México* 203.

Correa, Guillermo: testimony against him as judaizante given by Luis Nuñez Perez in 1642.

> AGN 414, fol. 73.

Correa, Isabel. *See* Isabel de Silva.

Correa, Jeronimo: testimony against him as judaizante.

> AGN 414, fol. 144.

Correa, Luis: b. Mexico [sic]; son of Diego Correa and Catalina Rivera. Judaizante.

> AGN 414, fol. 82.

Corvera, Juan Bautista: r. Guadalajara. Heretical propositions and escaping jail, suspicion of judío.

> AGN 4, proceso missing; Liebman, *Guide* 1038; Medina, *México* 55, 56; Toro, *Judíos* 137, 168-82 [which includes Corvera's poetry].

Cruz, Agustina de la: age 30; b. Atzcapotzalco; mulato; daughter of

Maria de Guzman and Andres de la Cruz, a Negro. Denounced as judaizante; claimed to know nothing of what she was accused; case suspended; freed on November 2, 1646.

Abec.

Cruz, Antonio de la: not a Jew but a slave of Thomas Nuñez de Peralta. Carrying messages for the Jews in the Holy Office cells.

AGN 396, No. 3.

Cruz, Francisco de la: not a Jew but a slave of Simon Vaez de Sevilla. Carrying messages for the Jews in the Holy Office cells.

Proceso at Washington State University.

Cruz, Isabel de la: died in the secret cells. Judío; relapsa; bones disinterred and burned.

Medina, *México* 195.

Cruz, Luis de la: not a Jew but a slave of Ines Pereira. Carrying messages for the Jews in the Holy Office cells.

Proceso at Washington State University.

Cruz, Maria de la: age 16; b. Mexico; slave of Carlos de Samano. Judío and blasphemy.

AGN 274, No. 3.

Cubas, Alonso: r. Tepotzlan; 1618 testimony. Suspicion of judaizante.

AGN 316, No. 37.

Cuello, Domingo: b. Almofala, Portugal, in the bishopric of Amego; dealer in cattle and *viandante,* traveler. Heresy and judaizante; reconciled, confiscation of property, sanbenito, life imprisonment.

Abec. [which indicates b. Praga and r. Michoacan]; AGN (Riva Palacio) 16, No. 2; García 5:99.

Cueva, Juana de la: wife of Pedro de Roja. Judaizante.

AGN 345.

DIAS. *See* DIAZ.

Diaz, Antonio: testimony by Luis Nuñez Perez. Judaizante.

AGN 414, fol. 83.

Diaz, Baltazar. *See* Baltazar del Valle.

Diaz, Catalina. *See* Margarita Morera.

Diaz, Diego: age 80; b. Villa de Ameda ca. 1579; son of Guimor Mendez, b. Ameda, Portugal; circumcised; "peasant farmer"; m. Ana Gomez, b. Madrid, after she had been reconciled by the Inquisition as judaizante. First arrested in 1642 for suspicion of judío; reconciled in 1649 auto, abjuration de vehementi, exile, confiscation of property, sanbenito; rearrested in 1656 as a relapso and judío, observer of Mosaic laws; relaxed alive in 1659 auto.

> Abec.; AGN 392, No. 1; AGN 394, No. 1; AGN 413, fols. 151, 152; AGN 573, No. 17; Medina, *México* 203, 249.

Diaz, Domingo. *See* Domingo Rodriguez.

Diaz, Francisco: b. Portugal; 1643 testimony of Simon Alvarez. Judaizante.

> AGN 417, No. 18.

Diaz, Gaspar: Portuguese; r. Telita; 1627 proceso. Judaizante in 1627.

> AGN 362, fols. 113-130.

Diaz, Gaspar. *See* Francisco de Campos Morales.

Diaz, Gonzalo: brother of Baltazar Diaz. Judaizante.

> AHN 1738, exp. 1.

Diaz, Gonzalo. *See* Gonzalo Diaz Santillan.

Diaz, Jorge: Portuguese; silversmith. Observer of Mosaic laws; fugitive; relaxed in effigy in 1601.

> Abec.; Medina, *México* 162; Toro, *Judíos* 62.

Diaz, Leonor: b. Seville; daughter of Ana Lopez; m. Francisco Rodriguez Deza; 1595 proceso. Judaizante; reconciled, confiscation of property, jail for six years.

> AGN 155, No. 3; García 5:95.

Diaz, Luis: Portuguese; silversmith. Judaizante; fugitive; relaxed in effigy in 1601.

> Abec.; AGN 161, No. 2; AGN 223, Nos. 33, 34, 35. Liebman, *Guide* 1059.

Diaz, Manuel: b. Fondon; brother of Andres Rodriguez; m. Isabel Rodriguez; son-in-law of Violante Rodriguez. Jewish parents; observer of Mosaic laws; tortured but did not confess; relaxed alive.

> Abec., AGN (Riva Palacio) 13, No. 2; García 5:104; Medina, *México* 112, 124; the proceso is to be found at the Henry C. Lea Memorial Library, University of Pennsylvania.

Diaz, Manuel (father of Ana de Campos). *See* Ana de Campos.

Diaz, Manuel a. Manuel Diaz de Castella: b. Rodrigo, Castile; peddler and shopkeeper; single. Observer of Mosaic laws.

> AGN 413, fols. 163, 164; AGN 414, No. 6A; AGN 415, fols. 104, 105, 347, 351-354, 455-458.

Diaz, Maria. *See* Luis de Burgos.

Diaz, Ruy a. Ruy Diaz de Lemos: b. Lisbon; handyman. Observer of Mosaic laws; freed from secret cells in 1606 under general papal pardon.
   Abec., AGN 276, No. 14.

Diaz, Simon: son of Manuel Diaz and Isabel Rodriguez. Reconciliado; denounced in 1613 for wearing silk and riding a horse.
   AGN 298, No. 6; AGN 404, No. 3.

Diaz de Caceres, Antonio: b. Villa de Saneta, bishopric of Coimbra; m. Catalina de Leon de la Cueva of the Carvajal family. Judaizante; tortured 1595; reconciled in 1601 auto; abjuration de vehementi; fined 1,000 duros of Castile.
   Abec., AGN 159, No. 1; Liebman, *Guide* 1057, 1067, 1202; Liebman, *Jews* 171, 172, 201; Medina, *México* 157, 160.

Diaz de Castella, Manuel. *See* Manuel Diaz.

Diaz Callero, Roque: 1642 testimony by Violante Suarez. Judaizante.
   AGN 415, fol. 431.

Diaz de Castillo, Manuel. *See* Manuel Diaz (b. Rodrigo).

Diaz Enriquez, Manuel: Portuguese; r. Guatemala. Judaizante; a criminal case also instituted against him.
   AGN 337, No. 7; Liebman, *Jews* 209-211. Cecil Roth (personal communication, October 28, 1965), wrote "Manuel Diaz Enriquez is apparently identical with Mattatiah Aboab, father of Isaac de Mattatiah Aboab (not to be confused with I. da Fonseca Aboab) who reverted to Judaism in Amsterdam in 1626."

Diaz de Espinosa, Simon a. Simon de Espinosa: accused in 1642 of being judaizante and an observer of Mosaic laws.
   AGN 405, No. 2; AGN 406, No. 1; AGN 413, fols. 97-100, 165, 166; AGN 414, Nos. 1, 6A; AGN 415, Nos. 1, 3, 5, 6; AGN 417, No. 18; AGN 453, fols. 404-408, 464-470.

Diaz Flores, Mari. *See* Gonzalo Flores.

Diaz de Limos, Ruy. *See* Ruy Diaz.

Diaz de Llerena, Rui: b. Llerena; had certificate of *limpieza de sangre* from Inquisition of Llerena. Denounced for being in New Spain when prohibited.
   Abec.

Diaz Machorro, Juana: 1614 testimony regarding her.
   AGN 278, No. 12.

Diaz Marquez, Antonio: b. Alvala, near Lisbon; merchant. Judaizante; confessed; sentenced in auto of March 25, 1601, as supporter and concealer of Jews; reconciled, confiscation of property, sanbenito. AGN 158, No. 4; Martínez del Rio 113; Medina, *México* 159; Toro, *Judíos* 12.

Diaz Mataraña, Amaro a. Amaro Diaz Mata: b. Camiña, Portugal; merchant; m. Margarita Morera (Moreira), b. Mexico and reconciled in auto of April 16, 1646. Judaizante; died in Mexico ca. 1641; relaxed in effigy on April 11, 1649.

> Abec. [where his birthplace is Villa de la Mirta]; AGN 372, No. 26; Medina, *México* 206; the proceso of Margarita Morera is at the Huntington Library.

Diaz de Montoya, Francisco a. Francisco Diaz de Yelbes: age 46; b. Casteloblanco; son of Diego Mendez de Elbes or Yelbes and Isabel Enriquez, b. Casteloblanco; both parents Hebrew New Christians; brother of Jorge Diaz de Montoya; circumcised; r. Manila; m. Nicolasa de Bañuelos of Manila; their three children r. in Manila. Judaizante; his father had sent him forged papers to prove that he was descended from "old Christians; caballeros, hidalgos of the families Acevedo and Vasconcelos"; confessed; reconciled on April 16, 1646, confiscation of property, sanbenito, abjuration de vehementi, jail for six months; exile from the Indies, the Philippines, Madrid, and Seville.

> Abec.; AGN 416, No. 37; AGN 435, fol. 404; AGN 499, fol. 517; García 28:49; Medina, *México* 114, 193.

Diaz de Montoya, Jorge a. Jorge Montoya: b. Casteloblanco; brother of Francisco Diaz de Montoya, b. Casteloblanco; formerly a prisoner of the Inquisition at Goa and reconciled there for false testimony; testimony against him came from Lima. Observer of Mosaic laws and judío; fugitive; relaxed in effigy in 1649 auto.

> Abec.; AGN 366, No. 4; AGN 404, No. 5; AGN 405, No. 7; AGN 415, fols. 58, 470; AGN 416, No. 37; Medina, *México* 205 [which states b. Holland]. Most of the proceso is at the Huntington Library.

Diaz Nieto, Diego: b. Oporto; son of Ruy Diaz Nieto. Observer of Mosaic laws and awaiting the Messiah; reconciled in auto of 1596, confiscation of property, sanbenito, jail for one year. Imprisoned a second time and appeared in auto of 1605; during the second trial it was revealed that he had been circumcised in Ferrara; reconciled again with life imprisonment, the first two years in jail to be taught Catholicism.

Abec.; AGN 159, No. 2; AGN 276, No. 14; García 5:98; Liebman, *Guide* 1084, 1223; Medina, *México* 124, 173 [which states
b. Ferrara, Italy]. Part of the proceso is at the Gilcrease Institute.

Diaz Nieto, Ruy (Rui): b. Oporto; had lived in the Jewish quarter of
Ferrara, Italy. Observer of Mosaic laws; reconciled in auto of March
25, 1601.

    Abec.; AGN 157, No. 1; AGN 271, No. 1; AGN 277, No. 2; AGN
279, No. 9; Medina, *México* 159.

Diaz Rojas, Manuel: 1642 testimony by Margarita Rivera.

    AGN 415, No. 1.

Diaz Santillan, Baltazar: age 32; Portuguese; son of Pedro Diaz Santillan
and Juana Esteves; circumcised; Bocanegra's *Relacíon* reports that
he was a "whole brother" of Francisco Lopez Diaz, el Chato, and of
Manuel Diaz Santillan, and a half brother of Gonzalo Diaz formerly
Santillan; shopkeeper; m. Ines Pereira; had a child, Pedro. Observer
of Mosaic laws; reconciled in auto of 1649, confiscation of property,
sanbenito, abjuration de vehementi, life imprisonment.

    Abec.; AGN 405, No. 9; Boconegra; Medina, *México* 203.

Diaz Santillan, Gonzalo: b. Casteloblanco; nephew (sic) of Baltazar
Diaz Santillan; formerly resided in Seville; single. Judaizante; died
and relaxed in effigy in 1649 auto.

    AGN 405, No. 9; AGN 431, fol. 559; Medina, *México* 408.

Diaz Santillan, Manuel a. Manuel Diaz Cantillana: accused in 1642.
Judío and judaizante.

    AGN 414, fol. 206; AGN 415, fols. 455, 501; Medina, *México*
195.

Diaz Santillan, Pedro. *See* Francisco Lopez Diaz and Baltazar Diaz Santillan.

Diaz de Silva, Barbola or Bartola. *See* Luis Nuñez Perez.

Diaz de Solis, Adan: proceso; suspicion of judiazante; 1661.

    AGN 512, No. 2.

Diaz Vaez, Diego: suspicion of judaizante, observer of Mosaic laws;
reconciled in 1648 auto.

    Medina, *México* 194.

DIEZ. *See also* DIAZ.

Diez, Domingo. *See* Domingo Rodriguez.

Diez de Lineo, Alvaro: grandson of Juan Garcia el Conde and Maria de
Alonso. Judaizante. A letter from Valladolid, Spain, gives his genealogy, as well as that of Pedro de Roja and Juana de la Cueva, and

states that they had all been judaizantes, and that Gonzalo Enriquez de Lineo had confessed before the tribunal at Llerena and delated against them.

AGN 345.

Dominguez, Sebastian. *See* Luis Mezquita Sarmiento.

Duarte, Clara. *See* Clara Antuñez.

Duarte, Diego. *See* Diego Fuentes.

Duarte, Isabel a. Isabel la de Antuñez: b. Seville ca. 1605; daughter of Marco Rodriguez Tristan and Ana Enriquez, b. Seville and reconciled in Mexico as judaizante; both parents were dead at the time of the proceso; widow of Diego Antuñez, gambler or juggler; had two children, Clara and Manuel. Observer of Mosaic laws; reconciled in auto of April 1646, confiscation of property, sanbenito, life imprisonment in Spain.

Abec.; AGN 278, Nos. 12, 14; AGN 392, No. 17; AGN 406, fol. 583; AGN 463, fol. 270; AGN 487, No. 21; AGN 500, No. 5; Liebman, *Guide* 1115, 1116; Medina, *México* 115, 193.

Duarte, Jorge a. Jorge de Leon: age 18; b. Mexico; son of Duarte de Leon Jaramillo and Isabel Nuñez; circumcised. Judaizante; reconciled in 1649 auto; sanbenito, confiscation of property, life imprisonment, abjuration de vehementi, 200 lashes.

AGN 431, No. 4; Medina, *México* 203.

Duarte, Juan a. Juan Duarte Espinosa: Portuguese. Observer of Mosaic laws; imprisoned in Oaxaca; reconciled.

AGN 389, No. 8; AGN 392, Nos. 7, 22; AGN 415, Nos. 4, 7; AGN 426; AGN 427, No. 14; AGN 434, fol. 216; AGN 447, fol. 372; AGN 498, No. 2. The greatest part of the proceso is at the Gilcrease Institute.

Duarte, Juan a. Juan Duarte Fernandez: age 37; b. Zabugal, bishopric and city of Lamego, Portugal; son of Antonio Fernandez and Guiomar Enriquez, both Hebrew New Christians; first cousin of Thomas Nuñez de Peralta; single; merchant in the interior of the viceroyalty; circumcised, but not known as a Jew in New Spain as he had changed his name. Judaizante; protested his inocence for six years while incarcerated; reconciled, abjuration de vehementi, 100 lashes, exile from the Indies, Seville, and Madrid, life imprisonment.

AGN 389, No. 8; AGN 392, Nos. 7, 22; AGN 393, No. 3; AGN 415, Nos. 4, 7; AGN 426, fol. 529; AGN 527, No. 14; AGN 434, fol. 216; AGN 447, fol. 372; AGN 498, No. 2.

Duarte, Maria. *See* Juan Cardoso.

Duarte Correa, Alberto: 1646 report from the Holy Office.
AGN 399, No. 12.

Duarte Espinosa, Juan. *See* Juan Duarte.

Duran Family: r. Tepeaca; all Jews; had emigrated from Llerena, Spain, where the elders had been burned at the stake; one family member was Fray Juan Duran. "Descendant of Jews."
AGN 356, fol. 90.

Enrique, Violante: sister of Enrique de Miranda and Francisco Home, both Jews; she is named in their case but no proceso was instituted against her.
AGN 398, No. 4.

Enriquez. *See also* Henriquez.

Enriquez, Ana: denounced in 1606. Not wearing sanbenito.
AGN 277, No. 6C.

Enriquez, Ana: m. Marcos Rodriguez Tristan; mother of Isabel Duarte a la Antuñez. Judaizante and observer of Mosaic laws; relaxed in effigy in 1649 auto.
AGN 405, No. 8; AGN 415, fols. 133, 157, 254, 276, 410; Medina, *México* 206.

Enriquez, Beatriz: 23; b. Mexico; r. Veracruz; daughter of Antonio Rodriguez Arias and Blanca Enriquez; sister of Micaela and Rafaela, also imprisoned by the Holy Office; m. Thomas Nuñez de Peralta. Observer of Mosaic laws; imprisoned July 13, 1642; reconciled in 1648 auto, confiscation of property, sanbenito, exile from the Indies, Madrid, and Seville.
Abec.; AGN 393, Nos. 1, 2; AGN 417, No. 16, fol. 542; AGN 463, fol. 266; García 28; Liebman, *Guide* 1124, 1136; Medina, *México* 117, 195.

Enriquez, Beatriz a. Beatriz Enriquez de la Paiba (Payba): b. Fondon; widow of Simon Rodriguez Paiba. Judaizante; relaxed December 8, 1596.
Abec.; AGN 153, No. 9; García 5:104; Liebman, *Guide* 1048, 1075, 1235; Medina *México* 112, 117; Toro 59.

Enriquez (Henriquez), Beatriz: 34; b. New Veracruz; daughter of Fernando Rodriguez, b. Aveiro, and Blanca Enriquez of Lisbon; sister of Rodrigo Fernandez Correa, a doctor; m. Thomas Mendez, b. Camiña, a merchant in New Veracruz; had two children, Bartolome and Ana. Observer of Mosaic laws; reconciled in 1647 auto, confiscation of property, sanbenito, abjuration de vehementi, 100 lashes, life imprisonment.

AGN 391, No. 1; García 28: 98; Medina, *México*, 116.

Enriquez, Benito: former r. Caracas or Maracaibo; 1649 proceso. Judaizante.

AGN 503, No. 7

Enriquez, Blanca: b. Seville; daughter of Francisco Lopez and Clara Enriquez; m. Antonio Rodriguez Arias; mother of Diego Rodriguez Arias, Micaela Enriquez, Rafaela, Catalina, and Juana. AGN procesos refer to her and her husband as "famous rabbis and dogmatists." Observer of Mosaic laws; relaxed in effigy in 1649 auto.

Abec.; Liebman, *Guide;* AGN 399, No. 3; AGN 404, Nos. 2, 3; AGN 405, Nos. 1, 9, 10; AGN 414, No. 2; AGN 415, No. 1; AGN 419, No. 38; AGN 427, No. 4; AGN 453, fol. 79; Medina, *México* 205.

Enriquez, Blanca: 50; b. Lisbon; r. Veracruz; daughter of Francisco Lopez Enriquez of Lisbon; m. Fernando Rodriguez; mother of Fernando Fernandez, Beatriz Henriquez (Enriquez), Clara Enriquez, Bachiller Rodrigo Fernandez Correa, Geronimo Miguel, (Jeronimo) Fernandez Correa, Isabel, Ana, and Francisco Lopez Correa; arrested in 1644. Judaizante; died in the secret cells; relaxed in effigy on April 11, 1649.

Abec.; AGN 404, No. 1; AGN 405, Nos. 6, 9; AGN 406, No. 1; AGN 414, Nos. 2, 6A; AGN 415, Nos. 3, 5; AGN 453, fol. 464; AGN 413, many fols.; AGN 499, fol. 130; Medina, *México* 408.

Enriquez, Blanca. *See* Pedro Lopez de Morales.

Enriquez, Catalina: b. Seville; daughter of Simon Paiba and Beatriz Enriquez de la Paiba; m. Manuel de Lucena; mother of Clara, Felipe, and Tomas. Observer of Mosaic laws; life imprisonment, reconciled, abjuration de vehementi.

Abec.; AGN 152, No. 4; Garcia 5:97; Toro, *Judíos* 11.

Enriquez, Catalina: age 80; b. Seville; daughter of Rodrigo Fernandez Salseda, merchant, and Inez Lopez, reconciled in Seville and later relaxed for having concealed Jews and being suspected of being a relapsa; both parents were Portuguese; widow of Pedro Arias Maldonado, b. Osuna, Andalucia, a merchant in Veracruz and Havana. Judío; died in the Inquisition cells; reconciled in effigy in the 1649 auto.

Abec.; AGN 399, No. 11; AGN 405, No. 1; AGN 414, No. 10; AGN 433, No. 7 [for Pedro Arias Maldonado]; Medina, *México*

202, 203. A major part of her proceso is at the Huntington Library; part of it is at AGN.

Enriquez, Catalina: b. la Torre de Moncorbo, Portugal; m. Francisco Nuñez; had a son, Francisco Nuñez Navarro. It is possible that she was not in New Spain in the 1640s but had been there previously.
  AGN 492, No. 5.

Enriquez, Clara: b. Fondon; daughter of New Christians; m. Francisco Mendez; mother of Justa Mendez. Observer of Mosaic laws; reconciled, confiscation of property, sanbenito, life imprisonment.
  Abec.; AGN 153, No. 7; AGN 279, No. 9; García 5:96; Medina, *México* 112, 124; Toro, *Judíos* 63.

Enriquez, Clara: daughter of Manuel de Lucena, relaxed in auto of 1596, and Catalina Enriquez, reconciled and freed in 1605; single. Observer of Mosaic laws.
  AGN 279, No. 9; *Procesos de Luis de Carvajal*.

Enriquez, Clara a. Clara a. la de Acosta: b. Veracruz, where she died; daughter of Fernando Rodriguez, b. Aveiro, Portugal, and reconciled in 1647 auto, and Blanca Enriquez, b. Lisbon and relaxed in effigy in 1649; single. Judaizante and observer of Mosaic laws; relaxed in effigy.
  Bocanegra; Medina, *México* 117, 408.

Enriquez (Henriquez), Clara: testimony against her in 1642. Judaizante.
  AGN 391, No. 10.

Enriquez, Clara. *See* Clara Antuñez.

Enriquez, Diego: b. Seville, son of Beatriz Enriquez de la Paiba and Simon Paiba; single. Judaizante and heresy; reconciled in 1590 auto; abjuration de vehementi, exiled. Rearrested in 1595 as a relapso, observer of Mosaic laws; ordered to the stake December 8, 1596. When informed on the evening of December 7, 1596 that he was to be burned the following day, he stated that "he wanted to die in the laws of Moses given by God." At dawn, however he took the cross and the garrote.
  García 5:105; Liebman, *Guide* 1048; Toro, *Judíos* 59. There is no record of the location of the proceso.

Enriquez, Gabriel: Portuguese; single; 1595 proceso. Judaizante.
  AGN 153, No. 2.

Enriquez, Gabriel. *See* Francisco Lopez Enriquez.

Enriquez, Guillermo: foreigner; denounced in 1690. Not wearing a sanbenito after reconciliation and for wearing silk.
  AGN 435, No. 13.

Enriquez, Guiomar: accused in 1642. Judaizante.

    AGN 407, No. 10.

Enriquez, Guiomar. *See* Juan Duarte a. Duarte Fernandez.

Enriquez, Isabel a. Isabel de la Huerta: b. Málaga, Spain, ca. 1607; daughter of Juan Mendez de Escobar, who was b. in San Vicente Davera and died in Texcoco, Mexico, and Ana Lopez de Chavez, who was b. in Osma, Galicia, and died in Puebla; r. Puebla; m. first Melchor Rodriguez de Huerta, then Pedro Gutierrez de Peralta. Judío and observer of Mosaic laws; called La Rosa among the Jews; imprisoned by the Holy Office between 1642 and 1647; reconciled in auto of January 23, 1647; confiscation of property, sanbenito, 100 lashes, life imprisonment in Spain; abjuration de vehementi.

    AGN 391, No. 10; AGN 393, No. 3; AGN 404, No. 5; AGN 414, Nos. 3, 10; AGN 415 Nos. 2, 6; AGN 418, No. 10; AGN 425, No. 12; García 28:114.

Enriquez, Isabel. *See* Francisco Lopez Enriquez.

Enriquez, Jeronimo: r. Zacatecas 1608. Suspicion of judío.

    AGN 283, No. 38.

Enriquez, Juana: 40; b. Seville; daughter of Blanca Enriquez and Antonio Rodriguez Arias; m. Simon Vaez Sevilla; mother of Gaspar Vaez Sevilla, hoped to be the Messiah, and of Leonor Vaez. Observer of Mosaic laws; arrested 1643; tortured twice; reconciled in 1649 auto, confiscation of property, sanbenito, life imprisonment, abjuration de vehementi.

    Abec.; AGN 381, No. 7; AGN 390, No. 11; AGN 400, No. 1; AGN 488, No. 5; Guijo, 40, 46; Medina, *México* 203.

Enriquez, Juana: r. Veracruz; m.. Anton Vaez; arrested in 1645; denounced by Antonio Mendez Chillon. Judaizante.

    AGN 381, No. 7; AGN 706, No. 48.

Enriquez, Leonor: testimony against her in 1645. Judaizante; reconciled; penanced in 1648 auto.

    AGN 421, No. 11; Medina, *México* 193, 195.

Enriquez, Louisa. *See* Duarte de Torres.

Enriquez, Manuel: 1646 proceso. Judaizante.

    AGN 413, No. 51.

Enriquez, Maria. *See* Maria Henriquez.

Enriquez, Micaela: 28; b. Mexico; daughter of Blanca Enriquez and Antonio Rodriguez Arias; m. Sebastian Cardoso. Observer of Mosaic laws; reconciled in 1648 auto, abjuration de vehementi, confiscation of property, sanbenito, life imprisonment.

Abec.; García 28:243; AGN 397, No. 2; AGN 405, Nos. 2, 9; AGN 406, No. 1; AGN 413, fols. 148-150; AGN 414, Nos. 3, 4, 6, 10; AGN 415, Nos. 1, 3; AGN 417, No. 16; AGN 418, no. 10; AGN 415, No. 12; AGN 453, fol. 430; AGN 483, fol. 381. Liebman, *Guide* 1135. Medina, *México* 119, 195, 218.

Enriquez, Pedro: b. Fondon; son of Simon Paiba and Beatriz Enriquez de la Paiba; single. Heresy and judío; reconciled in 1596 auto, 100 lashes, confiscation of property, five years in galleys without pay, sanbenito except when oarsman in galleys.

Abec.; AGN 154, No. 4; AGN 223, No. 32; García 5:100.

Enriquez, Pedro: denounced in 1629 by the comisario in Texcoco. Judaizante.

AGN 366 Texcoco.

Enriquez, Rafael: testimony by Clara Texoso. Judaizante.

AGN 405, No. 4.

Enriquez (Henriquez) Rafaela: b. Seville ca. 1605; daughter of Blanca Enriquez and Antonio Rodriguez Arias; m. Gaspar Juarez; mother of Blanca Juarez. Observer of Mosaic laws, reconciled in 1648 auto, confiscation of property, sanbenito, life imprisonment in Spain; abjuration de vehementi.

AGN 392, No. 5; AGN 402, No. 1; AGN 405, No. 8; AGN 413, fols. 54-60; Abec.; García 28:247; Liebman, *Guide;* AGN 415, fol. 76; AGN 417, No. 18; AGN 426, fol. 417; AGN 453, fol. 336; Liebman, *Guide* 1135, 1137; Medina, *México* 119, 195, 218.

Enriquez de Lineo, Gonzalo. *See* Alvaro Diez de Linio.

Enriquez Montillo, Diego. *See* Jorge Ramarez Montilla.

Enriquez de la Paiba, Beatriz. *See* Beatriz Enriquez.

Enriquez Saz, Pedro: 1596 testimony. Judío.

Martínez del Río 163.

Enriquez de Silva, Catalina. *See* Catalina de Silva Enriquez.

Enriquez de Silva, Francisco: no proceso against him but he denounced Duarte de Leon in 1639.

AGN 495, No. 14.

Enriquez de Silva, Isabel. *See* Isabel de Silva.

Enriquez Texoso, Beatriz. *See* Beatriz Texoso.

Ermitaño, Juan de Jesus Maria: a hermit. Judaizante; reconciled.

AHN 1738.

Espana, Simon de: testimony given by Luis Nuñez Perez in 1642. Judaizante.

AGN 414, fol. 119.

Espejo, Miguel de: r. Jalapa; 1755 proceso. Suspicion of judío.

AGN 978, No. 23.

Esperanza, Jeronima. *See* Esperanza Jeronima.

Espina, Isabel de: testimony by Thomas Nuñez Peralta in 1642. Judaizante.

AGN 415, fol. 323.

Espinola, Agustin de: b. Mexico; merchant; 1778 proceso. Suspicion of judaizante; seen attending synagogue in Kingston, Jamaica.

AGN 1133, No. 18.

Espinosa, Ana: b. Mexico; m. Juan Juarez de Figueroa; mother of Simon Juarez de Espinoza, Judaizante and observer of Mosaic laws.

González Obregón, *México* 693; Liebman, *Guide* 1109.

Espinosa, Bernardina de: b. Casteloblanco; m. Simon Rodriguez; mother of Pedro Espinoza.

Abec.

Espinosa, Clara de: testimony by Catalina de Silva Enriquez. Judaizante.

AGN 404, No. 1.

Espinosa, Francisco de: son of Simon Rodriguez; reconciliado; denounced by Cristobal Espinosa. Wearing silk.

AGN 339, No. 42.

Espinosa, Isabel de: arrested in 1642. Judaizante and observer of Mosaic laws.

AGN 393, No. 9; AGN 404, Nos. 1, 3; AGN 405, No. 69; AGN 406, fol. 46; AGN 415, fols. 380, 465; AGN 417, fol. 545.

Espinosa, Jorge a. Jorge Serrano. Judío; reconciled in the 1639 auto in Lima, 200 lashes, imprisonment in Spain; on his way to Spain escaped to Jamaica, then to Mexico where he became chief constable of Cuazualco. Rearrested ca. 1644 as relapso; reconciled in 1650.

AGN 406, No. 1; AGN 416, No. 41; Lewin, *Inquisición* 312-314; Medina, *México* 243.

Espinoza, Maria de: b. Spain; r. near Queretaro; m. Francisco Rodriguez. Descendant of Jews.

AGN 313, No. 5.

Espinoza, Pedro: age 45; b. Mexico; son of Simon Rodriguez, who was also reconciled, and of Bernardina de Espinosa, b. Burgos, Castile; m. Isabel Enriquez de Silva; administrator of the butcher shops in Sayula. Judaizante and observer of Mosaic laws; read the *Espejo de Consolación,* a revered book among the secret Jews; reconciled in 1646 auto; confiscation of property, sanbenito, abjuration de vehementi.

    Abec.; AGN 403, No. 1; AGN 498, No. 1; García 28:80; Medina, *México* 115, 193, 194.

Espinoza, Simon de. *See* Simon Diaz de Espinosa.

Esteves, Juana. *See* Francisco Lopez Diaz.

Fajardo, Gregorio. Judaizante.

    AGN 303, No. 67.

Farinas, Jose: b. Valladolid; 1785 proceso. Judío.

    AGN 1032, No. 7.

Febo, Catalina. *See* Francisco Febo.

Febo, Francisco; age 69; Portuguese; son of Juan Rodriguez Nuñez de Castro and Catalina Febo; single; died in secret cells. Observer of Mosaic laws; relaxed in effigy in 1649 auto.

    Abec.; AHN 1738, No. 1.

Felipe, Diego. Suspicion of judío.

    AGN 317, No. 32.

Fernan, Bartolome: Flemish; 1610 proceso. Suspicion of judaizante.

    AGN 473, fol. 248.

Fernandez. *See also* Hernandez.

Fernandez, Ana: b. Moral; r. Veracruz; m. Manuel Xuarez; aunt of Ana Gomez Botello. Judaizante; deceased; relaxed in effigy in 1635.

    Abec.; AGN 381, No. 5; AGN 382, No. 4; Medina, *México* 185.

Fernandez, Ana: m. Fernando Franco; mother of Francisca Franco. Judaizante.

    Abec.

Fernandez, Ana (b. Camiña). *See* Francisco Franco de Morera.

Fernandez, Antonio: Portuguese; r. San Luis Potosi; 1626 proceso. Suspicion of judaizante.

    AGN 1552, fol. 100.

Fernandez, Antonio. *See* Juan Duarte a. Duarte Fernandez.

Fernandez, Antonio: Portuguese; r. Tlaxcala; accused along with his wife in 1597 proceso. Judaizante; 1604 proceso: suspicion of judío.

    AGN 160, No. A; AGN 274, No. 2.

Fernandez, Beatriz: 1642 testimony. Judaizante.

    AGN 391, No. 10.

Fernandez, Clara. *See* Francisco Nieto Ramos.

Fernandez, Diego: testimony by Nuño de Figueroa a. Nuño Pereira in 1642. Judaizante.

AGN 413, No. 19.

Fernandez, Domingo: b. La Torre de Moncorbo; 1635 proceso. Heretical judaizante and observer of Mosaic laws; confessed; died in cells; reconciled in effigy in 1635.

Abec.; González Obregón, *México* 692.

Fernandez, Duarte. *See* Juan Duarte.

Fernandez, Enrique (Henrique): age 38; b. Villa de Santa Maria, Portugal; son of Simon Fernandez, cloth weaver, and Ana Rodriguez, b. Cea; both parents were Hebrew New Christians; brother of Isabel Nuñez; uncle of Simon Fernandez de Torres, b. Gobea, Portugal; r. Guadalajara; merchant; single. Judío and observer of Mosaic laws; reconciled as judaizante in 1646 auto; died in the secret cells; relaxed in effigy after his bones were disinterred in 1649 auto.

Abec.; AGN 392, No. 17; AGN 404, No. 1; AGN 405, No. 9; AGN 415, No. 5; Medina, *Mexico* 205. Most of the proceso is at the Gilcrease Institute.

Fernandez, Francisco. Judaizante.

AGN 223, No. 35 only has accusation and a copy of a letter from the Holy Office requesting information.

Fernandez, Gaspar. *See* Maria Rodriguez.

Fernandez, Isabel. *See* Francisco Botello.

Fernandez, Isabel. *See* Jeronimo Nuñez.

Fernandez, Isabel. *See* Luis Fernandez Tristan.

Fernandez, Jorge: testimony by Nuño de Figueroa a. Nuño Pereira in 1642. Judaizante.

AGN 413, No. 19.

Fernandez, Jose a. Jorge Fernandez: b. Salceda. Judío; reconciled 1601; confiscation of property, sanbenito, jail; confessed and took the cross after torture and was spared the stake.

Abec. AGN 160, No. 2; AGN 164, No. 7; AGN 254A, No. 10; AGN 271, No. 1; AGN 279, No. 9; Medina, *México* 159.

Fernandez, Jose Antonio: soldier. Circumcised and never baptized.

AGN 1203, No. 22.

Fernandez, Juan: testimony against him in 1602. Being the son of a reconciled person and for wearing silk.

AGN 452, fol. 207.

Fernandez, Luis. *See* Diego Nuñez a. Diego Pacheco.

Fernandez, Manuel: silversmith; 1616 proceso. Suspicion of judaizante.
Abec.; AGN 312, No. 11.

Fernandez, Simon. *See* Enrique Fernandez.

Fernandez, Simon. *See* Pedro Lopez a. Simon Fernandez.

Fernandez, Simon a. Simon Fernandez de Torres: age 36; b. Gobea,
Portugal; son of Diego Antuñez and Isabel Nuñez; merchant; r. Guadalajara. Observer of Mosaic laws; reconciled in 1646, sanbenito,
confiscation of property, abjuration de vehementi, jail for two years,
exile from the Indies, Madrid, and Seville.
    AGN 404, No. 1; AGN 405, No. 2; AGN 413, fols. 114, 115,
    250-258; AGN 414, No. 3, fol. 460; AGN 415, fols. 47, 448;
    AGN 453, fol. 85; AGN 503, No. 34.

Fernandez, Violante. *See* Gaspar Suarez.

Fernandez Angel, Luis: r. Maracaibo or Caracas; 1642 proceso. Judaizante.
    AHN 1738, exp. 1.

Fernandez Barraun, Manuel. *See* Juan Mendez (b. Sossel).

Fernandez Cardado, Antonio: b. Moral; son of Portuguese parents, both
reconciled; r. Pachuca; merchant; reputed to be very rich. Observer
of Mosaic laws; reconciled on April 2, 1635, confiscation of property, sanbenito, 200 lashes, five years in galleys.
    Abec.; AGN 381, No. 5; Medina, *México* 184.

Fernandez Cardado, Diego. *See* Isabel Nuñez.

Fernandez de Castro, Pedro a. Juan Fernandez de Castro: age 34; b.
Valladolid; son of Licenciado don Ignacio Aguado, a descendant of
Portuguese New Christians, b. Valladolid and attorney for the Royal
Chancery, and Mariana de Castro, b. Palencia, Spain; circumcised;
merchant; r. Mines of Chichicapa; m. Leonor Vaez, natural daughter
of Simon Vaez Sevilla, who resided in Pisa, Italy, and practiced
Judaism openly. Observer of Mosaic laws; reconciled in 1647 auto,
sanbenito, confiscation of property, abjuration de vehementi, life
imprisonment, 200 lashes, five years in galleys.
    Abec.; AGN 406, No. 1; AGN 409, No. 4; AGN 414, No. 6; AGN
    415, fols. 86, 328, 530; Liebman, *Jews* 76, 265; Medina, *México*
    117, 194.

Fernandez Chillon, Antonio. *See* Leonor Agurto.

Fernandez Correa, Geronimo (Jeronimo): b. Veracruz; son of Fernando
Rodriguez and Blanca Enriquez; r. San Francisco de Campeche; mer-

chant; single; had been a captain in the Spanish infantry. Judío; reconciled in 1647 auto, sanbenito, confiscation of property, abjuration de vehementi, jail for six months, exile.

Abec.; AGN 399, No. 12; AGN 404, No. 2; AGN 419, No. 37; García 28:113; Medina, *México* 116, 194. [Campeche was a port used for smuggling and for the entry of illegal immigrants: Geronimo was there to aid their entry and transport them to the outskirts of Veracruz.]

Fernandez Correa, Rodrigo: age 23; b. Veracruz; son of Fernando Rodriguez and Blanca Enriquez; circumcised; r. San Francisco de Campeche; single; bachiller of medicine. Judío and observer of Mosaic laws; reconciled in 1647 auto with other members of his family, abjuration de vehementi, sanbenito, confiscation of property, his medical degree was revoked and he was prohibited from ever practicing medicine, exile.

Abec.; AGN 399, No. 12; AGN 419, No. 41; García 28:128; Medina, *México* 194.

Fernandez de Elvas, Diego: died in cells. Relapso; bones were disinterred; relaxed in effigy.

Medina, *México* 195.

Fernandez de Fonseca, Miguel: no proceso. Judaizante.

AGN 413, No. 22.

Fernandez de Leon, Juan. *See* Joseph de San Ignacio.

Fernandez Pereyra, Ruy: 1644 proceso. Judaizante.

AGN 419, No. 18.

Fernandez Salseda, Rodrigo. *See* Inez Lopez and Catalina Enriquez.

Fernandez de Torres, Simon. *See* Simon Fernandez.

Fernandez Tristan; Captain Luis: b. Seville; son of Tristan Manuel (sic) and Isabel Fernandez, both b. Lisbon and Hebrew New Christians; brother of Violante Rodriguez; merchant; m. his niece Isabel Tristan (daughter of his sister Clara Tristan and Simon Lopez), relaxed alive in the 1649 auto; died at sea on a return trip to Mexico from the Philippines. Observer of Mosaic laws and dogmatist; relaxed in effigy in 1649 auto.

AGN 399, No. 13; AGN 414, fol. 284; Medina, *México* 205.

Ferreira, Andres: a clergyman; denounced by Manuel Gil de la Guarda in 1601. Judaizante.

AGN 256, No. 15N.

Figueroa, Isabel. *See* Nuño de Figueroa.

Figueroa, Juan de: denounced in 1611 by the comisario of Taxco. Judaizante.

    AGN 291, No. 5.

Figueroa, Nuño de a. Nuño de Pereira: age 39; b. Lisbon; son of Antonio de Tabera, b. Lisbon, and Isabel Figueroa, b. Hielbes [sic]; both parents died in Lisbon and both were Hebrew New Christians; circumcised; r. Guadalajara; merchant; single. Observer of Mosaic laws; tortured and confessed, reconciled in 1646 auto, confiscation of property, 200 lashes, abjuration de vehementi, exile.

    Abec.; AGN 392, No. 17; AGN 413, No. 19; AGN 415, Nos. 5, 6; AHN 1738, No. 1; García 28:78; Medina, *México* 115, 193.

Figueroa, Ponce de Leon Alvaro Ignacio de: Portuguese; 1714 proceso. Signs or marks of being judío.

    AGN 753, No. 4.

Flores, Diego: b. Fondon; encomendero in Xuchipilia, bishopric of Guadalajara. Suspicion of judío.

    Abec.; AGN 152, No. 1; Toro, *Judíos* 11.

Flores, Domingo: r. Tlaxcala; 1643 proceso. Suspicion of judío.

    AGN 418, No. 7.

Flores, Gonzalo a. Gonzalo Vaez Mendez: age 44; b. La Torre de Moncorbo; son of Francisco Vaez Mendez and Mari Diaz Flores, both also b. in La Torre de Moncorbo; merchant; single. Arrested in 1643; feigned insanity; demanded Jewish rations, new pots, and oil for cooking. Judaizante and observer of Mosaic laws; relaxed alive in 1649 auto.

    AGN 413, fols. 136-140; AHN 1738, No. 1; Medina, *México* 204.

Flores, Juan: r. Michoacan. Suspicion of judío in 1616.

    AGN 304, No. 29. *See also* Diego Fuentes.

Flores Ballinas, Juan: Portuguese, r. Chiapas; named with his wife and others in a 1667 proceso. Suspicion of judaizante.

    AGN 606, No. 7.

Fondevilla, Francisco de: Portuguese; r. Michoacan; 1637 accusation from the comisario in Michoacan. Suspicion of judaizante.

    AGN 376, No. 27.

Fonseca, Antonio de: accused in 1596 by Diego Nieto. Judaizante.

    AGN 159, No. 4.

Fonseca, Francisco de: 1646 proceso. Judaizante.

    AGN 425, No. 6.

Fonseca, Gaspar de a. Gaspar Mendez: b. Lisbon; r. Axutla, where he died; merchant; single. Observer of Mosaic laws; relaxed in effigy in 1649 auto.

> AGN 414, fol. 210. Most of the proceso is at the Huntington Library.

Fonseca, Hector de: b. Viseu, Portugal; r. Taxco; miner. Judaizante; reconciled in 1601 auto.

> Abec.; AGN 158, No. 1; AGN 271, No. 1; AGN 276, No. 14; AGN 279, No. 9; Medina, *México* 159; proceso at the American Jewish Historical Society according to PAJHS, vol. 9, p. viii.

Fonseca, Simon de: testimony of Luis Nuñez Perez. Judaizante.

> AGN 414, fol. 41.

Fonseca, Tomas de: b. Freyja Espadacinto; r. Tapujagua; miner. Judaizante.

> Abec. (which states case suspended; reopened about 1600; reconciled in 1601); AGN 158, No. 3; Liebman, *Guide* 1085; Medina, *México* 158 (which states "light punishment but life imprisonment since he was 80 years old"); *Libro Primero de Votos* 128, 153-54, 157-58, 184-85, 206-07, 213 (states first vote was reconsidered; abjuration de vehementi, fined 300 pesos); Toro, *Judíos* 12.

Fonseca, Tomas de a. Tomas Fonseca Castellanos: b. Visseu, Portugal; r. Taxco; commercial dealer and miner; arrested in 1590, but case suspended; rearrested in 1599. Judío and being a supporter and concealer of Jews. Relapso; relaxed alive in 1601 auto.

> Abec.; AGN 127, No. 1; AGN 156, No. 4; AGN 349, fols. 1-15; Liebman, *Guide* 1086; Medina, *México* 109, 160, 161; Toro, *Judíos* 12 (which gives 1595 as year of the first arrest).

Fonseca y Andrada, Manuel de. *See* Manuel Tavares.

Fonseca Enriquez, Simon del: previously reconciled for suspicion of judaizante. Relapso; relaxed in effigy.

> Medina, *México* 195.

Francis, Isabel de: 1642 proceso. Judaizante.

> AGN 453, fol. 485.

Francis, Maria de: 1642 proceso. Judaizante.

> AGN 453, fol. 487.

Franco, Fernando. *See* Ana Fernandez.

Franco, Francisca. *See* Ana Fernandez.

Franco, Hernando. *See* Francisco Franco de Morera.

Franco, Juan: jeweler. Sorcery, but trial revealed that he had been circumcised and his food prepared according to Mosaic laws; public and spiritual penance and fine.

> Abec. (which states that he was a cripple and cites the charge as blasphemy); AGN 38, No. 1; Greenleaf, *Mexican Inquisition* 113, 114, 117.

Franco, Juan: r. Nicaragua; mine operator; associate of Carlos Mala Espina; 1768 proceso. Judío and heresy.

> AGN 611, No. 4.

Franco, Miguel: b. Avieto, Portugal; doctor. Suspicion of judío; public penance, abjuration de vehementi, fine of 100 pesos.

> Abec.; AGN (Riva Palacio) 18, No. 5.

Franco de Morera, Francisco: age 46; b. Camiña, Portugal; son of Hernando Franco, b. Cobas, two leagues from Camiña, and Ana Fernandez, b. Camiña; circumcised; merchant; single; lived with great circumspection and apart from any of the Jewish communities in Mexico. Judío and observer of Mosaic laws; tortured; reconciled in 1647 auto, abjuration de vehementi, sanbenito, life imprisonment.

> Abec.; AHN 1738, No. 1; García 28:111; Medina, *México* 116, 194.

Franco, Pedro: denounced in 1606. Porging sheep.

> AGN 471, No. 28.

Frayle, Francisco: 1642 proceso; probably a fugitive. Judaizante.

> AGN 413, No. 19.

Fuentes, Diego a. Diego Duarte a. Juan Flores: r. Guadalajara. Judaizante.

> AGN 344, No. 2.

Gabriel, "Fulano" a. el Mozo: r. Real de Cuencame; 1625 proceso. Judaizante.

> AGN 510, No. 85.

Gama, Antonio de. *See* Catalina de Campos.

Gama, Blanca de: testimony against her after her death. Judaizante.

> AGN 391, No. 10.

Garcia, Francisco: 1722 proceso. Acts about rents and debts due him "a heretical apostate and Jew"; reconciled in effigy in Seville.

> AGN 796, No. 10.

Garcia, Ines: r. Celaya; 1614 testimony on Jewish affiliation.

> AGN 278, No. 12.

Garcia del Brocel, Juan: r. Puebla; 1649 proceso. Judaizante.

> AGN 503, No. 7.

Garcia Cabezuelo, Antonio: testimony against him in 1627. Suspicion of judío.

>AGN 360, fols. 181-195.

Garcia el Conde, Juan. *See* Alvaro Diez de Lineo.

Garcia de Santa Ana, Juan a. Juan Garcia de la Soria: r. Aguascalientes; denounced in 1604. Suspicion of judaizante.

>AGN 368, No. 78.

Garcia de la Soria, Juan. *See* Juan Garcia de Santa Ana.

Garcia de la Vega, Ana: m. Domingo Perez. Judío and judaizante; abjuration de vehementi, green cross.

>AHN 1030, fol. 274r.

Geronyma de Silva, Esperanza. *See* Esperanza Jeronima.

Gerrera, Cristobal de: Portuguese; r. Zacatecas; parents had died in Inquisition cells while awaiting trial. Descendant of Jews.

>AGN 356, fol. 154.

Gerrera, Luis de a. Simon Luis de Herrera y Enriquez: b. Seville; circumcised; formerly reconciled by the Holy Office of Seville for judío; rearrested 1690. Judaizante; reconciled in 1692 or 1696, abjuration de vehementi, confiscation of one-fourth of property, life imprisonment in Spain.

>Abec.; AGN 511, No. 1; AGN 682, No. 24.

Gierra, Bernabe. *See* Isabel de Ocampo.

Gil de la Guarda Manuel. *See* Andres Ferreira.

Gogorron, Palomeno: denounced in 1626. Descendant of Jews.

>AGN 1552, fol. 229. [In 1646 Antonio Arismena Gogorron testified against Maria de Aguilar, Pablo de Sola, and Francisco Lopez Lobo: AGN 425, No. 5.]

Gois de Matos, Fernando. *See* Francisco de Matos.

Gomez, Alberto Moisen. *See* Fernando de Medina.

Gomez, Ana: b. Madrid ca. 1606; daughter of Leonor Nuñez and Diego Fernandez Cardado; sister of Isabel Nuñez and half-sister of Maria Gomez; m. Gaspar Alvarez. Observer of Mosaic laws; reconciled in 1635 auto, jail for one year; rearrested as a relapsa; relaxed alive in 1649 auto.

>Abec.; AGN 381, No. 5; AGN 389, No. 10; AGN 404, No. 5; AGN 414, No. 2; Medina, *México* 119, 185.

Gomez, Ana. *See* Ana Gomez Botello.

Gomez, Ana. *See* Diego Diaz.

Gomez, Antonia. Observer of Mosaic laws; reconciled in 1648 auto.

AGN 416, No. 41; Medina, *México* 194. *See also* Sebastian Cardoso.

Gomez, Antonio: b. Villa Nueva de Poliman of Alberquez; merchant or innkeeper, Judaizante and observer of Mosaic laws; tortured; reconciled in 1601 auto.

    Abec.; AGN 160, Nos. 2, 13; AGN 254A, No. 40; AGN 285, No. 67 (petition to go to Amozoc to arrange his affairs).

Gomez, Antonio: b. Fondon; merchant; 1601 auto. Observer of Mosaic laws; the inquisitors noted that the charges had not been proved; five years in galleys, abjuration de levi, exile from New Spain.

    Abec.; AGN 279, No. 9.

Gomez, Bartolome: testimony by Catalina Enriquez; not found by the Inquisition.

    AGN 404, No. 1.

Gomez, Beatriz. *See* Tome Gomez.

Gomez, Catalina a. "la Cartuja." Observer of Mosaic laws; reconciled in 1648 auto.

    Medina, *México* 194.

Gomez, Cristobal: r. Los Reyes (sic); owned hacienda. Observer of Mosaic laws; relaxed in effigy in 1601.

    AGN 223, fol. 456; AGN 452, fol. 136; Medina, *México* 162.

Gomez, Diego: 1598 proceso. Judaizante.

    AGN 223, fol. 499.

Gomez, Duarte: r. Guatemala; denounced in 1627. Suspicion of judío.

    AGN 360, fol. 567.

Gomez, Francisco. *See* Thomas Lopez Monforte.

Gomez, Francisco Alvaro: r. Maracaibo. Judío.

    AHN 1738, No. 1.

Gomez, Garcia. Observer of Mosaic laws; reconciled in 1648 auto.

    Medina, *México* 194.

Gomez, Gonzalo: b. ca. 1490; r. Michoacan. Judaizante; reconciled, fined 400 gold pesos.

    AGN 2, No. 2; Greenleaf, *Mexican Inquisition* 46-72; Toro, *Judíos* 94.

Gomez, Ines. *See* Ana de Campos.

Gomez, Isabel. *See* Juan Gonzalez.

Gomez, Isabel. *See* Luis Mezquita Sarmiento and Francisco Amezquita.

Gomez, Juan: r. Puebla; m. Ana Lopez de Chavez. Heretical judaizante; died; relaxed in effigy.

    González Obregón, *México* 705.

Gomez, Maria: b. Mexico in 1616; daughter of Leonor Nuñez and Pedro Lopez a. Simon Fernandez; sister of Francisco Lopez Blandon; half-sister of Ana Gomez and Isabel Nuñez; sister-in-law of Luis Perez Roldan; m. Tomas Treviño de Sobremonte; had five children, two of whom were Rafael de Sobremonte and Leonor Martinez; arrested in 1635. Observer of Mosaic laws; reconciled; rearrested in 1644; relaxed in 1649 auto with her husband and other members of her family. [In the *Relación* of the 1649 auto, Bocanegra wrote that as she and other members of her family were at the platform of the stakes, they desired to give each other "el osculo de pas al modo Judaico," the kiss of peace in the Judaic manner. There is only one other instance known to this author in which the "kiss of peace" was referred to by the Inquisition and that was at the auto-da-fé in Lima on January 23, 1639, when Manuel Bautista Perez and his two brothers-in-law exchanged such kisses before they went to the funeral pyre. In Mexico, the ministers of the Holy Office restrained Maria and her family from this last mortal show of affection.]

    Abec.; AGN 381, Nos. 5, 9; AGN 426, No. 10; Liebman, *Jews* chapters 10-12, Medina, *México* 119, 185.

Gomez, Morales. *See* Fernando de Medina.

Gomez, Pedro. *See* Duarte Rodriguez a. Duarte Rodriguez Tejoso.

Gomez, Tome (Thome): age 45; b. Casteloblanco; son of Manuel Rodriguez, formerly of Seville and reconciled by the Holy Office, and Beatriz Gomez; r. Guadalajara; merchant; m. Catalina de Samaniego, b. Ahuacatlan, New Galicia, a province in New Spain. Judío and observer of Mosaic laws; confessed; reconciled on April 16, 1646, sanbenito, confiscation of property, abjuration de vehementi, 200 lashes, life imprisonment.

    Abec.; AGN 404, No. 4; AGN 405, No. 9; AGN 415, No. 3; García 28:88.

Gomez de Acosta, Manuel: r. Veracruz; 1635 proceso. Heretical judaizante.

    AGN 670, No. 83.

Gomez Alvarez, Francisco: r. Caracas or Maracaibo.

    AHN 1738, exp. 1.

Gomez Botello, Ana a. Ana Gomez: b. Villa de Riego; r. Pachuca; niece of Francisco Botello and of Ana Fernandez, the wife of Manuel Xuarez; m. Simon Burgos. Observer of Mosaic laws; reconciled in 1635 auto, abjuration de vehementi.

Abec.; AGN 381, No. 5 [where her name appears as Portillo]; Medina, *México* 185.

Gomez Cardoso, Rafael: accused in 1642. Judaizante.

AGN 453, fol. 34.

Gomez Carballo, Antonio: 1642 proceso. Judaizante.

AGN 453, fol. 39.

Gomez de Lima, Pedro: accused in 1649. Judaizante.

AGN 503, fol. 7.

Gomez Lobo, Luis: testimony by Maria de Rivera in 1642. Judaizante.

AGN 425, No. 12.

Gomez de Medina, Francisco. *See* Francisco Medina.

Gomez Navarro, Manuel: b. San Martin, Portugal. Judío.

Abec.; AGN 151, No. 6; Liebman, *Jews* 174-76; Martínez del Río, 122 (says relaxed alive); Medina, *México* 124 (states b. on frontier with Spain; sentenced 200 lashes, 6 years as galley slave, then life imprisonment in Seville).

Gomez Navarro, Maria: sister of Manuel Gomez Navarro. A proceso was started against her in 1593, and information was sought from other tribunals. Judaizante.

AGN 223, No. 32.

Gomez Pereira, Diego: Portuguese; r. Zacatecas; accused in 1626. Circumcised.

AGN 356, fol. 157.

Gomez de Silva: age 52; b. Herrera, Extramadura; son of Simon Lopez and Isabel of Casteloblanco; m. Elena de Silva; his daughter Isabel m. Antonio Carvallo. Judaizante; reconciled in auto of 1649, confiscation of property, sanbenito, abjuration de vehementi, jail for two years, exile from the Indies, Madrid, and Seville.

AGN 405, No. 2; AGN 405, No. 3 and fol. 505; AGN 415, fol. 402; AGN 417, fol. 528; Medina, *México* 203.

Gomez Silvera, Manuel: b. Morón; r. Sultepec. Observer of Mosaic laws and heretical judaizante; reconciled in 1601, 100 lashes, five years in galleys.

Abec. [cites b. Castile]; Medina, *México* 159; Toro, *Judíos* 63.

Gomez Texoso, Francisco: age 58; b. Valencia; son of Pedro Gomez Texoso and Violante Rodriguez; circumcised; r. Veracruz; captain of infantry, then a merchant; single; his grandmother gave him the name "Sad Manuel" because she foresaw that his days would be sad. Judío and observer of Mosaic laws; reconciled in 1646 auto, confiscation of property, sanbenito, abjuration de vehementi, life imprisonment, exile.

> AGN 414, No. 4; AGN 415, fol. 606; AGN 416, No. 15; AGN 453, fols. 71, 397; AGN 477, fol. 135; García 28:51; Medina, *México* 114, 193.

Gomez Texoso, Gabriel: son of Pedro Gomez Texoso and Violante Rodriguez. Observer of Mosaic laws.

> AGN 404, No. 2; AGN 415, fol. 166.

Gomez Texoso, Pedro a. Pedro Texoso: b. Seville; r. Veracruz; m. Violante Rodriguez; had nine children; d. Lima; accused in 1642. Judaizante.

> Abec.; AGN 503, No. 11.

Gomez Texoso, Rafael: b. Valencia; son of Pedro Gomez Texoso and Violante Rodriguez; single; broker acting as agent for market places; had an illegitimate daughter called Violante Texoso whose mother was Leonor de Flores; his daughter lived with him and followed his faith. Observer of Mosaic laws; died in the cells; relaxed in effigy in 1649 auto.

> Abec.; AGN 391, No. 10; AGN 405, No. 4; Medina, *México* 409.

Gonzalez, Alonso: Portuguese; servant of Alonso de Riviera. Judaizante.

> AGN 281, No. 16.

Gonzalez, Alvaro: b. Fondon; a fugitive. Judaizante; relaxed in effigy in 1601 auto.

> Abec.; AGN 161, No. 1; Medina, *México* 162.

Gonzalez, Antonio. Judaizante; reconciled.

> AHN 1738, No. 1.

Gonzalez, Beatriz: daughter of Juan Gonzalez, who had been condemned at Llerena by the Inquisition; r. Veracruz; m. Francisco Rodriguez, a barber; 1581 proceso. Judaizante.

> AGN 90, No. 38.

Gonzalez, Beatriz. *See* Diego Nuñez a. Diego Pacheco.

Gonzalez, Jose: 1700 proceso. Judaizante.

> AGN 713, No. 63.

Gonzalez, Juan: Portuguese; m. Isabel Gomez; father of Francisco Gomez Medina; denounced with his family in 1631. Judío; case suspended.

> AGN 373, No. 13.

Gonzalez, Juan. *See* Beatriz Gonzalez.

Gonzalez, Luis: mulatto; denounced in 1626. Observing Jewish rites.
  AGN 1552, fol. 155.

Gonzalez, Luis. Observer of Mosaic laws; reconciled in 1648 auto.
  Medina, *México* 194.

Gonzalez, Pedro: proceso states that he "could not eat the meat of a
  suckling pig." Suspicion of judaizante.
  AGN 435, No. 8; AGN 454, No. 18.

Gonzalez, Rufina: r. Campeche; accused in 1627. Porging.
  AGN 260, fol. 558.

Gonzalez, Simon: m. Violante Rodriguez; died prior to 1596. Judaizante.
  AGN 276, No. 14.

Gonzalez, Simon. *See* Francisco Nieto Ramos.

Gonzalez Bermegero, Garci: b. Spain. Judaizante and heresy; relaxed
  alive in 1579 auto. [He was the first Jew to be relaxed alive by order
  of the Tribunal of the Santo Oficio.]
  Abec.; AGN 59, No. 6; Liebman, *Jews* 73, 130, 139; Medina,
  México 76; Toro, *Judíos* 50.

Gonzalez de Escobar, Juan: testimony by Isabel de Silva in 1642. Judaizante.
  AGN 415, fol. 581.

Gonzalez Figueredo, Captain Diego: merchant in Veracruz; r. Orizaba.
  1691, 1693 procesos. Suspicion of judaizante.
  AGN 682, Nos. 5, 6.

Gonzalez Jamaica, Antonio: r. Veracruz; 1650 proceso. Suspicion of
  judaizante and statement about porging.
  AGN 399, No. 12; AGN 435, fol. 137.

Gonzalez de Saavedra, Andres: 1705 proceso. Suspicion of judaizante.
  AGN 546, Nos. 2, 3.

Gonzalves Sobrerro, Gaspar. *See* Elena de Silva.

Goya Matos, Fernando: testimony by Maria de Rivera in 1646. Judaizante.
  AGN 415, fol. 190; AGN 426, fol. 532.

Granada, Antonio de: 1642 testimony. Judaizante.
  AGN 391, No. 10.

Granada, Gabriel de: age 14; b. Mexico; son of Manuel de Granada,
  who died in China, and Maria de Rivera, b. Seville; grandson
  of Blanca Rivera; brother of Rafael de Granada; circumcised.
  Judaizante and observer of Mosaic laws; reconciled in 1646

auto, confiscation of property, sanbenito, jail for one year, exile from the Indies, Seville, and Madrid, abjuration de vehementi.

Abec.; AGN 405, Nos. 2, 7; AGN 413, fols. 86-88; AGN 414, fols. 141, 339; García 28:54; Medina, *México* 114, 191, 193; PAJHS, Vol. 7, 1889, has a verbatim translation of the entire proceso. [This proceso and many others (twelve boxes of originals) were taken by Colonel David Fergusson from Mexico and were destroyed by a fire in the Knox Warehouse in Seattle, Washington, in 1888.]

Granada, Isabel de: b. Spain; testimony by Isabel Tinoco and others in 1642. Judaizante.

AGN 406, fol. 51; AGN 453, fol. 471.

Granada, Manuel de: b. Seville; merchant; m. Maria de Rivera; died in China. Judío; relaxed in effigy in April 1649.

AGN 404, Nos. 1, 3; AGN 405, Nos. 6A, 9; AGN 414, Nos. 1, 3, 6, 10; AGN 415, Nos. 1, 6.

Granada, Rafael de: age 19; b. Mexico City; brother of Gabriel de Granada with the same parents and ancestry; student of rhetoric. Judaizante and observer of Mosaic laws; reconciled in 1646 auto with his brother, abjuration de vehementi, sanbenito, confiscation of property, jail for one year.

Abec.; AGN 289, No. 2; AGN 402, No. 2; AGN 404, No. 2; AGN 405, No. 2; AGN 413, fols. 89-91, 153, 154; AGN 414, fol. 135; García 28:81; Medina, *México* 191, 193.

Granados, Fabian: b. Lamego, Portugal. Heretic and judaizante; fugitive; relaxed in effigy in 1596.

Abec.; Medina, *México* 133; Toro, *Judíos* 59.

Guarda, Manuel de la: b. La Guarda; r. Manila. Observer of Mosaic laws; reconciled in 1601 auto.

AGN 160, No. 1; Toro, *Judíos* 12.

Guerra, Alonso a. Alonso Guerrera: 1599 proceso. Judaizante.

AGN 223, No. 32.

Guillermo, Juan: Irishman; r. Puebla; 1721 proceso. Suspicion of judaizante.

AGN 784, No. 3.

Gutierrez, Pedro: 1700 proceso; had been penanced by the Holy Office in Lima. Judaizante.

AGN 713, No. 59; Medina, *Lima* 2:187, 196.

Gutierrez de Peralta, Pedro: m. Isabel Enriquez a. Isabel de la Huerta, her second husband.
> García 28:114.

Guzman, Diego de. *See* Manuel Tavares.

Henero, Pedro: 1701 proceso. Judaizante.
> AGN 544, No. 22.

HENRIQUEZ. *See also* ENRIQUEZ.

Henriquez, Beatriz. Judaizante; reconciled.
> AHN 1738, exp. 1.

Henriquez, Benito: r. Maracaibo. Judío.
> AHN 1738, exp. 1.

Henriquez, Blanca: Observer of Mosaic laws; reconciled in 1648 auto.
> Medina, *México* 194.

Henriquez, Clara. *See* Clara Enriquez.

Henriquez, Guiomar: deceased. Judaizante; reconciled.
> AHN 1738, No. 1.

Henriquez, Justa: 1641 testimony by her nephew Francisco Home.
> AGN 391, No. 1.

Henriquez (Enriquez), Maria: 1642 testimony. Judaizante.
> AGN 391, No. 10.

Henriquez, Rafaela. *See* Rafaela Enriquez.

Henriquez, Vicente. *See* Francisco Home.

Heredia, Antonio de: b. Toledo; 1539 declaration. Suspicion of judío.
> AGN 40, No. 3E.

Hernandez, Beatriz: 1539 proceso. Judío.
> Greenleaf, *Zumarraga* 98 gives AGN 1, No. 19.

Hernandez, Beatriz: mother of Francisco Home; 1641 proceso. Judaizante.
> AGN 391, No. 1.

Hernandez, Beatriz. *See* Juan Mendez a. Juan Mendez de Escobar.

Hernandez, Domingo: accused in 1635. Judaizante.
> AGN 381, No. 5.

Hernandez, Enrique: testimony by Clara de Rivera. Judaizante.
> AGN 404, No. 5.

Hernandez, Felipe: shoemaker, 1606 proceso; fugitive. Judío.
> AGN 471, No. 61.

Hernandez, Francisco: brother of Manuel de Morales; m. Isabel Clara; 1595 proceso; fugitive. Judaizante; relaxed in effigy in 1601 auto.
> AGN 154, No. 3.

Hernandez, Garcia: Judío.
>AGN 1A, No. 18.

Hernandez, Gaspar. *See* Maria Rodriguez.

Hernandez, Iñez: sister of Manuel de Morales; m. Francisco Alvarez; a fugitive. Observer of Mosaic laws and judío; relaxed in effigy in 1596.
>Abec.; Medina, *México* 162.

Hernandez, Isabel Clara. *See* Isabel Clara.

Hernandez, Jorge: Portuguese; r. Tuxtla; sailor; 1574 proceso. Suspicion of judío.
>AGN 58, No. 1; Liebman, *Guide* 25; Toro, *Judíos* 10.

Hernandez; Manuel: 1598 proceso. Judaizante.
>AGN 223, fol. 499.

Hernandez, Miguel a. Miguel Hernandez de Almeyda: b. Viseu; r. Taxco; brother of Jorge de Almeyda; charged in 1590. Heresy and suspicion of judío; case suspended. Charged in 1595; fled. Judaizante; relaxed in effigy in 1601.
>Abec.; AGN 158, No. 2; Medina, *México* 162.

Hernandez, Pedro: m. Blanca de Morales; brother-in-law of licenciado Manuel de Morales; fugitive in 1595. Judío; relaxed in effigy in 1601.
>Abec.; AGN 153, No. 8.

Hernandez, Sebastian: denounced by Manuel de la Guarda in 1601. Suspicion of judaizante.
>AGN 256, No. 15N.

Hernandez de Almeyda, Miguel. *See* Miguel de Hernandez.

Hernandez de Alvor, Pedro: b. Canary Islands; 1538 proceso. Judío.
>AGN 30, No. 5; Medina, *México* 96; Toro, *Judíos* 9.

Hernandez de Cazala: 1554 proceso; denounced by Vicar of Zumpango. Suspicion of judaizante.
>AGN 30, No. 13; Toro, *Judíos* 116 [which gives the year as 1544].

Hernandez Serodia, Catalina. *See* Mathias Rodriguez de Olivera.

Hernandez Victoria, Diego: b. Oporto; r. Manila; 1597 proceso. Judaizante.
>AGN 162; AGN 163, No. 1; AGN 223, fol. 492; AGN 251, Nos. 1, 2; AGN 256, No. 15N: AGN 263, No. 1.

Herrador, Diego: shoemaker; 1577 proceso. Grandson of Jew relaxed in Spain.
>AGN 82, No. 35; Toro, *Judíos* 10.

Herrera, Antonio: arrested in 1604 in Acapulco. Judaizante.

AGN 368, No. 113.

Herrera, Antonio de: son of Francisco de Herrera; r. Cuautla; testimony given in 1650. Suspicion of judaizante.

AGN 435, fol. 265.

Herrera, Beatriz de. *See* Fernando Rodriguez.

Herrera, Cristobal de: r. Zacatecas; denounced in 1615. Suspicion of judío and teaching the law of Moses to Indians.

AGN 309, No. 4; AGN 486, fol. 68; Liebman, *Jews* 74, 75, 208.

Herrera, Francisco de: r. Cuautla. 1650 testimony concerning performance with his son Antonio of Jewish rites, et cetera.

AGN 435, fol. 254.

Herrero Osta, Xines de: r. San Luis Potosi; lawyer. Son of a woman who was relaxed in Spain after confessing; wore silk and had an entourage of Negro servants.

AGN 455, fol. 606.

Hidalgo y Castillo, Jose Maria: leader of Mexican independence. Judaizante, Lutheranism, apostasy, et cetera; killed in 1812 in Chihuahua after being defrocked.

Liebman, *Jews* 296.

Holgado, Alonso: companion of Francisco Alburquerque; arrested with him in 1627.

AGN 823, No. 21.

Home (Ome), Francisco a. Vicente Enriquez (Henriquez): age 52; b. San Vicente Davera; son of Gaspar Mendez, blacksmith, and Beatriz Hernandez, both of San Vicente Davera and Hebrew New Christians; brother of Enrique de Miranda, Pedro Lopez, Gaspar Mendez Piñero, and Violante Enriquez; uncle of Gaspar Robles; distantly related to Blanca Enriquez and Justa Mendez; circumcised; r. Mexico and Veracruz; m. his niece Maria Henriquez. Judío and observer of Mosaic laws; tortured and crippled as a result; died in the cell; bones disinterred and relaxed in effigy in 1649 auto.

Abec.; AGN 391, No. 1; AGN 405, No. 9; Medina, *México* 205, 218.

Huerta, Antonio de: Portuguese; r. Truxillo; denounced in 1639. Judío, judaizante, and illegal friendships.

AGN 388, No. 17.

Huerta, Isabel de la. *See* Isabel Enriquez.

Huerta, Manuel. *See* Miguel Nuñez Huerta.

Hurtado, Fray Francisco: accused in 1614 by the comisario of Jalapa. Being the son of relaxed persons and being an apostate.

AGN 301, No. 10A.

Ibernia, Juan de: r. Patzcuaro; 1700 proceso. Suspicion of judío.

AGN 543, No. 21.

Isabel (patronymic unknown): r. Canaria; 1694 proceso. Suspicion of judaizante.

AGN 529, No. 18.

Jacinto Bazan, Jorge. *See* Bazan, Jorge Jacinto.

Javares, Manuel. *See* Manuel Suarez.

Jeera, "Fulano": 1681 proceso. Suspicion of judío.

AGN 250, No. 41.

Jeronima (Geronyma), Esperanza a. Jeronima Esperanza a. Esperanza Geronyma de Silva: daughter of Juana Rodriguez; sister of Blanca Enriquez, the mother-in-law of Simon Vaez de Sevilla; she was named Esperanza because her parents hoped that she would sire the Messiah; when it appeared that this hope, known to the Jewish community affiliated with her family, would not be fulfilled, it was placed in her niece, Juana Enriquez; m. Sebastian Roman; r. Puebla. Judaizante and observer of Mosaic laws; relaxed in effigy in 1649 auto.

AGN 405, No. 9; AGN 406, No. 1; AGN 414, No. 10; AGN 415, Nos. 6, 7; Medina, *México* 408.

Jesus Maria, Juan de: r. Mexico. Observer of Mosaic laws.

AHN 1738, exp. 1.

Jimenez Piquero, Juan: silversmith; r. Puebla. Suspicion of judaizante in 1627.

AGN 360, fol. 564.

Jorge, Domingo: r. Veracruz; 1701 proceso. Judaizante.

AGN 718, fol. 300.

Jorge, Francisco: b. Benavente, Castile; r. Taxco. Judaizante, observer of Mosaic laws; fugitive; relaxed in effigy in 1596.

Abec.; AGN 223, fol. 409; Medina, *México* 133.

Jorge, Francisco: testimony by Blanca Rivera in 1642. Judaizante.

AGN 404, No. 4.

Jorge, Pedro: fought on the side of the Dutch against the Spaniards; 1645 testimony. Judaizante.

AGN 421, No. 11.

Jorge, Pedro: denounced in 1605. Judaizante.

AGN 277, No. 2.

Juan: mulatto; r. district of Villa de Lagos; 1690 proceso. Practiced
Jewish rites.

    AGN 435, fols. 32, 41, 54.

JUAREZ. *See also* SUAREZ and XUAREZ.

Juarez, Ana a. Ana Suarez: age 25; b. Mexico; daughter of Gaspar
Juarez, b. Lamego, Portugal, reconciled for judaizante, and Rafaela
Enriquez, reconciled in auto of 1648; m. first to Juan Mendez de
Villaviciosa, from whom she was divorced "por cierto impedi-
mento," impotency, or probably due to her grandmother's desire to
see her married to a more notable Jew; m. Francisco Lopez de
Fonseca; had a son. Observer of Mosaic laws and judío; confessed;
known as "Paloma Grande," Big Dove, among the Jews in the secret
cells; reconciled in 1648 auto, confiscation of property, sanbenito,
abjuration de vehementi, life imprisonment in Spain.

    AGN 410, No. 1; AGN 414, No. 7; García 28:194; Medina,
    México 117, 195.

Juarez (Suarez), Antonio: testimony by Clara de Rivera and Manuel
Rodriguez Nuñez in 1642. Judaizante.

    AGN 404, No. 5; AGN 414, No. 2; AGN 421, No. 11.

Juarez, Blanca. *See* Blanca Xuarez.

Juarez (Xuarez), Blanca: b. Mexico in 1626; daughter of Gaspar Juarez
and Rafaela Enriquez; niece of Simon Vaez Sevilla and Juana Enriquez and granddaughter of the "famous rabbis" Antonio Rodriguez
Arias and Blanca Enriquez; considered a great beauty; m. Jorge
Jacinto Bazan; considered saintly in the Jewish community; made
matzot for Passover; arrested in July 1642. Observer of Mosaic laws;
called "Paloma Chica," Little Dove, among the Jewish prisoners;
reconciled on March 30, 1648, abjuration de vehementi, sanbenito,
confiscation of property, exile, life imprisonment.

    Abec.; AGN 392, Nos. 3, 12; AGN 413, fols. 187, 188; AGN 414,
    fols. 252, 565; AGN 584, No. 17; García 28: 212; Medina,
    México 118, 195.

Juarez, Gaspar a. Gaspar Suarez a. Gaspar Xuarez: age 68; b. Lamego,
Portugal; son of Antonio Rodriguez and Violante Fernandez, both
of Maralabar, Portugal, and both Hebrew New Christians; merchant;
m. Rafaela Enriquez, b. Seville; father of Ana Juarez and Blanca
Juarez and of a natural daughter, Violante Suarez, b. in Lima, who
m. Manuel de Mella; jailed previously by the Inquisition in Seville

and Lima, but had not been sentenced; fell ill and died in the cell after confessing. Judío and observer of Mosaic laws; relaxed in effigy in 1649 auto.

> Abec.; AGN 392, No. 5; AGN 405, No. 2; AHN 1738, No. 1; Medina, *México* 203.

Juarez, Manuel. *See* Manuel Xuarez.

Juarez, Melchor: b. Spain; secretary to Bishop Juan de Palafox y Mendoza, of Puebla. Judío, judaizante, and bigamy; case not concluded; the bigamy charge was dismissed, as his wife in Spain had died before the investigation.

> AGN 374, No. 6; AGN 416, No. 38; Liebman, *Guide* 1070; Medina, *México* 193.

Juarez, Violante. *See* Violante Suarez.

Juarez de Espinoza, Simon: age 28; b. Mexico; son of Juan Juarez de Figueroa, b. Lisbon, and Ana Espinosa, b. Mexico; circumcised; merchant; m. Juana Tinoco; converted to Judaism in order to marry Juana. Judío and judaizante; confessed; reconciled on April 16, 1646.

> Abec.; AGN 441, No. 4; García 28:82; Liebman, *Guide* 1109, 1132; Medina, *México* 116, 193.

Juarez de Figueroa, Ines. *See* Diego Suarez de Figueroa.

Juarez de Figueroa, Julio. *See* Ana Espinosa.

Juarez de Figueroa, Nuño. *See* Nuño de Silva.

Lais, Jorge. *See* Jorge Baez.

Lamport, Don Guillen de a. Guillermo de Lombard: known as "the crazy Irishman"; mentioned in the letters included in the proceso of Diego Ximenez de la Camara. Judaizante; relaxed in 1659 auto, contrary to the advice of the Suprema.

> AGN 416, fols. 434, 466.

Lanzarote, Fernando. *See* Fernando Rodriguez.

Laponte, Justa: testimony by Thomas Nuñez Peralta. Judaizante.

> AGN 414, fol. 457.

Launguaran, Juan: b. Bordeaux. Lutheranism and Judaism; convicted of judaizante; reconciled in auto of August 9, 1795.

> Liebman, *Guide* 1176.

Leon, Catalina de. *See* Francisca de Carvajal.

Leon, Fray Cristobal de: r. Manila; denounced himself in 1667. Son of penanced people and usurers.

> AGN 608, No. 4.

Leon, Diego de: r. Zacetecas; 1626 testimony. Descendant of Jews.
  AGN 356, fol. 155.
Leon, Duarte de. *See* Duarte de Leon Jaramillo.
Leon, Enrique de: former r. Caracas or Maracaibo; denounced in 1649.
  Judaizante.
  AGN 503, fol. 107. [For additional testimony see summary of
  Ursula Zib, AHN 1738, No. 1.]
Leon, Gonzalo de: goldsmith. Grandchild of persons relaxed in Spain.
  AGN 59, No. 7.
Leon, Jorge de: 1646 proceso. Judaizante.
  AGN 426, fol. 530.
Leon, Jorge de. *See* Jorge Duarte.
Leon, Jose de: brother of Lopez de Leon Mendoza y Alencastro; r.
  Durango; 1701 proceso. Suspicion of judaizante.
  AGN 718, fol. 88.
Leon, Juana de: testimony by Gaspar de Robles in 1641. Judaizante
  and observer of Mosaic laws.
  AGN 390, No. 11.
Leon, Juan Ponce de. *See* Pedro Ponce de Leon Ayola.
Leon, Manuel de: b. San Martin de la Vega, near Toledo, Spain; son of
  reconciled parents; 1669 proceso and criminal case. Observer of Mo-
  saic laws; reconciled in 1678 auto.
  AGN 612, No. 1; Robles, vol. 1, 236.
Leon, Manuel de: r. Pachuca; merchant; 1693 proceso. Suspicion of
  judío.
  AGN 689, fol. 486; González Obregón, *México* 712.
Leon, Maria de: b. Mexico; daughter of Ana de Carvajal and Cristobal
  Miguel; m. Diego Nuñez; had four children: Luis, Manuel, Beatriz,
  and Cristobal, who were 11, 7, 4, and 1 in 1632. Judaizante.
  Abec.; AGN 372, No. 21; AGN 404, No. 1.
Leon, Simon de: age 17; brother of Ana and Antonia Nuñez. Observer
  of Mosaic laws; reconciled in 1647 auto; confiscation of property,
  sanbenito, abjuration de vehementi, jail for one year.
  Abec.; AGN 426, fol. 524; García 28:263; Medina, *México* 195.
  The major portion of the proceso is at Washington State
  University.
Leon Carvajal, Ana de. *See* Ana de Carvajal.
Leon y de la Cueva, Catalina de: b. Benavente; daughter of Francisca de
  Carvajal; m. Antonio Diaz de Caceres; mother of Leonor de Caceres.

Observer of Mosaic laws; apprehended twice, 1589 and 1595; relaxed in 1596 auto.

Abec.; AGN 12 (Riva Palacio), No. 1; AGN 223, No. 31; García 5:106-07; Liebman, *Enlightened* 10, 23, 29, 31, 33, 58, 76, 81; Liebman, *Jews* ch. 8; Medina, *México* 94.

Leon Jaramillo (Xaramillo), Duarte de: b. Casteloblanco ca. 1591; son of Francisco Antuñez and Antonia Nuñez, both b. in Casteloblanco and reconciled by the Inquisition in Lisbon; m. Isabel Nuñez; arrested ca. 1628. Suspicion of judío; tortured; case suspended on December 12, 1628; rearrested in 1635; reconciled, abjuration de vehementi, fined 20 pesos; rearrested 1642. Observer of Mosaic laws and relapso; relaxed alive in 1649 auto.

Abec.; AGN 381, No. 5; AGN 426, No. 7; AGN 453, fol. 129; AGN 495, No. 14; Medina, *México* 119, 184, 185, 194, 204. Part of the proceso is at the Thomas Gilcrease Institute.

Leon Jaramillo, Francisco de: age 15; b. Mexico; son of Duarte de Leon Jaramillo and Isabel Nuñez; circumcised. Judío; tortured; reconciled on January 23, 1647; rearrested for not having made a full confession; 200 lashes, confiscation of property, sanbenito, jail for twelve years.

Abec.; AGN 426, fol. 525; AHN 1738, No. 1; García 28:109; Medina, *México* 117, 195.

Leon Mendoza y Alencastro, Lopez de: b. Toledo; brother of Jose del Leon; r. Guadalajara; three procesos. Suspicion of judío (1692 and 1696) and judaizante (1701).

AGN 685, fol. 559; AGN 718, fols. 88, 93.

Lescano, Fernando: 1685 proceso. Suspicion of judaizante.

AGN 660, No. 2.

Lima, Pedro de: r. San Felipe in 1604. Suspicion of judío.

AGN 368, No. 9.

Linares, Captain Domingo de. Suspicion of judío; accused of working his slaves on Christian holidays and saying that there is no hell.

AGN 416, No. 14.

Lombard, Guillermo de. *See* Don Guillen de Lamport.

Lopez, Alonso: Portuguese; 1639 testimony. Suspicion of judaizante.

AGN 367, No. 4.

Lopez, Ana a. Ana Arenas Lopez: b. Casteloblanco or Fondon; m. Diego Lopez Regalon; 1595 proceso. Judío; reconciled, confiscation of property, sanbenito, life imprisonment.

AGN 155, No. 2; AGN 252A, No. 2; AGN 279, No. 9: García 5:96.

Lopez, Antonio: b. Seville; son of Diego Lopez Regalon and Ana Arenas Lopez, a confessed Jewess. Suspicion of judío and concealing Jews; reconciled in 1601, confiscation of property, sanbenito.

> Abec.; AGN 368, No. 105 [where mention is made of the fact that he did not complete his punishment]; AGN 277, No. 6C; AGN 279, No. 9.

Lopez, Beatriz: b. Lisbon; r. Veracruz; m. Francisco Mendez, b. Tomar. Observer of Mosaic laws; never apprehended.

> AGN 391, No. 10; AGN 413, fols. 178-183; AGN 425, fol. 525.

Lopez, Blas: Portuguese; r. Guadalajara; merchant; converted to Judaism in order to marry Juana del Bosque. Judaizante; escaped; relaxed in effigy in 1649 auto.

> AGN 413, fols. 82-85; AGN 415, fol. 499; AGN 418, No. 10; Medina, *México* 205.

Lopez, Constanza. *See* Tomas Lopez Monforte.

Lopez, Diego: b. San Vicente Davera; single; Jewish ancestry. Judaizante; reconciled in 1596 auto.

> Abec.; AGN 223, No. 35; Garcia 5:101. Medina, *México* 169 [reports that he was later arrested for illegally entering the house of the Holy Office and received 100 lashes].

Lopez, Diego: r. Zacatecas; denounced in 1617. Judaizante and irreverence.

> AGN 316, No. 22.

Lopez, Diego: b. San Vicente Davera; single; accused in 1642. Descendant of Jews.

> AGN 391, No. 10. The proceso is at the Gilcrease Institute.

Lopez, Diego (b. Monsanto). *See* Francisco Lopez Enriquez.

Lopez, Domingo: deceased when testimony against him was given in 1642. Judaizante.

> AGN 391, No. 10.

Lopez, Duarte: Portuguese; brother of Antonio Bravo; 1663 proceso; denounced by residents of San Miguel, Guatemala in 1670 or 1677. Suspicion of judío, judaizante.

> AGN 594, No. 4; AGN 633, No. 6.

Lopez, Elena. *See* Elena de Silva.

Lopez, Felipa: daughter of Diego Lopez Regalon and Ana Lopez; no record of a proceso against her, but in 1593 the inquisitor stated that she was accused of being a Jew.

AGN 223, No. 32.

Lopez, Felipa. *See* Manuel Carrasco.

Lopez, Inez: b. Seville; sister of Francisco Lopez Enriquez and Ana Enriquez; r. Veracruz; m. Rodrigo Fernandez Salseda, a Portuguese merchant, who had resided in Seville; mother of Catalina Enriquez, reconciled in 1649; reconciled by the Holy Office in Seville many years previously. Judaizante and observer of Mosaic laws; relaxed in effigy in 1649.

Abec.; AGN 405, fol. 565; AGN 414, fol. 130; Medina, *México* 408.

Lopez, Juan. *See* Melchor Rodriguez Lopez.

Lopez, Juan: 1610 proceso. Suspicion of judaizante.

AGN 473, fol. 199.

Lopez, Juana. *See* Manuel de Acosta.

Lopez, Manuel: r. Puebla; m. Luisa Mendez; father of Manuel Alvarez de Arellano, who was reconciled in 1647. Suspicion of judío and judaizante.

Abec.; AGN 281, No. 47.

Lopez, Manuel a. Manuel Lopez Coronel: b. Bayone, Galicia; r. Veracruz; broker; m. Lenor Nuñez (b. Seville). Judío; died prior to auto of 1649; relaxed in effigy.

Liebman, *Guide* 1167; González Obregón, *México* 708.

Lopez, Mateo: Portuguese; deceased; 1680 proceso. Suspicion of judío.

AGN 520, No. 2.

Lopez, Mayor: Portuguese; m. Francisco Blandon; "close relative of her mother-in-law." Judaizante and dogmatist; relaxed in effigy in 1649.

AGN 1738, fol. 158; Gonzalez Obregón, *México* 708, Medina, *México* 408.

Lopez, Pedro a. Simon Fernandez: Portuguese; the second husband of Leonor Nuñez. Suspicion of judío in 1618; reconciled; recharged in 1632 as a dogmatist and observer of Mosaic laws; a proceso was opened against his memory and fame; relaxed in effigy in 1649.

AGN 381, No. 5; Liebman, *Jews* 221, 260.

Lopez, Pedro a. brother of Francisco Home, Gaspar Mendez a. Gaspar Piñero and Enrique de Miranda; testimony against him in 1641.

AGN 391, No. 1.

Lopez, Philipa: testimony naming her as a Jewess.
 Proceso of Catalina Enriquez at the Huntington Library.
Lopez, Simon a. Simon Lopez de Guarda (Aguarda): b. Guarda, Portu-
 gal; peddler. Observer of Mosaic laws.
 AGN 405, No. 1; AGN 426, fol. 528. The proceso is at the
 Huntington Library.
Lopez, Simon a. Simon Ramirez; 1635 testimony. Judaizante.
 AGN 381, No. 7.
Lopez, Simon. See Gomez de Silva.
Lopez, Simon. See Isabel Tristan and Ana Tristan.
Lopez, Simon. See Marcos del Valle.
Lopez de Aguarda, Gonzalo: testimony by Catalina Enriquez de Silva.
 Judaizante.
 AGN 404, No. 1. The proceso is at the Huntington Library.
Lopez de Altavista, Francisco: 1642 testimony. Judaizante.
 AGN 391, No. 10.
Lopez Blandon, Antonio: b. Madrid; r. Guadalajara; both parents had
 been relaxed in effigy in Portugal as judíos. Judaizante, dogmatist,
 and teacher of Mosaic laws; died prior to sentence; relaxed in effigy
 in 1635.
 Abec.; AGN 381, No. 5; Medina, *México* 184.
Lopez Blandon, Francisco. See Francisco Blandon.
Lopez Bravo, Juan: r. Guatemala. Suspicion of judaizante in 1615.
 AGN 308, No. 96.
Lopez Cardado, Isabel: b. Medina del Campo, Spain; r. Pachuca; m.
 Baltasar del Valle. Observer of Mosaic laws; reconciled in 1626; rear-
 rested in 1634; reconciled; life imprisonment; died within two
 months, having been twice on the torture rack.
 Abec.; AGN 380, No. 1; AGN 381, No. 5; Medina, *México* 184.
Lopez de Chavez, Ana: b. Burgo (Burgos) de Osma, Castile; r. Puebla,
 where she died; daughter of Isabel Alvarez; m. Juan Mendez de
 Escobar; mother of Isabel Enriquez also known as "de la Huerta"; a
 friend of Justa Mendez. Observer of Mosaic laws; relaxed in effigy in
 1649. *See also* Juan Gomez.
 Bocanegra; González Obregón, *Mexico* 705; Medina, *México* 408.
Lopez Coronal, Diego a. Diego Lopez Nuñez a. Diego Coson: b. Seville;
 son of Leonor Nuñez; r. Campeche; 1646 proceso. Judaizante.
 Abec.; AGN 423, No. 1.
Lopez Coronel, Manuel. See Manuel Lopez a. Manuel Lopez Coronel.

Lopez Correa, Francisco: age 27; b. and r. Veracruz; son of Fernando Rodriguez and Blanca Enriquez; single. Observer of Mosaic laws and judaizante; reconciled in 1647, sanbenito, confiscation of property, abjuration de vehementi; jail for one year.

AGN 399, No. 13; AGN 419, No. 34; AGN 425, No. 12; García 28:108; Medina, *México* 116, 194.

Lopez Correa, Miguel: accused in 1644. Judaizante.

AGN 419, No. 63.

Lopez Diaz, Francisco a. el Chato: age 41; b. Casteloblanco; son of Pedro Diaz Santillan, lessee of royal rents, and Juana Esteves, reconciled by the Holy Office in Seville; both parents b. Casteloblanco and Hebrew New Christians; brother of Baltazar Diaz Santillan; single; merchant; came to New Spain in 1637; related how the Jews in the provinces sent money to Mexico City for the aid and support of the poor Jews in the city; had attended Jewish religious services in Seville where one man served as rabbi and a prayer book in Hebrew was used; the men prayed wearing hats and the women wore large headdresses; he was known as "Tobacco" while in the secret cells. Judío and observer of Mosaic laws; reconciled in 1648, confiscation of property, sanbenito, abjuration de vehementi, 200 lashes, five years in galleys, after which he was to report to the Suprema for further penance.

Abec.; AGN 393, No. 10; AGN 404, Nos. 1, 3; AGN 405, fol. 587; AGN 413, fols. 101-04; AGN 414, Nos. 6, 6A, 8; AGN 453, fol. 65; Garcia 28:222; Liebman, *Guide* 1206. Medina, *México* 195. In the proceso of Simon Lopez at the Huntington Library, reference is made to Francisco Lopez with further information concerning him and Judaism.

Lopez Enriquez, Francisco: b. Seville; son of Diego Lopez, b. Monsanto, Portugal, r. Seville, and Clara Enriquez, b. Ocrato, Portugal; grandson on his mother's side of Gabriel Enriquez and Justa Mendez, both of Ocrato, all Hebrews; cousin of a Manuel Alvarez, reconciled in Mexico in auto of March 25, 1601; m. Isabel Enriquez, who died in Cadiz; died at an unspecified date from a fall from a mule. Judaizante; reconciled; pardoned by the Pope's Bull in 1605; relapso; relaxed in effigy in 1649.

Abec.; AGN 223, Nos. 33, 34; AGN 254A, No. 4C; AGN 277, No. 2; AGN 405, fol. 16; AGN 414, No. 3; AGN 415, No. 2; AHN 778, fol. 224; Medina, *México* 112, 174, 408.

Lopez Enriquez, Francisco. *See* Blanca Enriquez (b. Lisbon).

Lopez Enriquez, Juan: b. Casteloblanco; testimony by Maria de Rivera in 1642. Judaizante.

AGN 415, fols. 92, 267.

Lopez de Fonseca; Francisco a. Francisco Mendez: b. Botan, Portugal; son of Enrique Lopez Mendez, who was relaxed in Coimbra as a judaizante, and Isabel de Olivares or Olivera, both parents were b. in Melo, Portugal; his mother escaped the Inquisition and resided in San Juan de Luz, France, where she was a practicing Jewess; circumcised; r. Veracruz; m. Ana Juarez, b. Mexico; died on the ship en route to Spain; while in jail, he observed all the fasts, the Sabbaths, and Rosh Chodesh (inauguration of the New Moon). Observer of Mosaic laws; reconciled in 1646 auto; confiscation of property, sanbenito, abjuration de vehementi, life imprisonment.

AGN 391, No. 10; AGN 405, No. 8; AGN 410, No. 2; AGN 413, fol. 169; AGN 414, fols. 103, 131; Medina, *México* 203.

Lopez de Granada, Diego: testimony by Blanca Rivera. Judaizante.

AGN 404, No. 4.

Lopez de Guarda, Juan: testimony by Maria Rivera and Thomas Nuñez de Peralta in 1642. Judaizante.

AGN 415, fols. 202, 323.

Lopez de Guarda, Simon. *See* Simon Lopez.

Lopez Home, Pedro: r. Guadalajara; accused in 1642. Observer of Mosaic laws.

AGN 391, No. 10; AGN 397, No. 2.

Lopez de Huerta, Luis: testimony by Blanca de Rivera in 1642. Judaizante.

AGN 405, fol. 519.

Lopez de Llerena, Margarita. *See* Blanca Mendez.

Lopez Lobo, Francisco: r. San Luis Potosi; 1646 proceso. Suspicion of judaizante.

AGN 425, No. 5.

Lopez Lucena, Diego: testimony by Manuel Rodriguez Nuñez in 1642. Judaizante.

AGN 414, fol. 164.

Lopez Mejia, Juan: r. Veracruz; 1728 proceso. Suspicion of judaizante.

AGN 821, No. 14.

Lopez Mendez, Enrique. *See* Francisco Lopez de Fonseca.

Lopez de Mendizabal, Bernardo: the Spanish governor of New Mexico, where he antagonized the Church; m. Teresa de Aguirre y Roche, who belonged to a noble, Spanish family; his maternal grandmother had been relaxed as a judío, denounced in 1663; his wife had also been denounced for suspicion of judío in 1664, but was acquitted due to her lineage. Judío; died in the cells, where he had been since 1661; acquitted posthumously in 1671.

Abec.; AGN 594, No. 1; Liebman, *Jews* 22, 283.

Lopez Mesa, Alvaro: came from Cartagena to New Spain. Accused in 1639; fled and returned to New Granada, where he was apprehended and tried in 1642. Judaizante; reconciled, confiscation of property, sanbenito, abjuration de vehementi.

AGN 388, No. 7; AHN 1021, fols. 51R, 58-64R; Medina, *Cartagena* 206. See *also* Alvaro Lopez Mesa in Cartagena.

Lopez Monforte; Pedro: son of Francisco Gomez and Constanza Lopez of Monforte; r. Mines of Fresnillo; died before accusation; a proceso was opened against his memory and fame. Observer of Mosaic laws; relaxed in effigy in 1649 auto.

Abec.; AGN 668, No. 4; Medina, *México* 409.

Lopez Monforte, Tomas: age. 35; b. Monforte, son of Francisco Gomez, merchant, and Constanza Lopez; both parents died in Seville. Judío and judaizante; reconciled in 1646, confiscation of property, sanbenito, abjuration de vehementi, life imprisonment.

AGN 415, No. 1; AGN 418, No. 6; Medina, *México* 194.

Lopez de Morales, Antonio a. Antonio Lopez: b. Seville; nephew of Manuel de Morales; actor and singer; fugitive. Judío and observer of Mosaic laws; tortured; relaxed in effigy in 1596.

AGN 168, No. 1; AGN 1490, No. 1 [which indicates b. Celorico, Portugal]; García 5:109; Liebman, *Jews* 157, 308; Toro, *Judíos* 59.

Lopez de Morales, Pedro: age 49; b. Ciudad Rodrigo, Castile; son of Juan Morales, merchant, b. Troncoso, Portugal, administrator of the rents for the king in Ciudad Rodrigo, and Blanca Enriquez, b. Travazos, Portugal; both parents were New Christians; r. Ixtla, near Guadalajara; miner; m. his second cousin in Madrid according to the Jewish law; remarried in Mexico; had one daughter. Judío and observer of Mosaic laws; reconciled in 1647, 200 lashes, sanbenito, confiscation of property, life imprisonment.

García 28:124; Liebman, *Guide* 1126; Medina, *México* 117, 194.

Lopez de Noroña, Felipe: m. Clara de Rivera; arrested in 1642. Judaizante.

AGN 398, No. 3; AGN 404, No. 5; AGN 415, No. 7.

Lopez, Nuñez: 1642 testimony by Isabel Antuñez. Judaizante.

AGN 415, fol. 366.

Lopez Nuñez, Diego. See Lopez Coronal a. Coson.

Lopez Nuñez, Manuel: b. Seville; brother of Isabel Tristan and Pedro
Lopez Nuñez; merchant; single. Judaizante and observer of Mosaic
laws; died prior to sentence; relaxed in effigy in auto of April 11,
1649.

Abec.; AGN 401, No. 5; AGN 405, No. 9; AGN 422, No. 12
[refers to a Manuel Lopez, noting that the testimony is incom-
plete]; Medina, México 409; González Obregón, Mexico Viejo
708.

Lopez Nuñez, Pedro. See Isabel Tristan.

Lopez de Orduña, Antonio: age 27; b. Seville; r. Guadalajara; son of
Fernando Vaez Torres, b. Casteloblanco, and Isabel Rodriguez, b.
Seville; his father was buried in Utrera, Spain; his mother died in
Seville; both parents were Hebrew New Christians; circumcised; merchant and deputy mayor of the Mines of Chichicapa. Observer of
Mosaic laws; confessed to judío and judaizante; reconciled in 1646,
abjuration de vehementi, confiscation of property, sanbenito, exile;
he was to report to the Suprema in Seville within one month after
his arrival in Spain to have it fix the place of his imprisonment for
one year.

AGN 404, No. 6; AGN 414, No. 5; AGN 499, fol. 4; AHN 1738,
No. 6; García 28:42; Liebman, Guide 1108; Medina, México 113,
193; Jiménez Rueda, 123.

Lopez Ramirez; Ramon: 1643 testimony of Micaela Enriquez. Judaizante.

AGN 418, No. 10.

Lopez Regalon, Diego a. Felipe Lopez: b. Fondon; merchant; m. Ana
Lopez; had two children, Antonio Lopez and Felipa Lopez; Had
been a prisoner of the Inquisition in Los Reyes, Peru, arrested 1597;
tortured in spite of his illness and died in the secret cells. Judaizante
and observer of Mosaic laws; relaxed in effigy in 1601.

Abec.; AGN 160, No. 12; Medina, México 159, 162.

Lopez Rivera, Diego: b. Casteloblanco; m. Blanca Rivera; 1632 proceso;
died prior to arrest. Judaizante; relaxed in effigy in 1649;

AGN 375, No. 1; AGN 415, fol. 573; Medina, México 408.

Lopez Sevilla, Francisco. See Gonzalo Vaez.

Lopez de Tepozotlan, Thomas: Portuguese; r. Teposotlan; died before accusation; 1650 proceso opened against his memory. Observer of Mosaic laws.

AGN 504, No. 3.

Lopez Tristan, Pedro: testimony by Clara Texoso. Judaizante.

AGN 405, No. 4.

Lorenzo, Blanca. *See* Baltasar Rodriguez.

Lorenzo, Gaspar: charged by the Jesuit P. D. de Guzman and the comisario of Sinaloa in 1639. Judío.

AGN 386, No. 2.

Lozado, Diego: b. Lemos, Galicia; r. Guadalajara. Suspicion of judío; case suspended in 1625.

Abec.; AGN 355, No. 1; AGN 356, No. 105.

Lozano, Juan: r. Puebla; 1597 proceso. Blasphemy.

AGN 161, No. 3; Toro, *Judíos* 13.

Lucena, Francisco a. Ugena: r. Puebla; 1627 testimony. Judío.

AGN 360, fol. 564.

Lucena, Gaspar de: brother of Manuel de Lucena. Judaizante.

AGN 223, No. 33, fol. 268.

Lucena, Isabel de: testimony between 1611 and 1616. Judaizante.

AGN 223, No. 35.

Lucena, Manuel de: b. San Vicente Davera ca. 1564; merchant; r. Pachuca; m. Catalina Enriquez, daughter of Beatrix Enriquez, father of Simon de Paredes. Concealer of heretical judaizantes, observer of Mosaic laws, and dogmatizer; relaxed in 1596.

Abec.; AGN 152, Nos. 3, 4; García 5:105; Liebman, *Jews* 168, 171; Revah, vol. 1 (N.S.) 1959-60; Toro, *Judíos* 58.

Lucena, Maria de. Judaizante.

AGN 223, No. 33, fol. 268 [no other record of a proceso].

Lucena, Simon: b. Casteloblanco; testimony by Maria de Rivera in 1642. Judaizante.

AGN 415, fol. 250.

Lucena Baez, Damian de: r. Puebla. Suspicion of judío; reconciled in 1648 auto, sanbenito, confiscation of property.

Medina, *México* 195.

Lucerna, Simona: m. Marcos Rodriguez. Judaizante.

AGN 179, No. 3.

Luis, Alfonso. *See* Francisco Luis.

Luis, Francisco: b. Santa Baya das Donas, Galicia; son of Alfonso Luis and Lucia Perez de Ocastelo, descendants of New Christians; circumcised; innkeeper; single; 1646 proceso. Judaizante; well-versed in the Bible; knew all about the procedures of the Holy Office; a second proceso was opened denying that there had not been sufficient evidence for the punishment imposed earlier; appeared in auto of 1649, when he was 70 years of age; reconciled; fined 1,000 Castilian ducats for extraordinary expenses of the Holy Office.

>Abec.; AGN 426, fol. 531; AGN 435, No. 4 [1690 is given as the date of this proceso].

>Medina, *Mexico* 203.

Luna, Bernardo de: b. Lisbon, r. Michoacan; 1598 proceso. Judaizante; reconciled in 1601 auto; confiscation of property, sanbenito, 200 lashes, life imprisonment.

>Abec.; AGN 164, No. 3; Liebman, *Guide* 1087; Medina, *México* 158.

Luna, Bernardo: accused of eating kid during Lent.

>AGN 112, fol. 112.

Machado, Antonia: daughter of Juan Machado; granddaughter of Antonio Machado; reconciled in 1601; 1604 proceso. Descendant of Jews and wearing silk clothes with gold fringe.

>AGN 273, No. 16.

Machado, Antonio: b. Lisbon; tailor; declared to be a rabbi by the Inquisitors as his house was used as a synagogue; tortured and died prior to sentence. Judío and dogmatizer; relaxed in effigy on March 25, 1601.

>Abec.; AGN 273, No. 16; AGN (Riva Palacio) 16, No. 3; Medina, *México* 97, 159, 162.

Machado, Francisco a. Francisco Rodriguez de Molina: son of Leonor Machado; grandson of Antonio Machado. Wearing silk.

>AGN 274, No. 11.

Machado, Isabel: b. Portugal; daughter of Antonio Machado. Judaizante; reconciled on March 25, 1601.

>Abec.; AGN 279, No. 9 [contains her request to go free]; AGN (Riva Palacio) 55, No. 3; Medina, *México* 159.

Machado, Juan: son of Antonio Machado; doctor; died prior to sentence. Descendant of Jews; relaxed in effigy in 1601.

>Medina, *México* 162.

Machado, Leonor: b. Portugal; daughter of Antonio Machado; m. Gonzalez Rodriguez de Molina; mother of Francisco Machado. Descendant of Jews.

Abec.; Liebman, *Jews* 26.

Machado, Lorenzo: b. Villa Villaneuva de Portiman, Portugal; r. Mines of San Luis Potosi. Heretical judaizante; denying the resurrection of the flesh ten years previously; reconciled in 1601, confiscation of property.

Abec.; Medina, *México* 157; Toro, *Judíos* 62.

Machorro, David. *See* Antonio Narvaez.

Machorro, Solomon. *See* Juan Pacheco de Leon.

Machucca, Diego: b. Duero; 1537 proceso. Suspicion of judío.

AGN 22, No. 9; Greenleaf, *Zumárraga* 98.

Maderos, Francisco. Judío.

AGN 161, No. 7; Liebman, *Guide* 1037; Toro, *Judíos* 13 [cites as Mederos].

Madrigal, Diego de: r. Puebla; always swore by the God of Israel; 1602 testimony and proceso. Suspicion of judío.

AGN 452, fol. 278.

Magdalena, Juana: b. Topatalcingo; mulatto; m. Josef de Valencia. Heresy for saying that she did not have to believe in hell and that at the mass she was eating bread and wine; reconciled in 1603 auto, two years reclusion in a church to be taught Christianity.

Abec.; González Obregón, *Mexico* 690.

Magdalena, Maria: b. Barbary, Africa; had been reconciled by the Inquisition in Cordoba. Relapsa; bones disinterred and burned.

Medina, *México* 195.

Mala Espina, Carlos: r. Nicaragua; mine operator; 1768 proceso. Judío.

AGN 611, No. 4.

Maldonado, Catalina: testimony by Catalina Enriquez de Silva. Judaizante.

AGN 404, No. 1; AGN 413, fols. 209-216, 294-297; AGN 415, fol. 146.

Mantillo, Gonzalo de: r. Campeche; accused in 1642. Judaizante.

AHN 1738, fol. 116.

Manuel, Tristan. *See* Luis Fernandez Tristan.

Maria, Ana: 1612 proceso. Suspicion of judío or judaizante.

AGN 455, fol. 805.

Marin, Maria: b. Mexico; r. Cholula; denounced in 1650 along with her siblings. Using silk, bearing arms, riding horses, and being a grand-child of penitents who had been relaxed in effigy.

AGN 435, fol. 322.

Marquez, Catalina. *See* Antonio Rodriguez Arias.

Marquez, Domingo: chief constable of Tepeaca; 1660 processo. Judai-zante.

AGN 460.

Marquez, Juan: r. Tepeaca; 1662 processo. Suspicion of judío.

AGN 439, No. 22.

Marques de Leon, Francisco: denounced in 1632 along with his father by his wife Catalina Ortiz. Suspicion of judío.

AGN 376, No. 2.

Martinez, Leonor: age 14; b. Mexico; daughter of Tomas Treviño de Sobremonte and Maria Gomez. Observer of Mosaic laws; reconciled in 1648, abjuration de vehementi, exile, was to be boarded with a minister of the Holy Office until a ship left for Spain.

Abec.; AGN (Riva Palacio) 20, No. 6; García 28; 9, 23; Liebman, *Guide* 1138; Medina, *México* 118, 120, 195.

Martinez, Nicolas: candlemaker; 1764 proceso. Suspicion of judío.

AGN 1041, No. 11.

Martinez de la Torre, Juan: r. Chiapas; 1596 information. Suspicion of judío.

AGN 157, No. 3A.

Martinez de Villagomez, Leonor. *See* Tomas Treviño de Sobremonte.

Matos, Francisco de a. Fernando Gois de Matos; r. Mexico City; testi-mony by Isabel Antuñez in 1642; died in the cells. Judaizante.

AGN 415, fol. 398, AHN 1738, No. 1.

Medina, Antonio de: Portuguese; r. Mines of Tora, Guadalajara; testi-mony from Lima. Suspicion of judaizante; reconciled in 1630, ab-juration de vehementi, 100 lashes, fine of 2,000 pesos.

Abec.; AGN 360, No. 4; Medina, *México* 176.

Medina, Fernando de a. Fernando de Medina y Merida a. Isac de Medina a. Alberto Moisen Gomez a. Morales Gomez; b. France; circumcised; had been before Holy Office in Seville; 1690 proceso. Judaizante; 1695 proceso for judaizante, relaxed alive in 1699.

AGN 681, No. 1, AGN 704, No. 3: Medina, *México* 278, 279, 415.

Medina, Francisco a. Francisco Gomez de Medina, El Tuerto: circumcised; captain and supervisor of textile sweat shops; accused in 1642. Judaizante.

> AGN 413, fols. 159, 160; AGN 414, fol. 244; AGN 419, fol. 413; AGN 415, fol. 244; AGN 453, fol. 606; AHN 1738, No. 1; Medina, *México* 203.

Medina, Isabel de: testimony by Catalina Enriquez de Silva in 1642. Judaizante.

> AGN 415, fol. 516.

Medina, Isac de. *See* Fernando de Medina.

Medina, Manuel de: Portuguese; r. Guadalajara; tailor; 1667 proceso. Suspicion of judío and blasphemy.

> AGN 606, No. 6.

Medina, Pedro de: testimony by Francisco de Victoria from Lima; 1630 proceso. Judaizante.

> AGN 366, No. 4.

Medina y Merida, Fernando. *See* Fernando de Medina.

Mejia, Francisco: r. Tepeaca; arrested in 1626. Suspicion of judío.

> AGN 356, fol. 34; only the second part of his proceso has been found.

Melendez, Lope Manuel:

> r. Guanajuato 1717. Suspicion of being a descendant of Jews.
> AGN 767, No. 35.

Melandez, Mencia: r. Celaya; 1614 testimony.

> AGN 278, No. 12.

Mella, Gregorio de. *See* Manuel de Mella.

Mella, Isabel de: testimony by Isabel de Silva in 1642. Judaizante.

> AGN 415, fol. 588.

Mella, Manuel de: age 54; b. Huelva, Condado; son of Gregorio de Mella, merchant in Malaga, and Violante Rodriguez, b. Ledesma close to Zamora; goldsmith; r. Guadalajara; first m. in Spain to Beatriz Rodriguez de Alba, b. Seville, who died; came to Mexico in 1624 with the reputation of being "a fine Jew"; m. his second wife Violante Suarez; his home served as the synagogue of the Jews in that area; had been reconciled in Seville. Observer of Mosaic laws; reconciled in auto of March 30, 1648, confiscation of property, sanbenito, life imprisonment, 200 lashes, abjuration de vehementi.

> Abec.; AGN 399, No. 9; AGN 403, No. 2; AGN 405, Nos. 3, 9; AGN 413, fols. 141-147; AGN 414, fol. 280; AGN 415, fols. 41,

372, 508; AGN 543, fol. 150; García 28:239; Medina, *México* 119, 195.

Melo, Francisco de. *See* Duarte de Castaño.

Mena, Luis de: 1642 testimony. Judaizante.

AGN 391, No. 10.

Mendez, Antonio: b. Portugal, reared in Jeva, Andalucia; r. Pachuca; servant; arrested 1598. Judaizante; tortured, confessed, reconciled in 1601 auto.

Abec.; AGN 254A, No. 9 [which records a charge of wearing silk clothes in 1604]; AGN 276, No. 14; AGN (Riva Palacio) 17, No. 3; Medina, *México* 159.

Mendez, Beatriz: Portuguese; m. Manuel Fernandez; mother of Juan Mendez; 1642 testimony. Judaizante.

AGN 391, No. 10.

Mendez, Clara: denounced in 1629 by the comisario in Texcoco. Judaizante.

AGN 366 Texcoco; AGN 421, No. 11.

Mendez, Enrique: 1646 proceso. Judaizante.

AGN 419, No. 30.

Mendez, Francisco. *See* Clara Enriquez (b. Fondon).

Mendez, Francisco. *See* Beatriz Lopez.

Mendez, Francisco. *See* Francisco Lopez de Fonseca.

Mendez, Francisco: 1642 testimony by Rafaela Enriquez and Luis Nuñez Perez.

AGN 405, No. 8; AGN 413, fols. 169, 170; AGN 414, No. 1.

Mendez, Gaspar a. Gaspar Piñero: b. San Vicente Davera; brother of Francisco Home; r. Guadalajara. Judío and observer of Mosaic laws; died in cell; relaxed in effigy in 1649.

AGN 391, No. 1, 10; AGN 410, No. 5; Medina, *México* 408.

Mendez, Gaspar. *See* Gaspar de Fonseca.

Mendez, Guimor. *See* Diego Diaz.

Mendez, Henrique. *See* Enrique de Miranda.

Mendez, Isabel. *See* Juan Mendez de Villaviciosa.

Mendez, Juan: Portuguese; r. Havana; candy manufacturer; arrested 1596. Judaizante; reconciled.

AGN 209, No. 1.

Mendez, Juan: age 35; b. Sossel; son of Manuel Fernandez Barraun, notary of the ecclesiastical vicar of Sossel near Ebora, and Beatriz Mendez; circumcised; r. Puebla; single; tailor. Judío and observer of Mosaic laws; reconciled in 1648 auto, abjuration de vehementi, exile.

Abec.; García 28:189; Medina, *México* 117, 195.

Mendez, Juan a. Juan Mendez de Escobar; b. San Vicente Davera; son of Juan Mendez of Estremoz, Portugal, and Beatriz Hernandez of San Vicente Davera, both Hebrew New Christians; peddler; m. Ana Lopez de Chavez, a daughter of Isabel Alvarez; died in Texcoco; was noted as a learned and observant Jew. Judío; reconciled 1648, abjuration de levi, jail in Spain.

Abec.; AGN 393, No. 3; AGN 414, No. 3; AHN 1738, No. 1; Medina, *México* 117, 195, 408.

Mendez, Julio: b. Villaviciosa, Portugal; descendant of New Christians; merchant. Heretical judaizante; reconciled in 1647 auto.

González Obregón, *México* 697.

Mendez, Justa: b. Seville, parish of San Salvador, ca. 1576; Portuguese ancestry; daughter of Francisco Mendez, b. Ocrato, and Clara Enriquez, b. Fondon; her name appears frequently in Inquisition records between 1596 and 1649. Observer of Mosaic laws; reconciled in 1596 auto, confiscation of property, jail; relaxed in effigy in 1649.

Abec.; AGN 154, No. 1; AGN 156, No. 3; AGN 277, No. 6C; AGN 366 Texcoco; AGN 373, No. 28; AGN 393, No. 6; AGN 415, No. 2; AGN 417, No. 16; AGN (Riva Palacio) 20, No. 2; Liebman, *Guide* 1151; Medina, *México* 112, 124, 409. *See also* Isabel Nuñez.

Mendez, Laureano: 1646 proceso. Judaizante.

AGN 419, No. 44.

Mendez, Leonor. *See* Thomas Mendez.

Mendez, Luisa: m. Manuel Lopez; mother of Manuel Alvarez de Arellano. Descendant of Jews.

Abec.

Mendez, Manuel. *See* Margarita de Rivera.

Mendez, Pedro. *See* Manuel Coronel.

Mendez, Thomas: age 43; b. Camina, Portugal; son of Francisco Rodriguez, penanced by the Inquisition in Lisbon, and Leonor Mendez; first cousin of Manuel Coronel; r. Veracruz; merchant; m. Beatriz Henriquez a. Enriquez; had two children, Bartolome and Ana. Judaizante; reconciled on January 23, 1647, abjuration de vehementi, sanbenito, confiscation of property, 200 lashes, exile.

Abec.; AGN 399, No. 12; AGN 405, No. 4; García 28:130; Medina, *México* 194.

Mendez, Violante: a. Violante Mendez Cardado: b. Madrid; sister of Ana Gomez; m. Marcos del Valle; r. Toluca in 1650. Observer of

Mosaic laws; reconciled in 1635, confiscation of property, jail for two years; denounced later for saying that her sister had been relaxed though she had not been a relapsa.

Abec.; AGN 381, No. 5; AGN 435, No. 37; Medina, *México* 184.

Mendez Cardado, Violante. *See* Violante Mendez.

Mendez Chillon, Antonio: son of Beatriz Lopez and Francisco Mendez; r. Veracruz. Observer of Mosaic laws; reconciled in 1647 auto, sanbenito, confiscation of property, abjuration de vehementi, exile; ordered to report to the Supreme Court in Seville within one month after landing in Spain to learn further punishment.

Abec.; AGN 414, fols. 103, 131; García 28:97; Medina, *México* 116, 194.

Mendez de Escobar, Juan. *See* Juan Mendez.

Mendez Esporan, Juan: r. Manila; denounced himself and his mother on his deathbed. Being Jews and observers of Mosaic laws.

AGN 293, No. 28.

Mendez Huerta, Isabel: 1642 testimony by Isabel Tinoco. Judaizante.

AGN 406, fol. 60; AGN 415, fol. 553.

Mendez Marino, Diego: b. Tangier; r. Veracruz; mariner and broker [the word "marino" in his name indicates that he was a mariner]; m. Juana de Alvarado of New Granada. Observer of Mosaic laws; tortured, freed in 1647.

Abec.; AGN 399, No. 12; AGN 406, fol. 49.

Mendez de Miranda, Manuel: age 50; b. Lisbon; r. Veracruz; m. Isabel de Acosta. Observer of Mosaic laws; reconciled in auto of 1649, confiscation of property, sanbenito, abjuration de vehementi, fine of 200 Castilian ducats, exile from the Indies.

Abec.; AGN 389, No. 8; AGN 399, No. 12; Medina, *México* 203.

Mendez de Sevilla, Diego. *See* Luisa de Mercado.

Mendez de Silva, Diego: 1642 proceso. Judaizante.

AGN 453, fol. 54.

Mendez de Villaviciosa, Juan: age 43; b. Villaviciosa; son of Pablo Nuñez de Franco and Isabel Mendez, Hebrew New Christians; m. Ana Juarez but later divorced. Observer of Mosaic laws; reconciled in auto of 1647, sanbenito, confiscation of property, abjuration de vehementi, 200 lashes, five years in galleys, life imprisonment.

Abec.; AGN 393, No. 3; AGN 414, No. 3; AGN 415, Nos. 1, 4; AGN 416, No. 1; García 28:116; Medina, *México* 116, 194. The major part of the proceso is at the Gilcrease Institute.

Mendoza, Juan de a. Juan de Torres Mendoza: b. Spain; r. Queretaro; arrested in 1621. Suspicion of judaizante.

AGN 339, fol. 1.

Mendoza, Justa: 1642 proceso. Judaizante.

AGN 453, fol. 413.

Mener, Luis: Franciscan monk. Suspicion of judío.

AGN 126, No. 6; Toro, *Judíos* 10 lists him as guardian of the convent at Aguacatlan in Michoacan.

Mercado, Felipa de: sister of Isabel de Mercado and Maria de Mercado; 1646 testimony. Suspicion of judío.

AGN 360, fol. 88; Chinchilla Aquillar, 61, 184.

Mercado, Isabel de: b. Granada; sister of Maria and Felipa de Mercado. Suspicion of judío.

AGN 360, fol. 88, Chinchilla Aquillar 61, 184.

Mercado, Luisa de: b. Seville; m. Diego Mendez de Sevilla; New Christian. Judaizante.

Abec.; Medina, *México* 113 [where her birthplace is La Guarda.]

Mercado, Maria de: The records contain her nephew Ruiz de Cordova's letter to her and her sisters and their reply. Suspicion of judío.

AGN 360, fol. 88, Chinchilla Aquillar, 61, 184.

Mercado, Pedro de a. Pedro de Guevaro: b. Madrid; son of Doctor Mercado, physician in Madrid and related to many penanced by the Inquisition in Seville; served as spy for the Jews in Mexico; a learned man. Either as actor or usher he gave two seats in the first rows for a theatrical performance to two Jews who had been reconciled by the Holy Office "while Catholics and honored people were standing" and later he took the Jews to his home and feted them; a fugitive. Observer of Mosaic laws; relaxed in effigy in 1649.

Abec.; AGN 395, No. 1; AGN 414, fol. 197; Medina, *México* 205.

Merino, Fernando. Observer of Mosaic laws.

AHN 1738, No. 1.

Mexia, Francisca: mentioned several times in proceso of Antonio Benites for porging.

AGN 356.

Mezquita, Fernando de: 1644 proceso. Judaizante.

AGN 419, No. 27.

Mezquita (Amezquita), Francisco: b. Segovia; son of Lope de Mezquita and Isabel Gomez, both b. Segovia and Hebrew New Christians; brother of Luis Mezquita Sarmiento; 1630 testimony from Lima. Judaizante; relaxed in effigy in 1649 auto.

> AGN 366, No. 4; Medina, *México* 408.

Mezquita, Lope de: 1642 testimony of Bartolome Alfaro. Judaizante. AGN 425, No. 12.

Mezquita Sarmiento, Luis a. Luis Amezquita Sarmiento: age 50; b. Segovia, Castile; son of Lopez (sic–Lope?) de Mezquita, b. Seville, and Isabel Gomez, of Mexico, both Hebrew New Christians; merchant; single; caught while trying to escape to Spain. Judaizante and observer of Mosaic laws; reconciled in 1646 auto, confiscation of property, sanbenito, 200 lashes, exile from the Indies, Seville, and Madrid.

> AGN 389, No. 8; AGN 399, No. 2; AGN 413, No. 19; AGN 414, Nos. 1, 2; AGN 415, No. 5; AGN 499, No. 4; García 28: 65; Medina, *México* 193.

Miguel, Cristobal: former reconciliado. Accused of wearing silk about 1604.

> AGN 368, No. 56; AGN 592, No. 19; Liebman, *Guide* 1159.

Miguel, Cristobal. *See* Maria de Leon.

Millan, Francisco: b. Villa de Hutera, near Seville, ca. 1500; m. Isabel Sanchez, b. Jerez; six minor children in Spain with mother; innkeeper; claimed he could not write; arrested in 1538; charged judío, judaizante in Lisbon. Judío; confessed; reconciled in 1539 auto, abjuration de vehementi, sanbenito, exile from New Spain and the Indies. [He did not leave Mexico, however, and was rearrested.]

> Abec.; AGN 30, No. 9; Greenleaf, "Francisco Millan," 184; Greenleaf, *Mexican Inquisition* 70.

Mirabel, Mariana de: denounced in 1602. Porging.

> AGN 452, No. 8.

Miranda, Cristobal de: r. Merida, Yucatan; dean of cathedral at Merida; denounced by Bishop de Landa in 1575. Jewish ancestors had been relaxed.

> AGN 55, No. 4; AGN 75, No. 3; AGN 79, No. 10; AGN 80, No. 17; AGN 82, Nos. 32, 35; AGN 83, No. 4. Lengthy proceso was never terminated.

Miranda, Enrique (Henrique) de a. Henrique Mendez; Portuguese; son of Gaspar Mendez and Beatriz Hernandez, both of San Vicente Davera; brother of Francisco Home; r. Guadalajara; merchant; 1642 proceso. Judío; died prior to sentence; relaxed in effigy in 1649.

> Abec.; AGN 391, No. 1; AGN 398, No. 4; AGN 414, No. 10.

Miranda, Pedro de: b. Antequera; 1664 proceso. Suspicion of judío.

> AGN 599, No. 12.

Moisen Gomez, Alberto. *See* Fernando de Medina.

Molina, Gonzalo de: b. Taxco; grandson of Antonio Machado. Judaizante and descendant of Jews; reconciled; 1611-1614 testimony for wearing silk, bearing a sword, and riding a horse.

> AGN 223, fol. 355; AGN 308, No. 1. Lewin, *Inquisición* 305 contains a transcript of part of the proceso.

Montero, Elena. *See* Simon Montero.

Montero, Simon: age 49; b. Casteloblanco; son of Francisco Antuñez and Antonia Nuñez, both b. Casteloblanco; his mother, the daughter of Isabel Rodriguez and Diego Enriquez, had been reconciled by the Holy Office in Lisbon; full brother of Duarte de Leon Jaramillo, relaxed in 1649; full brother of Jorge de Leon, the husband of Beatriz Enriquez, "well known in Seville," where she and her husband had resided; circumcised; m. Elena Montero, b. Seville, daughter of Hebrew New Christians; first came to New Spain in 1633; arrested ca. 1634. Judaizante; freed by the Holy Office in Mexico ca. 1635; left for Spain and then went to France, Pisa, and Rome, where he studied Judaism and was ordained as a rabbi by the Jewish community of Rome, officiated at the funeral of Justa Mendez and saw that her funeral shroud was made of pure linen from Rouen; rearrested in 1644. Relapso; relaxed in 1649 auto.

> Abec.; AGN 381, No. 5; AGN 404, No. 4; AGN 426, fol. 525; Medina, *México* 119, 184, 205, 207.

Montes, Simon: 1642 proceso. Judaizante.

> AGN 453, fol. 115.

Monteverde, Antonio: r. Zacatecas; 1693 proceso. Suspicion of judío.

> AGN 689, No. 5.

Montoya, Jorge. *See* Jorge Diaz de Montoya.

Morales, Antonio de: Portuguese; doctor; nephew of Manuel de Morales; escaped with his uncle; a fugitive. Judío; relaxed in effigy.

> Abec. gives 1596 as the date of the auto; AGN 168, No. 1, and Toro, *Judíos* 13 indicate 1599 as the date of his arrest.

Morales, Beatriz de a. Beatriz de Rivera: 1599 proceso. Judaizante.

> Abec. [charge cited as bigamy]; AGN 223, fol. 269; Medina, *México* 170 [charge is listed as bigamy].

Morales, Blanca de: sister of Manuel de Morales; m. Pedro Hernandez; a fugitive. Judaizante; relaxed in effigy in 1601.

AGN 152, No. 8; Medina, *México* 123.

Morales, Diego de: b. Seville; brother of Gonzalo de Morales; 1525 arrest by secular courts for blasphemy. Blasphemy, suspicion of judío; public penance, mass, abjuration de vehementi, fine.

Abec. [cites r. Mexico]; AGN 1, No. 6; Greenleaf, *Mexican Inquisition* 30-32; Liebman, *Jews* 115, 138; Toro, *Judíos* 124 [states r. Guatemala].

Morales, Gonzalo de: b. Seville; brother of Diego de Morales; shopkeeper; Jewish lineage. Heresy, judaizante; relaxed alive October 17, 1528.

Abec.; Greenleaf, *Mexican Inquisition* 33; Liebman, *Guide* 1040; Medina, *México* 95.

Morales, Juan de: 1646 proceso; confessed to Judaism. Judaizante.

AGN 423, No. 2; AHN 1738, No. 1.

Morales, Juan. *See* Pedro Lopez de Morales.

Morales, Manuel de: b. Portugal; doctor in Venice prior to coming to New Spain and after his escape; m. Isabel Perez. Judaizante.

Abec.; AGN 127, No. 3; Liebman, *Guide* 1072; Liebman, *Jews* 25, 58, 144-46, 151, 169, 173, 181, 270; Medina, *México* 101, 110, 133; Toro, *Judíos* 51. *See also* Antonio de Morales, Blanca de Morales, and Isabel Clara.

Morales Gomez, Alberto. *See* Fernando de Medina.

Moreno, Fernando: b. Lisbon; r. Miguatlan; tortured and abused by Inquisitor Peralta. Judaizante.

AHN 1738, No. 1; Medina, *México* 227 [contains a large part of the report].

Moreno, Geronimo: a Holy Office report.

AGN 399, No. 12.

Morera (Moreira), Margarita: age 36; b. Mexico; daughter of Pascual Morera, capmaker, b. Camiña, and Catalina Diaz, b. Seville; m. first Amaro Diaz Matarana; m. second Pedro de Castro, b. Seville; tortured; confessed; interesting account of manner in which the Jews of Mexico City were called to synagogue for prayer or special meetings. Judío and observer of Mosaic laws; reconciled in 1646, abjuration de vehementi, sanbenito, confiscation of property, life imprisonment.

The proceso is at the Huntington Library.

Morera, Pascual. *See* Margarita Morera.

Moro, Gerardo: attorney for Royal Court; 1729 proceso. Judío.
   AGN 1169, No. 8.

Moron, Juan: r. Puebla; a high cleric; 1703 proceso. Judío.
   AGN 722, No. 27.

Mosquera, Blas. Judío; striking a priest.
   AGN 31, No. 1; Liebman, *Guide* 1025; Medina, *México* 96.

Muñoz, Diego. *See* Diego Alvarado.

Muñoz Perez, Luis. *See* Luis Nuñez Perez.

Muñoz de Sandoval, Agustin: a military captain; 1695 proceso. Judaizante.
   AGN 560, No. 7.

Narvaez, Antonio a. David Machorro: father of Juan Pacheco de Leon; died in Havana ca. 1639; proceso against his fame and memory. Judaizante.
   AGN 503, No. 7.

Navarro, Francisco: 1598 proceso. Judaizante.
   AGN 223, fol. 496.

Nieto, Francisco. Judío; reconciled.
   AHN 1738.

Nieto Ramos, Francisco: b. Casteloblanco; son of Simon Gonzalez of Casteloblanco, who had been imprisoned by the Holy Office in Seville; m. Clara Fernandez in Seville, who died; m. then Isabel Nuñez in Mexico; all Hebrews. Observer of Mosaic laws; reconciled in 1649 auto, confiscation of property, sanbenito, 200 lashes, exile from the Indies, Madrid, and Seville.
   Abec.; AGN 389, No. 8; AGN 391, No. 1; AGN 414, No. 2; Medina, *México* 203.

Noguera, Crisobal: r. Cuautla. Suspicion of judaizante.
   AGN 301, No. 54; AGN 471, No. 51.

Nuñez, Ana: age 13; b. Mexico; daughter of Duarte de Leon Jaramillo and Isabel Nuñez. Observer of Mosaic laws; reconciled in 1648 auto, sanbenito, abjuration de vehementi, exile from the Indies, Seville, and Madrid.
   Abec.; AGN 426, fol. 524; García 28:197; Medina, *México* 117, 119. Part of the proceso is at Washington State University and part is at the Gilcrease Institute.

Nuñez, Andres: b. Mogodouro; a servant; fugitive. Judaizante; relaxed in effigy; captured in Peru and sentenced there; was in Lima auto of December 10, 1600.

>Abec.; AGN 159, No. 3; AHN lib. 1029, fols. 53R-55R; Medina, *México* 162; Toro, *Judíos* 12.

Nuñez, Antonia: age 15; b. Mexico; daughter of Duarte de Leon Jaramillo and Isabel Nuñez; sister of Ana Nuñez. Observer of Mosaic laws; reconciled in 1648 auto, sanbenito, confiscation of property, abjuration de vehementi, two years in jail, exile from the Indies, Seville, and Madrid.

>AGN 426, fol. 523; García 28:201; Liebman, *Jews* 258; Medina, *México* 117, 195.

Nuñez, Antonio: 1594 proceso. Judaizante.

>AGN 223, fols. 458, 499.

Nuñez, Antonio: son of Duarte de Leon Jaramillo and Isabel Nuñez; brother of Ana Nuñez and Francisco de Leon Jaramillo; the data concerning his circumcision and other matters are in the proceso of his father.

>Liebman, *Guide* 1200.

Nuñez, Beatriz: b. Guarda; m. Francisco Rodriguez; testimony by her son, Manuel Rodriguez Nuñez, in 1642. Judaizante.

>AGN 414, fol. 164.

Nuñez, Clara: age 23. Observer of Mosaic laws; reconciled in 1648 auto, confiscation of property, sanbenito, abjuration de vehementi, exile from the Indies, Madrid, and Seville.

>AGN 389, No. 8; AGN 291, No. 10 [where reference is made to another Clara Nuñez who died before 1642]; García 28:216; Medina, *México* 118. The proceso is at the Gilcrease Institute.

Nuñez, Diego a. Diego Nuñez Batoca: m. Juana Rodriguez, the mother of Clara de Silva. Judaizante and observer of Mosaic laws; died in cell; relaxed in effigy in 1649 auto.

>Abec.; AGN 453, fol. 91.

Nuñez, Diego a. Diego Pacheco: age 52; b. Valverde ca. 1591; son of Luis Fernandez, merchant, and Beatriz Gonzalez, both of Guarda, Portugal, and both Hebrew New Christians; r. Querétaro; merchant; m. Maria de Leon; had four children; arrested in 1632; his pseudonym while in jail was Mecate. Judaizante; reconciled; rearrested as judaizante; died prior to sentence; relaxed in effigy in 1649 auto.

>Abec.; AGN 372, No. 21; AGN 413, fol. 279; AGN 414, fol. 241; AGN 415, fol. 199; AGN 417, fol. 468; AGN 419, fol. 252; AGN 453, fol. 91; Medina, *México* 205.

Nuñez, Francisca: b. Mexico; daughter of Justa Mendez and Francisco Nuñez a. Rodriguez; m. Juan de Roxas. Judío and observer of Mosaic laws; deceased; relaxed in effigy in 1649 auto.

> Abec.; AGN 391, No. 1; AGN 405, Nos. 1, 9; AGN 415, fols. 142, 256; AGN 500, No. 8.

Nuñez, Francisco. *See* Francisco Nuñez Navarro.

Nuñez, Geronimo. *See* Nuñez Huerta, Miguel.

Nuñez, Guiomar a. Guiomar Rodriguez. Observer of Mosaic laws.

> AGN 391, No. 10.

Nuñez, Isabel: b. 1610, Bordeaux, France; daughter of Leonor Nuñez and Diego Fernandez Cardado; m. Luis Perez Roldan. Observer of Mosaic laws; reconciled on April 2, 1635; rearrested 1642; relaxed in effigy in 1649 auto.

> AGN 381, Nos. 5, 7; Liebman, *Jews* 245; Medina, *México* 119, 185, 204, 205.

Nuñez, Isabel: b. Mexico; daughter of Justa Mendez and Francisco Nuñez; m. Duarte de Leon Jaramillo; mother of Ana, b. 1635; Antonia Nuñez, b. ca. 1631; Simon de Leon, b. ca. 1634; Antonio Nuñez; Jorge, b. ca. 1638; Francisco de Leon Jaramillo; Clara de Leon, b. ca. 1637. Observer of Mosaic laws; sentenced in 1635 auto; a new proceso was opened against her in 1642 for being an observer of Mosaic laws and dragging a statue of Christ.

> Abec.; AGN 391, No. 1; AGN 401, No. 1; AGN 414, No. 2; AGN 415, No. 4; Medina, *México* 119, 200, 208.

Nuñez, Isabel. *See* Francisco Nieto Ramos.

Nuñez, Isabel. *See* Simon Fernandez a. Simon Fernandez de Torres.

Nuñez, Jeronimo a. Geronimo de Roxas: age 34; b. La Guarda; son of Rodrigo Nuñez, b. Linares, Portugal, and Isabel Fernandez, b. La Guarda; both parents died in La Guarda and both were Hebrew New Christians; half-brother of Agustin de Rojas; circumcised; servant in the mines of Zacatecas; single. Judío and observer of Mosaic laws; reconciled in 1646 auto, sanbenito, confiscation of property, jail for one year, exile.

> AGN 404, No. 1; AGN 415, Nos. 1, 3; AGN 417, No. 18; AGN 453, fol. 107; García 28:54; Medina, *México* 114, 193.

Nuñez, Leonor: b. Madrid; r. Ixmiquilpan; m. three times; had three daughters, Isabel Nuñez and Ana and Maria Gomez, and a son, Francisco Blandon; denounced in Peru; arrested in Mexico. Observer of Mosaic laws; reconciled in auto of 1635, two years jail, confiscation of property, relaxed alive in 1649 auto.

Abec.; AGN 379 (2 procesos); AGN 381, No. 5; AGN 404, No. 4; AGN 419, No. 35; AGN 426, No. 7; Liebman, *Jews* 221, 222, 245, 247, 260, 261; Medina, *México* 184, 204.

Nuñez, Leonor: over age 70; b. Seville; daughter of Gaspar de Agurto and Maria Nuñez; r. Veracruz; widow of Manuel Coronel, a broker of Veracruz. Observer of Mosaic laws; reconciled in 1646 auto, abjuration de vehementi, sanbenito, two years jail, exile from Veracruz and within twenty leagues around it, two years service in hospital in Mexico, to be taught Christianity after jail term.

AGN 404, No. 4; AGN 419, No. 35; García 28:66; Medina, *México* 205.

Nuñez, Leonor. *See* Antonio Caravallo.

Nuñez, Manuel: b. Portugal; r. Tabasco in 1604. Judaizante.

AGN 368, No. 58; AGN 414, fol. 47.

Nuñez, Maria. *See* Leonor Nunez (b. Seville).

Nuñez, Mariana. *See* Mariana de Carvajal.

Nuñez, Miguel. *See* Miguel Nuñez Huerta.

Nuñez, Miguel: father-in-law of Luis de Carvajal y de la Cueva; agent for the king of Portugal in Santo Domingo in the slave traffic.

AGN 11 (Riva Palacio) No. 3. Proceso of Luis de Carvajal, el Viejo.

Nuñez, Rodrigo. *See* Agustin de Rojas and Jeronimo Nuñez.

Nuñez, Simon: 1646 proceso. Judaizante.

AGN 419, No. 32.

Nuñez, Thomas: b. Bayone, Galicia; accused in 1639. Observer of Mosaic laws.

AGN 387, No. 16.

Nuñez de Agurto, Leonor. Judaizante.

AHN 1738.

Nuñez Baca, Diego. *See* Jorge Jacinto Bazan.

Nuñez Batoca, Diego. *See* Diego Nuñez a. Diego Nuñez Batoca.

Nuñez Caceres, Simon: b. Portugal; r. Guatemala. Judío.

AGN 308, fols. 352-368; AGN 312, No. 7; Chinchilla Aguilar, 183.

Nuñez Caravallo, Manuel. *See* Manuel Rodriguez Nuñez.

Nuñez Diaz, Gaspar: b. Cartagena. Judaizante.

AGN 405, No. 2; AGN 413, fols. 3, 4, 206, 208; AGN 414, Nos. 7, 10; AGN 415, fol. 284.

Nuñez de Franco, Pablo. *See* Juan Mendez de Villaviciosa.

Nuñez Huerta, Miguel a. Miguel Nuñez a. Manuel de Huerta: age 38; b. Cubillana, Portugal; son of Geronimo Nuñez, b. Somar, and Beatriz Rodriguez of Fondon, both parents Hebrew New Christians; merchant trading between Havana and New Spain; m. Margarita de Rivera; his cousin Gabriel Rodriguez had been reconciled in Lisbon as a judaizante. Judío and observer of Mosaic laws; died in the secret cell after confessing; relaxed in effigy in 1649 auto.

    Abec.; AGN 390, No. 11; AGN 404, Nos. 1, 2, 4, 5; AGN 405, No. 3; AGN 414, No. 3; AGN 415, Nos. 1, 6; AGN 421, No. 2; AGN 453, fol. 46; Medina, *México* 192, 205.

Nuñez de Leon, Juan: age 48; b. Villa de Cea, Spain; official of the Royal Mint; father of seven children; 1596 proceso. Suspicion of judaizante, alumbrado or illuminati; convicted for being "suspected of practicing the law of Moses;" reconciled in auto of April 20, 1603, abjuration de vehementi, fine of 5,000 Castillian ducats for extraordinary expenses of the Holy Office.

    AGN 210, No. 2.

Nuñez de Luna, Licenciado Pedro: curator of church, 1647 information from Temascaltepec. Judaizante.

    AGN 391, No. 2.

Nuñez de Montalvan, Pedro: r. Tlaxcala; 1576 proceso. Descendant of Jews.

    AGN 81, No. 17; Medina, *México* 76; Toro, *Judíos* 10.

Nuñez Navarro, Francisco a. Francisco Nuñez: age 43; b. Villa de Chazin, Portugal; son of Francisco Nuñez, b. and d. in Chazin, and Catalina Enriquez, b. La Torre de Moncorbo, both Hebrew New Christians; circumcised; bachelor; peddler; r. Guadalajara; testimony by Rafaela Enriquez, Violante Juarez, and Isabel Antuñez. Observer of Mosaic laws; confessed; reconciled in auto of 1646, sanbenito, confiscation of property, abjuration de vehementi, life imprisonment.

    Abec.; AGN 414, fol. 256; AGN 415, fols. 418, 441; AGN 492, No. 5; Medina, *México* 114, 193.

Nuñez de Ocaña, Beatriz. *See* Diego de Ocaña.

Nuñez de la Paz, Felipa. Suspicion of judaizante; reconciled in 1648 auto.

    Medina, *México* 194.

Nuñez de Peralta, Thomas: b. Cubillan ca. 1604; son of Jorge Vaez Alcaceria, a leather tanner, and Isabel Rodriguez, both of Cubillan;

circumcised; trader and merchant in Zacatecas and in the interior of the country; m. Beatriz Enriquez; first cousin of Juan Duarte a. Juan Duarte Fernandez. Observer of Mosaic laws and judío; reconciled in 1646 auto; confiscation of property, sanbenito, 200 lashes, life imprisonment, exile from the Indies.

> Abec.; AGN 392, No. 7; AGN 395, No. 5; AGN 396, No. 3; AGN 419, No. 9; AGN 498, No. 2; García 28:84; Medina, *México* 116, 193.

Nuñez Perez, Luis a. Luis Muñoz Perez: age 30; b. Samamede, near Lisbon; son of Manuel Rodriguez Acuña a. Manuel de Abeña and Barbola Diaz Silva, both Hebrew New Christians; his mother was born in Lisbon; circumcised; single; seller of cocoa and peanuts. Observer of Mosaic laws and heretical judaizante; reconciled in 1646, sanbenito; confiscation of property, abjuration de vehementi, life imprisonment.

> AGN 401, No. 4; AGN 406, fol. 71; AGN 412, No. 2; AGN 415, No. 7; AGN 416, No. 41; AGN 426, No. 7; AGN 453, fol. 59; García 28:64; González Obregón, *México* 695. [In his proceso is a copy of an agreement between Holland and Portugal.]

Nuñez de Roxas, Augustin. *See* Augustin de Rojas.

Nuñez de Segovia, Alvaro: b. Portugal; m. Cridonia de Campos; died in Havana en route from Spain to New Spain. Observer of Mosaic laws; relaxed in effigy in 1649.

> Abec.; AGN 405, Nos. 1, 9; AGN 415, Nos. 4, 5: AGN 418, No. 10; Medina, *México* 408.

Nuñez Viceo, Diego: 1702 proceso. Judaizante.

> AGN 721, No. 7.

Obandajo, Diego. *See* Diego Perez.

Ocampo, Isabel de: sister of Beatriz Gonzalez, who m. Francisco Rodriguez; r. Veracruz; m. Bernabe Gierra, sword cutter; 1581 proceso.

> AGN 90, No. 38.

Ocaña, Diego de: b. Seville; Jewish lineage; notary and scribe in Mexico; m. Beatriz Nuñez de Ocaña; father of Leonor Xuarez de Ocaña and García Suarez de Ocaña. Heresy, judío; reconciled.

> Abec.; Greenleaf, *México* 35, 36; Liebman, *Guide* 1041; Medina, *México* 95. Ocaña's will appears in AGN *Publicaciones VII*.

Ocaña, Diego de: son of Leonor Xuarez de Ocaña, daughter of Diego de Ocaña, reconciled 1528, condemned to wear sanbenito for a short time.

> Medina, *México* 95.

Olivarez, Fray Benito: accused in 1635. Judaizante.
AGN 381, No. 5.
Olivera (Oliveres), Isabel de. *See* Francisco Lopez de Fonseca.
Olivares, Juan: 1642 testimony by Clara Texoso. Judaizante.
AGN 404, No. 2.
Olivares, Tomasa. *See* Esteban Zerecedo.
Oliver, Don de: m. Antonia de Rivera; 1640 letter from the comisario at Taxco regarding him and his wife. Suspicion of judaizante.
AGN 389, No. 12A.
Olivera, "Fulano": b. Antequera; 1664 proceso. Suspicion of judío.
AGN 599, No. 12.
Ome, Diego: b. Portugal; r. Chiapas; denounced in 1623 for having given instructions to be washed according to the Jewish ritual when he died. Judaizante.
AGN 345, No. 37; Chinchilla Aquilar, 184.
Ome, Francisco. *See* Francisco Home.
Oporto, Francisco: 1642 testimony. Judaizante.
AGN 391, No. 10.
Ordaz, Leonor de: r. Cuautla; 1612 proceso. Suspicion of judaizante and witchcraft.
AGN 455, fol. 196.
Ordoñez, Manuel: b. Seville; 1717. Suspicion of judío.
AGN 775, No. 3.
Orozco, Jorge: referred to in a letter written by the Holy Office to the Suprema containing a report of the status of seven Jews.
AGN 416, No. 41.
Orta, Jorge de: arrested in Acapulco in 1622. Judaizante.
AGN 335, No. 42.
Ortega, Melchor: accused in 1632. Judaizante.
AGN 375, No. 3.
Ortiz, Juan: 1571 proceso. Suspicion of judío.
AGN 49, No. 8; AGN 51, fol. 17.
Pacheco, Andres: 1601 proceso. Suspicion of judío.
AGN 452, fol. 292.
Pacheco, Diego. *See* Diego Nuñez.
Pacheco, Gaspar. *See* Gaspar Rodriguez.
Pacheco de Leon, Juan a. Salomon Machorro: b. either Antequerra, Spain, or Leghorn, Italy; son of Antonio Narvaez David Machorro of Italy; came to New Spain in 1639 with his father who had been engaged to be the spiritual leader of the Simon Vaez Jewish commu-

nity but died in Havana; r. Queretaro; single; tested by Blanca Enriquez, who approved of him as a rabbi. Observer of Mosaic laws; reconciled in auto of July 10, 1650, confiscaton of property, sanbenito, eight years in galleys, life imprisonment.

AGN 416, Nos. 40, 41; Guijo, 111 [Guijo, a witness to the autoda-fé, states that Pacheco de Leon received 300 lashes and ten years in the galleys]; Liebman, *Jews* 24, 230, 267-272; Medina, *México* 243.

Paduano, Francisco: using Jewish ceremonies; 1613.

AGN 478, fol. 415.

Paiba (Payba), Simon a. Simon Rodriguez Paiba: b. Lisbon; m. Beatriz Enriquez; father of Pedro and Diego Enriquez; died prior to sentence. Heretical judaizante; bones disinterred, relaxed in effigy in 1601.

Liebman, *Guide* 1095; Medina, *México* 180; proceso is at the Gilcrease Institute.

Pardo, Nuño: testimony by Manuel Rodriguez Nuñez. Judaizante.

AGN 414, fol. 150.

Paredes, Simon de: r. Texcoco; son of Manuel de Lucena; denounced by Holy Office in Texcoco in 1629. Judío; relaxed alive in 1635.

Abec.; AGN 366, Texcoco.

Paz, Alvaro de: b. Portugal; r. San Miguel, Guatemala; 1677 processo. Judaizante.

AGN 633, No. 6.

Pascual, Juan: r. San Salvador. For saying he had a lamb hidden.

Chinchilla Aquilar, 184.

Peña, Ana de la: r. Tepeaca; 1662 proceso. Suspicion of judío.

AGN 439, No. 22.

Peña, Blas de la: 1642 testimony by Blanca Rivera. Judaizante.

AGN 405, fol. 513.

Peña, Sebastian de la a. Sebastian Cardoso: b. San Juan de Pesquera (sic), bishopric of La Guarda; Jewish ancestry; single. Observer of Mosaic laws; reconciled, sanbenito, confiscation of property, life imprisonment with the first two years to be spent in a monastery where he was to be taught Christianity.

AGN 155, No. 4; AGN 167, No. 3; AGN 271, No. 1; AGN 276, No. 14; García 5:98; Medina, *México* 124, 169.

Peñaloes, Luis de: r. Acapulco. Suspicion of judío.

AGN 452, fol. 330.

Peñaloso Betanzos, Francisco: vicar; 1647 information from Temascaltepec. Judaizante.
> AGN 391, No. 2.

Peralta, Antonio de: relaxed in effigy previously; 1642 proceso. Judaizante.
> AGN 416, No. 40.

Peregrino, Gabriel. *See* Juan Cardoso.

Pereira, Baltasar. Judaizante; case suspended. AHN 1738.

Pereira, Gaspar de: b. Bayonne; arrested in 1623. Judaizante.
> AGN 344, No. 4.

Pereira, Ines: age 23; b. Ixmiquilpan, Mexico; daughter of Gaspar Alvarez, Portuguese, and Ana Gomez; niece of Tomas Treviño de Sobremonte; m. Baltazar Díaz Santillan; some Jews believed that she would give birth to the Messiah. Observer of Mosaic laws; reconciled in 1649 auto, confiscation of property, sanbenito, "perpetual jail for ten years."
> Abec.; Medina, *México* 203.

Pereira, Nuño. *See* Nuño de Figueroa.

Pereira Cardoso, Gaspar: believed to have been mayor of Cartago, Costa Rica, then part of the province of Guatemala; 1610 proceso. Judaizante.
> AGN 474, fol. 333.

Pereiras, Los: r. Antequera; bakers; 1612 proceso. Sons of parents penanced by the Holy Office.
> AGN 455, fol. 356.

Pereyra, Diego: r. Puebla; 1601 testimony. Suspicion of judaizante.
> AGN 467, No. 6.

Pereyra Lobo, Captain Mathias: 1662 proceso; Suspicion of judío.
> AGN 439, No. 24.

Perez, Anton: denounced in 1617. Suspicion of judaizante.
> AGN 315, No. 5C.

Perez, Antonio: Portuguese; r. Oaxtepeque; laborer; denounced in 1650; testimony that T. Treviño de Sobremonte had been a good Jew to die in his law and for statements about Sebastian Vaez de Acevedo.
> AGN 435, fol. 265; AGN 435, No. 1.

Perez, Diego a. Diego Obandajo. Judaizante.
> AHN 1738, No. 1.

Perez, Duarte. Judaizante; reconciled.
> AHN 1738.

Perez, Fernando. Judaizante; reconciled.
AHN 1738.

Perez, Gonzalo; b. Oporto, Portugal; studied judaism. Observer of Mosaic laws; abjuration de levi, 100 lashes in auto of February 24, 1590.
Abec.; Liebman, *Jews* 144, 276.

Perez, Isabel: b. Portugal; m. Manuel de Morales; a fugitive. Observer of Mosaic laws and judío; relaxed in effigy on December 8, 1596.
Abec.; Toro, *Judíos* 59.

Perez, Juan: denounced in 1643; escaped from the cells of the Holy Office. Judaizante.
AHN 585, No. 51.

Perez, Juana. Judaizante; reconciled.
AGN 1738.

Perez, Mathias: accused in 1614 by the comisario of Guadalajara. Suspicion of judaizante.
AGN 301, No. 21.

Perez, Nuño: 1642 proceso. Judaizante.
AGN 415, fol. 193; AGN 453, fol. 570.

Perez, Violante. Judaizante; reconciled.
AHN 1738.

Perez de Albuquerque, Diego: b. Bordeaux; r. Puebla; arrested April 16, 1624; tortured. Judaizante, observer of Mosaic laws; reconciled in 1630 auto, confiscation of property, sanbenito, 100 lashes, six years in galleys, life imprisonment in Seville.
Abec.; AGN 348, No. 5; Medina, *México* 175.

Perez Arias, Gabriel: r. Mexico. Judaizante.
AHN 1738.

Perez del Bosque, Isabel: r. Mexico City. Judaizante.
AHN 1738, No. 1.

Perez del Bosque, Maria: r. Mexico City. Judaizante.
AHN 1738, No. 1.

Perez Caldero, Gonzalo: r. Hueotzingo; 1610 proceso. Judaizante.
AGN 287, No. 6.

Perez Carello, Manuel: testimony by Luis Nuñez Perez in 1642.
AGN 414, fol. 97.

Perez Correa, Rodrigo. Judaizante; reconciled.
AHN 1738.

Perez Ferro, Gonzalo: b. Villaflor, Portugal; single. Suspected observer of Mosaic laws; 100 lashes, exile. Did not leave New Spain; was reapprehended and reconciled in 1601.

Abec.; AGN 126, No. 11.

Perez Nuñez, Manuel. Judaizante; reconciled.

AHN 1738.

Perez de Ocastelo, Lucia. *See* Francisco Luis.

Perez Roldan, Luis: age 50; b. Mexico; son of Francisco Rodriguez a. Francisco Nuñez, who abjured de vehementi in auto of 1596, and Justa Mendez, reconciled in the 1596 auto and relaxed in effigy in 1649; brother of Francisca Nuñez and Isabel Nuñez, reconciled on April 21, 1649; circumcised; m. Isabel Nuñez, who was relaxed in the same auto. Judaizante and observer of Mosaic laws; reconciled in 1649 auto, exile from the Indies, 200 lashes; confiscation of property, sanbenito. Did not leave Mexico; was apprehended in 1656 for not wearing his sanbenito; his excuse was that he had become a thread salesman and customers would not buy from him when he wore it; was in 1659 auto; 100 lashes, jail until he could be put on a boat going to Spain.

Abec.; AGN 381, Nos. 5, 7; AGN 401, No. 3; AGN 414, fol. 164; AGN 415, fol. 118; AGN 487, No. 14; AGN 572, No. 10; Medina, *México* 203, 205, 247.

Perez de Salazar, Heronimo: r. Puebla. Suspicion of judaizante.

AGN 283, No. 49.

Perez Tristan, Marcos. Judaizante; reconciled.

AHN 1738.

Perez de Villadiego, Diego: 1690 proceso. Suspicion of judaizante.

AGN 435, No. 5.

Perpente Joannes, Basilio: b. Spain; miner. Paganism, judaism, and being an apostate.

AGN 770, No. 1.

Pimentel, Jose a. Juan Joseph Pimentel: r. Acapulco; 1717 proceso. "Signs of being a Jew."

AGN 767, No. 13; AGN 777, No. 33; For more complete sources see Jose Diaz Pimienta of Cartagena.

Pinero, Gaspar. *See* Gaspar Mendez.

Pliego, Hernando. *See* Fernando Alvarez Pliego.

Pomar, Jeronimo: b. Majorca; m. Maria de la Vega, b. Spain, in Campeche; 1746 proceso. Judío.

AGN 912, No. 19.

Ponce, Alonzo de: arrested 1604. Judío.
    AGN 274, No. 17.
Ponce de Leon, Juan. *See* Pedro Ponce de Leon Ayala.
Ponce de Leon Ayala, Pedro: son of Juan Ponce de Leon, relaxed in
    person by Inquisition in Seville; 1584 proceso. Descendant of Jews.
    AGN 126, No. 5.
Potello, Antonio: r. Manila; 1642 proceso; he held goods of Simon
    Vaez Sevilla. Judaizante.
    AGN 416, No. 2.
Prieto de Villegas, Antonio: r. Guatemala; arrested in Cartagena. Judío.
    AGN 354, fols. 97-101.
Quiñonez, Diego: b. Spain; r. Cuautla; a lieutenant; 1727 proceso.
    Judío.
    AGN 817, No. 21.
Quiñonez, Francisco: r. Guanajuato; 1715 proceso. Suspicion of judío.
    AGN 760, No. 44.
Ramirez, Isabel. *See* Jorge Ramirez Montilla.
Ramirez, Simon. *See* Simon Lopez.
Ramirez de Guzman, Fernando de a. Juan Ramirez de Guzman a. Juan
    Antonio de Leal Guzman: r. Guadalajara; 1711 proceso. Suspicion
    of judío.
    AGN 737, No. 4.
Ramirez Lopez, Juan: b. Casteloblanco; 1642 testimony by Maria de
    Rivera. Judaizante.
    AGN 415, fol. 297.
Ramirez Montilla, Jorge: age 31; b. Montilla del Marquesado de Priego,
    Andalucia; son of Diego Enriquez Montilla, b. Portugal, d. Seville,
    and Isabel Ramirez, b. Carmona, Andalucia, d. Seville, both Hebrew
    New Christians; his mother's brother was Duarte Leon de Jaramillo;
    r. Querétaro; circumcised; merchant. Judío and observer of Mosaic
    laws; reconciled in auto of 1648, abjuration de vehementi, fined
    2,000 ducats for extraordinary costs of the Holy Office.
    Abec.; García 28:190; Medina, *México* 117, 195.
Ramirez de Montilla, Manuel a. Manuel Ramirez de Montero: b. Mon-
    tilla del Marquesada de Priego; r. Mexico; merchant; died on a trip to
    the Philippines. Observer of Mosaic laws; relaxed in effigy in 1649
    auto.
    Abec.; Medina, *México* 409.
Ramirez de Portella, Manuel: accused in 1642. Judaizante.
    AGN 407, No. 4.

Ramos, Manuel: came to Lima; friend of Luis de Carvajal, el Mozo; "one of the group of Jews;" arrested ca. 1608; absolved in 1611. Judaizante.

> AHN lib. 1029, fols. 454-456R.; García de Prodian 241.

Rasen, Francisco a. Francisco Razin: Frenchman from Normandy; accused in 1643. Judío and Calvinism.

> The proceso is at the Huntington Library.

Raspiera, Nicolas de la: accused in 1635. Judaizante.

> AGN 381, No. 5.

Raymundi y Arengo, Santiago. *See* Santiago Azcazibar.

Renaldos, Jusepe: b. Spain; r. Tlaxcala; admitted that he had never been baptized. Suspicion of judaizante.

> AGN 301, No. 42A.

Reyes, Gaspar de los: b. Seville; pharmacist. Judío; 1572 auto, lashes, and exile.

> Abec. lists as grandson of relaxed; AGN 52, No. 1; Toro, *Judío* 9.

Reza, Maria de: r. Acapulco; 1612 proceso. Suspicion of judaizante.

> AGN 455, fol. 287.

RIBERA. *See* RIVERA and RIVERO.

RIOS. *See also* RODRIGUEZ.

Rios, Gabriel: b. Cercedas, Portugal; descendant of Jews; r. Zacatecas; merchant. Heretical judaizante; reconciled in effigy in 1591.

> Abec. [which has a Gabriel Rodriguez for 1591, b. Portugal and reconciled in effigy for being an observer of Mosaic laws]; Medina, *México* 109 [which states that a Gabriel Rodriguez had escaped the Inquisition and it was learned that he had died and was reconciled in effigy]; Toro, *Judíos* 52.

Rios, Pedro. *See* Pedro Rodriguez.

Riosas, Pedro. *See* Pedro Rodriguez.

RIVERA. *See also* RIVERO.

Rivera, Ana de: testimony by Clara de Texoso. Observer of Mosaic laws.

> AGN 404, No. 2.

Rivera, Antonia de: r. Taxco; m. Don de Oliver; 1640 letter from the comisario at Taxco with information regarding her and her husband. Suspicion of judaizante.

> AGN 389, No. 12A.

Rivera, Beatriz de. *See* Beatriz de Morales.

Rivera, Blanca de a. Blanca Mendez: b. Seville; daughter of Enrique Rodriguez Obregon, b. Llerena, Spain, a broker of Negroes from

Angola to New Spain, and Margarita Lopez de Llerena; came to
Mexico in 1621; widow of Diego Lopez Rivera, b. Casteloblanco and
a merchant there; had six children including Maria, Margarita, Catalina, Clara, and Isabel. Judío and observer of Mosaic laws; reconciled
in 1646 auto, confiscation of property, sanbenito, 100 lashes, life
imprisonment in Spain.

> Abec.; AGN 390, No. 11; AGN 391, No. 10; AGN 396, No. 4;
> AGN 399, Nos. 5, 7, 11; AGN 401, No. 4; AGN 404, No. 4; AGN
> 405, Nos. 8, 9; AGN 406, No. 1; AGN 413, fols. 189-191,
> 217-219, 265-271; AGN 414, Nos. 6, 9; AGN 415, No. 4; AGN
> 417, No. 16; AGN 426, No. 7; AGN 453, fol. 531; AGN 500, No.
> 6; AGN (Riva Palacio) 56, No. 3; 68; García 28:44; Medina,
> *México* 115, 191, 193.

Rivera, Catalina: age 27; b. Seville; daughter of Diego Lopez Rivera, b.
Castille and relaxed in 1649 auto, and Blanca Rivera a. Mendez,
reconciled in 1646; m. Diego Correa; aunt of Rafael and Gabriel de
Granada; died in cell. Judaizante; relaxed in effigy in 1649.

> Abec.; AGN 391, No. 10; AGN 396, No. 4; AGN 405, No. 1;
> AGN 413, fols. 205-258; AGN 414, Nos. 7, 8, 9; AGN 415, No.
> 1; AGN 417, fol. 522; AGN 453, fol. 525; Medina, *México* 205.

Rivera, Clara de. Judaizante.

> AGN 256, No. 11.

Rivera, Clara de: age 26; b. Seville; daughter of Diego Lopez Rivera and
Blanca Rivera a. Mendez; m. Felipe Lopez de Noroña; confessed and
died in the secret cells. Judaizante and observer of Mosaic laws;
reconciled in 1646, relaxed in effigy in a private auto in 1649 after
her bones were disinterred.

> Abec.; AGN 396, No. 4; AGN 404, No. 1; AGN 405, Nos. 1, 2, 3,
> 9; AGN 406, fol. 501; AGN 413, Nos. 19, 32; AGN 414, Nos. 1,
> 6Z, 8; AGN 415, fol. 378; AGN 417, fol. 523; AGN 453, fols.
> 11-31, 475-76; AGN 487, No. 20 [which mentions a daughter];
> Medina, México 116, 191, 194.

Rivera, Isabel de: age 25; b. Seville; daughter of Diego Lopez Rivero
and Blanca Rivera a Mendez; maker of hoop skirts. Judío and observer of Mosaic laws; reconciled in 1646 auto, confiscation of property, sanbenito, abjuration de vehementi, 200 lashes, exile, life imprisonment.

> Abec.; AGN 393, No. 4; AGN 396, Nos. 1, 4; AGN 399, Nos. 4,
> 5, 7; AGN 401, No. 4; AGN 404, Nos. 1, 5; AGN 406, fols. 16,
> 286-353, 537; AGN 413, fols. 220-234, 259-264; AGN 414, Nos.

5, 6, 6A; AGN 415, Nos. 1, 2; AGN 453, fol. 481; García 28:58; Medina, *México* 115, 191, 193.

Rivera, Margarita de: b. Seville; daughter of Diego Lopez Rivera and Blanca Rivera a. Mendez; m. Miguel Nuñez Huerta. Judío; reconciled in 1646 auto, sanbenito, confiscation of property, abjuration de vehementi, life imprisonment in Seville.

AGN 369, No. 16; AGN 394, No. 2; AGN 405, Nos. 1, 8, 9; AGN 408, No. 1; AGN 414, No. 6; AGN 453, fols. 151-470, 533, and others; García 28:67-70; Liebman, *Guide* 1122; Medina, *México* 113, 115, 191, 193.

Rivera, Margarita de: b. Seville; daughter of Manuel Mendez. Judaizante.

AGN 399, No. 12.

Rivera (Ribera), Maria de: age 38; b. Seville; daughter of Diego Lopez Rivero of Casteloblanco and Blanca Rivera; sister of Margarita, Catalina, Isabel, and Clara de Rivera; widow of Manuel de Granada; mother of Rafael and Gabriel de Granada. Judío; died in the cells of the Holy Office; relaxed in effigy in April 1649.

AGN 393, No. 3; AGN 396, No. 4; AGN 401, No. 4; AGN 403, No. 3; AGN 404, Nos. 1, 2, 5, 6; AGN 405, Nos. 6A, 8, 9; AGN 413, fols. 89-91, 153, 154; AGN 414, Nos. 1, 6, 6A, 8, 9; AGN 415, Nos. 1, 2, 4, 5; AGN 417, No. 16; AGN 440, No. 3; AGN 453, fols. 467, 468, 521, 565; AGN 498, No. 4; AGN 499, No. 4.

Rivera Maldonado, Catalina: 1642 testimony. Judaizante.

AGN 391, No. 10.

Rivero, Juan: b. Portugal; ironworker; two procesos. Judaizante.

AGN 429, No. 13; AGN 436, No. 16.

Robledo, Gaspar de: 1642 testimony against him. Judaizante.

AGN 413, No. 32.

Robles, Antonio: 1642 proceso. Judaizante.

AGN 499, No. 4.

Robles, Gaspar de: age 32; b. Guarda or San Vicente Davera; Jewish parents; confessed and testified against others. Judaizante and observer of Mosaic laws; reconciled in 1646 auto.

Abec.; AGN 390, No. 1; AGN 404, Nos. 5, 9; AGN 415, Nos. 6, 7; AGN 453, fol. 94; AGN 498, No. 2; Liebman, *Jews* 225, 254.

Rocabal, Pedro la a. Pedro la Rozaval: r. Puebla. Suspicion of judío and Lutheranism.

AGN 150, No. 6; Toro, *Judíos* 10.

Rodriguez, Alvaro: Portuguese; nicknamed Achocado, the hoarder.

Judaizante; fugitive; relaxed in effigy in 1601.
>   Abec.; AGN 161, No. 12.

Rodriguez, Ana. *See* Enrique Fernandez.

Rodriguez, Ana. *See* Melchor Rodriguez Lopez.

Rodriguez, Andres: b. Fondon; r. Texcoco; merchant; single; fasted Mondays and Thursdays. Observer of Mosaic laws and judaizante; reconciled, confiscation of property, 200 lashes, five years in galleys without pay, sanbenito, life imprisonment in Seville.
>   Abec.; AGN 155, No. 1; AGN 252, No. 1; García 5:103; Liebman, *Guide* 1045, 1074; Toro, *Judíos* 59.

Rodriguez, Anton: 1601 proceso; denounced by Manuel Gil de la Guarda. Judaizante.
>   AGN 256, No. 15N.

Rodriguez, Antonio: brother of Domingo Rodriguez. Judaizante; reconciled.
>   García 5:108; Liebman, *Guide* 1100; Toro, *Judíos* 59.

Rodriguez, Antonio: b. San Vicente Davera; single. Heretical judaizante; relaxed in effigy in 1596.
>   Martínez del Río 115; Toro, *Judíos* 65.

Rodriguez, Antonio. *See* Antonio Caravallo.

Rodriguez, Antonio. *See* Antonio Rodriguez of Cartagena.

Rodriguez, Antonio. *See* Gaspar Suarez.

Rodriguez, Baltasar: 1581 declaration; son of Blanca Lorenzo, who had been reconciled by the Inquisition in Spain. Descendant of Jews.
>   AGN 125, No. 25.

Rodriguez, Beatriz. *See* Miguel Nuñez Huerta.

Rodriguez, Beatriz: aunt of Francisco Home; 1641 testimony against her by Manuel de Mella and others. Judaizante.
>   AGN 391, No. 1; AGN 405, No. 6A.

Rodriguez, Blanca: 1642 testimony by Blanca de Rivera and Manuel Rodriguez Nuñez. Judaizante.
>   AGN 405, fol. 562; AGN 414, fol. 160.

Rodriguez, Clotilde. *See* Clara Texoso.

Rodriguez, Constanza: b. Seville; m. Sebastian Rodriguez, born San Vicente Davera; 1595 proceso. Judaizante and observer of Mosaic laws; confiscation of property, sanbenito, life imprisonment.
>   Abec.; AGN 154, No. 2; AGN 276, No. 14; AGN 277, Nos. 6C, 7A; AGN 279, No. 9; García 5:96; Liebman, *Guide* 1099; Medina, *México* 124; Toro, *Judíos* 11.

Rodriguez, Diego a. Diego Bandejo: Portuguese; his parents were Hebrew New Christians; a member of his family had been imprisoned by the Holy Office in Lima, and before that other members of his family had been imprisoned by the Inquisition in Lisbon; a fugitive. Observer of Mosaic laws; relaxed in effigy in 1649.

Abec.; Bocanegra [which lists Diego Rodriguez a. Obandajo]; González Obregón, *México* 709.

Rodriguez, Domingo: Portuguese; r. Ciudad Real, Guatemala; removed the landrecilla from a roasted lamb. Suspicion of judío.

AGN 285, fol. 111; Chinchilla Aquilar 183.

Rodriguez, Domingo a. Domingo Diaz a. Diez: b. Mexico; r. Puebla in 1622. Judío and observer of Mosaic laws; reconciled, confiscation of property, sanbenito, five years in galleys, life imprisonment.

AGN 391, No. 1. Most of his proceso is at Huntington Library.

Rodriguez, Domingo a. Domingo Rios: b. Portugal; brother of Antonio Rodriguez; r. Manila. Judaizante; reconciled; body was disinterred and burned in the 1596 auto.

Abec.; García 5:108; Liebman, *Guide* 1032, 1049, 1071, 1100; Toro, *Judíos* 59.

Rodriguez, Duarte: b. Villana (sic), bishopric of La Guarda, Portugal; single; merchant. Observer of Mosaic laws; reconciled in 1596 auto, confiscation of property, sanbenito, 100 lashes.

Abec.; AGN 157, No. 3; AGN 160, No. 2; AGN 223, No. 33; AGN 279, No. 9; García 5:102.

Rodriguez, Duarte a. Duarte Rodriguez Tejoso: b. Alpedrina, Portugal; son of Baltazar Rodriguez and Mencia Rodriguez, both b. Alpedrina; first cousin of Rodrigo Vaez Pereira who was relaxed alive in 1639 Lima auto; r. Veracruz; merchant; m. Clara Texoso, b. Lima, Peru, and reconciled on January 23, 1647; father of Pedro Gomez, b. Veracruz; sentenced by the Holy Office in Lima but escaped; his home in Veracruz served as the Jewish communal center for prayer and Jewish culture; apprehended in Mexico. Judaizante; reconciled on January 23, 1647, abjuration de vehementi, sanbenito, confiscation of property, 200 lashes, life imprisonment.

Abec.; AGN 393, No. 3; AGN 404, No. 2; AGN 415, No. 1; AGN 421, No. 8; AGN 453, fol. 393; García 28:103; Part of the proceso is at the Gilcrease Institute.

Rodriguez, Elena. *See* Jorge Jacinto Bazan.

Rodriguez, Esperanza: age 64; b. Seville; daughter of Isabel, a Negress

who died in Seville, and Francisco Rodriguez, a Hebrew New Christian; mulatto with white skin; seamstress; widow of Juan Baptista
del Bosque, a German sculptor and carpenter who died in Guadalajara, also judío; mother of: Diego, m. to a person of noble descent;
Juana del Bosque, m. to Blas Lopez, a Portuguese; Juan del Bosque;
and Maria del Bosque; had been freed by her former mistress Catalina Enriquez, a Jewess, then in the Inquisition cells for being an
observer of Mosaic laws. Judío and observer of the laws of Moses;
confessed; reconciled, confiscation of property, sanbenito, life imprisonment in Spain.

   Abec.; AGN 391, No. 10; AGN 407, No. 8; AGN 408, No. 2;
   AGN 414, No. 5; AGN 415, Nos. 6, 7; AGN 419, No. 6; AGN
   427, No. 6; Medina, *México* 193.

Rodriguez, Felipa. *See* Manuel Coronel.

Rodriguez, Fernando: age 58; b. Haveiro, Portugal; son of Fernando
Lanzarote and Beatriz de Herrera, both of Haveiro; r. Puebla and
Veracruz; merchant and broker in the slave trade; his home in Veracruz served for many years as a hostel for the secret Jews immigrating in New Spain; circumcised; m. Blanca Enriquez; had eight children. Judío and observer of Mosaic laws; reconciled in auto of January 23, 1645, abjuration de vehementi, 200 lashes, confiscation of
property, sanbenito, life imprisonment.

   Abec.; AGN 405, No. 8; AGN 413, fols. 74-81; AGN 419, Nos.
   19, 40 and fols. 507-513; García 28:106; Medina, *México* 194.

Rodriguez, Francisco: b. San Vicente Davera; single; shoemaker. Judaizante; reconciled in auto of December 8, 1596, abjuration de levi,
convicted of concealing Jews, for which he received 100 lashes and
two years of exile from Mexico City.

   Abec.; AGN 160, No. 1; AGN 223, No. 35; AGN 254A, Nos. 4A,
   4B; Medina, *México* 101; Toro, *Judíos* 12 and 59 [states relaxed
   in effigy in 1597 auto].

Rodriguez, Francisco: b. Casteloblanco; father of Manuel Rodriguez,
who appeared in the auto of 1649; r. Panuco, Huejtla, and Queretaro; m. Beatriz Nuñez. Judaizante; reconciled, confiscation of property, sanbenito.

   AGN 289, No. 3A; AGN 308, No. 35; AGN 366, No. 5; AGN
   414, fol. 213; AGN 419, No. 56.

Rodriguez, Francisco. *See* Maria de Espinoza.
Rodriguez, Francisco. *See* Beatriz Gonzalez.

Rodriguez, Francisco. *See* Thomas Mendez.

Rodriguez, Francisco. *See* Esperanza Rodriguez.

Rodriguez, Francisco. *See* Manuel Rodriguez Nuñez.

Rodriguez, Francisco a. Francisco Nuñez: b. San Vicente Davera; m. Justa Mendez. Judaizante.

> AGN 156, No. 3; AGN 391, No. 1; AGN 254A, No. 4A; Toro, *Judíos* 12 quotes AGN 157, No. 5, March 1596, and states that he was a fugitive, which is incorrect; Toro, *Judíos* 59 gives the same name and birthplace and indicates relaxed in effigy.

Rodriguez, Francisco a. Francisco Rodriguez de Seas or Ceas or Desa or Deza: Portuguese; silversmith; m. Leonor Diaz. Judizante; fugitive; relaxed in effigy in 1601.

> Abec.; AGN 155, No. 3 [cites b. Seville]; González Obregón *México* [states b. San Vicente Davera].

Rodriguez, Fructuoso. *See* Mathias Rodriguez de Olivera.

Rodriguez, Gabriel: b. Portugal; dealer. Heresy and judaizante; reconciled in effigy.

> Abec.

Rodriguez, Gabriel. *See also* Gabriel Rios.

Rodriguez, Gabriel a. Gabriel Pacheco: b. Fondon, Portugal; Jewish parents; nephew of Francisco Rodriguez, Duarte, and Andres Rodriguez. Judaizante and observer of Mosaic laws; confessed; reconciled, confiscation of property, sanbenito, jail for four years, spiritual penance.

> AHN 1029, fols. 49V-50V.

Rodriguez, Gabriel a. Gabriel Rodriguez Arias: b. Veracruz; son of Antonio Rodriguez Arias and Blanca Enriquez; accused in 1642. Judaizante; relaxed in effigy in 1649 auto.

> AGN 399, No. 16; AHN 1738.

Rodriguez, Gaspar: r. Caracas. Judaizante.

> AHN 1738, No. 1.

Rodriguez, Gaspar. *See* Melchor Rodriguez.

Rodriguez, Gaspar a. Gaspar Rodriguez de Segura; accused in 1642; considerable testimony; likely a fugitive. Judío.

> AGN 414, fol. 80; AGN 415, fols. 121, 412; AGN 425, fol. 531.

Rodriguez, Geronimo: b. San Vicente Davera; r. Puebla. Aiding and concealing heretical Jews; reconciled 1602, abjuration de vehementi.

> AGN 425, fol. 215; Medina, *México* 123.

Rodriguez, Gonzalo: 1644 proceso. Judaizante.

> AGN 419, No. 17.

Rodriguez, Guillermo: son of Violante Rodriguez; merchant; accused in
1608. Judaizante.

> Medina, *México* 112. [Medina gives as his source Bocanegra's
> *Relación* of the 1647 auto, but no mention of either mother or
> son is made in it.]

Rodriguez, Guiomar. *See* Guiomar Nuñez.

Rodriguez, Hernando: Holy Office report to Spain.

> AGN 399, No. 12.

Rodriguez, Isabel: b. Salceda; daughter of Violante Rodriguez; m.
Manuel Diaz who was relaxed in 1596 auto; did not believe in Jesus.
Judaizante; reconciled, sanbenito, confiscation of property, life im-
prisonment.

> Abec.; AGN (Riva Palacio) 13, No. 1 AGN 271, No. 1; AGN 277,
> No. 6C; AGN 279, No. 9; Martínez del Río 115; García 5:98;
> Medina, *México* 112, 124, 194. Part of the proceso is at the Lea
> Memorial Library.

Rodriguez, Isabel. *See* Francisco de Campos Morales.

Rodriguez, Isabel. *See* Thomas Nuñez de Peralta.

Rodriguez, Isabel: testimony by Blanca Rivera and others. Observer of
Mosaic laws.

> AGN 391, No. 10; AGN 404, No. 4.

Rodriguez, Isabel. *See* Antonio Lopez de Orduña.

Rodriguez, Jorge: b. Portugal; brother of Domingo Rodriguez; r. Manila; dealer. Judaizante; reconciled.

> Abec.; Liebman, *Guide* 1032, 1071.

Rodriguez, Jorge a. Jorge Ruiz: b. Seville; r. Pachuca; miner. Judaizante; reconciled in 1593; accused of being a relapso in 1601; 200
lashes and ten years in galleys, early confession saved him from the
stake.

> Medina, *México* 159.

Rodriguez, Juan: b. Portugal; soapmaker; fugitive. Observer of Mosaic
laws and judaizante; relaxed in effigy in 1601.

> Abec.; AGN 157, No. 2; Toro, *Judíos* 12, 62.

Rodriguez, Juan: 1642 testimony by Isabel de Silva. Judaizante.

> AGN 415, fol. 602.

Rodriguez, Juana a. Juana de los Angeles: b. Lisbon; daughter of Diego
Lopez Rivera and Blanca Rivera a. Mendez, both Hebrew New Chris-
tians; m. Diego Nuñez Batoca; mother of Clara de Silva, Esperanza
Jeronima, and Blanca Enriquez, the wife of Antonio Rodriguez

Arias; died in Mexico in the late 1620s. Observer of Mosaic laws; relaxed in effigy in 1649.

AGN 405, No. 9; AGN 415, No. 1; Medina, *México* 205, 409.

Rodriguez, Leonor: b. Fondon; m. Manuel Alvarez. Judaizante; reconciled in 1601, abjuration de vehementi, fine.

Abec.; AGN 252A, No. 2C; Medina, *México* 157. The main proceso is at the Huntington Library.

Rodriguez, Manuel: b. Fondon [in the jurisdiction of la Villa de Cubillan, bishopric of La Guarda, Portugal]; peddler. Observer of Mosaic laws; reconciled, sanbenito, confiscation of property, jail for six years.

Abec. [which lists only one case for a Manuel Rodriguez who was in the 1596 auto]; AGN 156, No. 1; Liebman, *Guide* 1001.

Rodriguez, Manuel: r. Zacatula; denounced in 1609. Suspicion of judío.

AGN 285, No. 41.

Rodriguez, Manuel. *See also* Tomé Gomez.

Rodriguez, Marcos: m. Simona Lucerna. Judaizante.

AGN 179, No. 3.

Rodriguez, Maria: accused in 1642. Judío.

AGN 404, No. 7; AGN 415, fols. 204, 374; AGN 453, fol. 56.

Rodriguez, Maria; Portuguese; m. Gaspar Hernandez a. Fernandez, Portuguese; denounced by a Franciscan monk. Judío and dogmatist; relaxed in effigy in auto of 1635.

Abec.; AGN 281, No. 39; AGN 381, No. 5; Medina, *México* 185.

Rodriguez, Melchor a. Melchor Rodriguez de Huerta: b. Alpedrina, bishopric of La Guarda; son of Gaspar Rodriguez and Violante Rodriguez; first cousin of Duarte Rodriguez, son of Mencia Rodriguez, Melchor's father's sister; first cousin of Rodrigo Vaez Pereira, son of Leonor Rodriguez of Monsanto or Alpedrina, the sister of Baltasar Rodriguez; m. Isabel Enriquez called "de Huerta"; accused in 1634; died prior to sentence. Concealer of Jews; relaxed in effigy.

AGN 377, No. 20; AGN 413, No. 19; AGN 415, fol. 157; AGN 419, No. 35; AGN 426, fol. 519; Medina, *México* 409. For his relatives, see Medina, *Lima* 2:52, 53, 94, 135; Palma 1219.

Rodriguez, Mencie. *See* Duarte Rodriguez.

Rodriguez, Micaela: testimony by Pedro Espinoza in 1642.

AGN 414, fol. 402.

Rodriguez, Miguel. *See* Miguel de Carvajal.

Rodriguez, Pedro a Pedro Rios a. Pedro Riosas: b. Fondon; Jewish ancestry. Judío and observer of Mosaic laws; reconciled in auto of 1596, four years in galleys without pay, sanbenito and life imprisonment in Seville after completing term on the galley.

Abec.; AGN 223, No. 32; Garcia 5:99; Gonzalez Obregón, *México* 683; Toro, *Judíos,* 88, 60.

Rodriguez, Rafael Crisanto Gil: Spaniard; r. Guatemala; circumcised; Franciscan monk; circumcised two friends; 1788 proceso. Judaizante; reconciled; relapsed; sentenced to be relaxed in 1795 but the sentence was commuted to life imprisonment at last moment and he was the only prisoner in the Holy Office cells when Mexico became independent in 1821.

AGN 1191, fols. 157-229; AGN 1234, fol. 67; Liebman, *Jews* 295, 296; Medina, *México* 316.

Rodriguez, Sebastian: b. San Vicente Davera; m. Constanza Rodriguez; father of Domingo Rodriguez a. Diaz. Observer of Mosaic laws; reconciled in 1596, confiscation of property, sanbenito, life imprisonment.

Abec.; AGN (Riva Palacio) 13, AGN 276, No. 14; AGN 279, No. 9; No. 3; García 5:98; Liebman, *Guide* 1099; Martínez del Río 115.

Rodriguez, Sebastian: 1601 proceso; denounced by Manuel Gil de la Guarda. Judaizante.

AGN 256, No. 15N.

Rodriguez, Simon: Portuguese; Jewish parents; his mother wore sanbenito in Portugal; merchant; believed to be the father of Ana Espinosa, b. Mexico, reconciled in 1646, and of Pedro Espinosa. Judaizante.

AGN 153, Criminal Branch vol. 685; AGN 160, No. 2; AGN 223, No. 19; AGN 685; Medina, *México* 159, 180 [which quotes a letter of May 15, 1615, sent by the Holy Office to the Supreme Court indicating that he was the father of Ana and Pedro Espinosa].

Rodriguez, Simon: r. Casteloblanco; m. Bernardina Espinosa; father of Pedro Espinosa.

AGN 414, fol. 185.

Rodriguez, Simon. *See* Luis de Burgos.

Rodriguez, Simon. *See* Violante Rodriguez.

Rodriguez, Violante: b. Villa de la Salceda, Portugal; Jewish ancestors; widow of Simon Rodriguez. Observer of Mosaic laws, awaiting the

Messiah, and concealing heretics; reconciled, confiscation of property, sanbenito, life imprisonment.

> Abec.; AGN 271, No. 1; AGN 276, No. 14; García 5:95; Liebman, *Guide* 1052; Medina, *México* 112, 124; Toro, *Judíos* 60.

Rodriguez, Violante: b. Seville; sister of Luis Fernandez Tristan; famous Jewess; r. for some time in Mexico, then Veracruz where she died; m. Pedro Gomez Texoso, had nine children; was the grandmother of many Jews penanced by the Holy Office. Observer of Mosaic laws.

> AGN 404, 3; AGN 453, fol. 99; Medina, *México* 409.

Rodriguez, Violante. *See* Juan de Roxas.

Rodriguez, Violante. *See* Manuel de Mella.

Rodriguez, Acuña, Manuel. *See* Luis Nuñez Perez.

Rodriguez Alfaro, Gaspar a. Gaspar de Alfar: accused in 1642. Judaizante.

> AGN 392, No. 17; AGN 401, Nos. 3, 4, 5; AGN 413, fols. 192-195; AGN 415, Nos. 1, 3; AGN 417, fol. 560. [There was a Gaspar Alfar a. Gaspar de los Reyes, a non-Jew, sent to the galleys in 1646.]

Rodriguez Alva, Beatriz: testimony by Blanca Juarez. Judaizante.

> AGN 418, No. 10.

Rodriguez Arias, Antonio: b. Seville; son of Catalina Marquez of Seville; broker; m. Blanca Enriquez, "famosa dogmatista y rabina"; father of Juana, Gabriel, Diego Rodriguez Arias; Rafaela, Catalina, Micaela, and Beatriz; all daughters bore the patronymic of Enriquez in Mexico; died prior to arrest. Judío and observer of Mosaic laws; his bones were disinterred; relaxed in effigy in 1649 auto.

> Abec.; AGN 405, No. 9; AGN 406, No. 1; AGN 413, fols. 61-63; 128-130, 161-163; AGN 415, No. 3; AGN 423, No. 3; AGN 427, No. 4; AGN 434, fol. 26; Medina, *México* 408.

Rodriguez Arias, Diego: b. Seville ca. 1604; son of Blanca Enriquez and Antonio Rodriguez Arias; circumcised; in jail his pseudonym was Gigote, which means minced meat or hash. Observer of Mosaic laws; reconciled in 1648 auto, confiscation of property, sanbenito, abjuration de vehementi, exile, life imprisonment.

> AGN 392, No. 3; AGN 414, fol. 169; AGN 427, Nos. 4, 5, 10; AGN 487, No. 15; García 28:220; Medina, *México* 118, 195.

Rodriguez Arias, Gabriel. *See* Gabriel Rodriguez.

Rodriguez Arias, Simon. *See* Simon Rodriguez Vaez.

134 INQUISITORS AND JEWS

Rodriguez del Bosque, Maria a. Maria del Bosque: b. Guadalajara, Mexico; daughter of Esperanza Rodriguez and Juan Baptista del Bosque; mulatto; single; r. Mexico City. Judío and observer of Mosaic laws; reconciled in 1646 auto, confiscation of property, sanbenito, abjuration de vehementi, jail for six months, exile from the Indies.
AGN 413, fols. 64, 65; AGN 414, fol. 128; AGN 427, No. 6.

Rodriguez Botello, Diego. *See* Francisco Botello.

Rodriguez de Carassco, Antonio: b. Seville; 1602 proceso; denounced by Clara de Rivera. Judaizante.
AGN 256, Nos. 11, 15N.

Rodriguez Carrasco, Francisco. *See* Manuel Carrasco.

Rodriguez Castaño, Isabel: r. Zacatecas; 1626 testimony. Descendant of Jews.
AGN 356, fol. 156.

Rodriguez de Carvajal, Baltazar: b. Benavente, Castile; son of Francisca de Carvajal and Francisco Rodriguez de Matos; single; fugitive. Observer of Mosaic laws; relaxed in effigy in 1590.
Abec.; AGN (Riva Palacio) 12, No. 3; Liebman, *Enlightened* 23, 28, 29, 31, 56, 62-66, 73, 74, 147; Medina, *México* 101; *Procesos de Carvajal;* Toro, *Judíos* 57.

Rodriguez Ceas, Francisco. *See* Francisco Rodriguez.

Rodriguez Deza, Francisco. *See* Leonor Diaz.

Rodriguez Falero, Gaspar: 1642 testimony. Judaizante.
AGN 415, fol. 49.

Rodriguez Garcia, Diego. *See* Jose de Villauriti.

Rodriguez de Gresta, Melchor: r. Mexico. Judaizante; reconciled.
AHN 1738.

Rodriguez de Herrera, Hernando: b. Cubillan, Portugal. Judaizante.
AGN 127, No. 1; AGN 149, No. 2 [which states b. Fondon]; AGN 223, No. 31.

Rodriguez Horta, Manuel: 1642 testimony by Manuel Rodriguez Nuñez. Judaizante.
AGN 414, fol. 189.

Rodriguez de Huerta, Melchor. *See* Melchor Rodriguez.

Rodriguez Juarez (Xuarez), Juan: b. Lisbon; son of Juan Rodriguez Juarez, b. Leira, Portugal, and Luisa de Castro, b. Lisbon; both parents were New Christians; circumcised; merchant; single. Observer of Mosaic laws; reconciled in auto of January 23, 1647, confiscation of property, sanbenito, abjuration de vehementi, life imprisonment.

Abec.; AGN 392, No. 17; AGN 399, No. 12; AGN 425, No. 12; AGN 584, No. 15; García 28:119; Medina, *México* 117, 194.

Rodriguez de Ledesma, Francisco: b. Salamanca or new Ledesma; came to Mexico from Cartagena. Observer of Mosaic laws; reconciled in auto of April 20, 1603, confiscation of property, sanbenito.

AGN (Riva Palacio) 17, No. 2; García 5:94; Liebman, *Guide* 996, 1092; Medina, *México* 171.

Rodriguez Lopez, Melchor: age 40; b. Cubillan, Portugal; son of Juan Lopez, b. Guimaraes, Portugal, and Ana Rodriguez, b. Cubillan, both Hebrew New Christians; his uncle had been penanced as judaizante in Portugal; single; r. in Angola, Laguna, Teneriffe, then he came to New Spain and r. in Mexico City and Zacatula, where he raised cocoa. Judío and observer of Mosaic laws; reconciled in auto of March 30, 1648, abjuration de vehementi, sanbenito, confiscation of property, fine of 3,000 Castilian ducats.

Abec.; AGN 395, Nos. 3, 4; AHN 1738, No. 1; García 28:192; Medina, *México* 117, 195.

Rodriguez de Matos, Ana. *See* Ana de Caravajal.

Rodriguez de Matos, Francisco: b. Medina del Campo; m. Francisca de Carvajal; died ca. 1585. Denounced as a rabbi; bones disinterred and burned in 1590.

Abec.; Lea, *Spanish Dependencies* 208 [where he is described as a rabbi and dogmatizer]; Liebman, *Jews,* ch. 8; Martínez del Río, 22-43; Toro, *Judíos* 57.

Rodriguez de Matos. Manuel. *See* Miguel Rodriguez de Matos.

Rodriguez de Matos, Miguel a. Manuel Rodriguez de Matos: b. Spain; son of Francisco Rodriguez de Matos and Francisca de Carvajal; fugitive. Judaizante; relaxed in effigy on December 8, 1596.

Toro, *Judíos* 58.

Rodriguez Matus (Matos), Pedro a. "Los Reyes": son of Antonio Rodriguez Matos; r. Comayagua and Caretero (sic); blacksmith; married in Lisbon; came to Mexico ca. 1635; denounced in 1632 by the precentor of the cathedral; denounced himself in 1646. Judaizante.

AGN 376, No. 6; AGN 425, No. 6.

Rodriguez de Molina, Francisco. *See* F ancisco Machado.

Rodriguez de Molina, Gonzalez. *See* Leonor Machado.

Rodriguez Nuñez, Antonio: 1642 testimony. Observer of Mosaic laws.

AGN 391, No. 10; AGN 415, No. 1; AGN 453, fol. 44.

Rodriguez Nuñez, Manuel a. Manuel Nuñez Caravallo: age 34; b. Casteloblanco; son of Francisco Rodriguez, b. in Casteloblanco, who died in the secret cells of the Holy Office in Seville, and Beatriz Nuñez, b. Guarda. Judío and observer of Mosaic laws; reconciled in 1646, confiscation of property, sanbenito, abjuration de vehementi, jail for two years, exile from the Indies, Madrid, and Seville.

   AGN 405, fol. 580; AGN 406, fol. 586; AGN 413, fols. 235-238; AGN 414, fol. 191; AGN 415, fol. 105; Brenner 17; García 18:73; Medina, *México* 193.

Rodriguez Nuñez, Simon: Portuguese; had resided in Seville; believed to have been reconciled by the Inquisition in Seville for judío. Relapso; bones disinterred and burned.

   Medina, *México* 195.

Rodriguez Nuñez de Castro, Juan. *See* Francisco Febo.

Rodriguez Obregon, Enrique: b. Llerena of Extremadura; broker or shipper of Negroes from Angola to New Spain; father of Blanca Mendez, as she was known in Spain, or Blanca de Rivera, as she was known in New Spain.

   Medina, *México* 113.

Rodriguez de Olivera, Mathias (Matias): age 51; b. San Salvador de Laens (sic), near Duero, 55 leagues north of Lisbon; illegitimate son of Fructuoso Rodriguez, b. Lima, and Catalina Hernandez Serodia, b. Laens; both parents New Christians; trader; single. Observer of Mosaic laws; tortured; reconciled in auto of 1649, abjuration de vehementi, exile, fine of 6,000 Castillian ducats.

   Abec.; AGN 409, No. 1; AGN 414, No. 7; Medina, *México* 203.

Rodriguez Paiba, Simon. *See* Simon Paiba.

Rodriguez de Seas, Francisco. *See* Francisco Rodriguez.

Rodriguez de Segura, Gaspar. *See* Gaspar Rodriguez a Gaspar Rodriguez de Seguna.

Rodriguez de Silva, Juan: b. Portugal; single. Judaizante; escaped; relaxed in effigy December 8, 1596.

   AGN 153, No. 10; Garcia 5:110; Liebman, *Guide* 1083; Medina, *México* 133; Toro, *Judíos* 11.

Rodriguez Sobremonte, Tomas: r. Zacatecas; denounced in 1639 by the comisario of Zacatecas. Judío.

   AGN 388, No. 19.

Rodriguez Tavares, Jorge: 1646 proceso. Judaizante.

   AGN 419, No. 57.

Rodriguez Tejoso, Duarte. *See* Duarte Rodriguez.

Rodriguez Tristan, Marco: m. Ana Enriquez; father of Isabel Duarte a. la Antuñez; 1644 proceso. Judaizante.

    Abec.; AGN 415, fol. 280; AGN 419, No. 29.

Rodriguez Vaez, Simon a. Simon Rodriguez Arias: 1642 testimony by Juana Enriquez. Judaizante.

    AGN 414, fol. 525.

Roel, Gracia. *See* Fray Lorenzo Altamirano.

Roja, Pedro de: captain; letter from Inquisition Court of Valladolid. Judaizante.

    AGN 345.

Rojas, Augustin de a. Augustin de Roxas a. Augustin Nuñez de Rojas: b. Guarda; illegitimate son of Rodrigo Nuñez, b. Linares, a fugitive from the Inquisition in Portugal and relaxed in effigy; half-brother of Jeronimo Nuñez a. de Roxas; merchant and peddler; m. Leonor de Rojas; hung himself in the secret cells; Observer of Mosaic laws and judío; relaxed in effigy in 1649 auto.

    AGN 395, No. 2; AGN 413, fols. 277-279; AGN 492, Nos. 3, 6; AGN 584, No. 1; Medina, *México* 114, 205.

Rojas, Alonso de: Accused in 1694 of porging; denounced by Manuel de la Guarda and the jail warden in 1605. Judaizante.

    AGN 276, No. 14; AGN 368, No. 32.

Rojas, Antonio: Denounced by Manuel de la Guarda and the jail warden in 1605. Judaizante.

    AGN 276, No. 14.

Rojas, Antonio de. Papers found on him when imprisoned.

    AGN 429, No. 5.

Rojas, Juan de. *See* Juan de Roxas.

Rojas, Leonor de a. Leonor de Roxas a. Leonor Vaez a. Leonor Baez; b. Casteloblanco ca. 1616; daughter of Francisco Lopez Sevilla a. Simon Rodriguez and Maria Aeres a. Arias, sister of Gonzalo Vaez; niece of Simon Vaez Sevilla; m. Augustin de Rojas; had two children, Rodrigo and Francisco; Observer of Mosaic laws; tortured; she was called "the Baker" while in prison, reconciled in the Convent of Santo Domingo on April 21, 1649, instead of being a participant in the auto of April 11, 1649, due to confessions made at the eleventh hour, abjuration de vehementi, confiscation of property, sanbenito, 200 lashes, life imprisonment.

Abec.; AGN 393, No. 10; AGN 399, No. 1; AGN 404, No. 3; AGN 405, Nos. 7,9; AGN 414, No. 9; AGN 417, No. 16; Medina, *México* 200, 208.

Rojas Ayara, Francisco de: Judaizante.
AGN 416, fol. 440.

Roman, Sebastian: b. Seville; m. Jeronima Esperanza; peddler; assisted in synagogue services outside of Spain; a learned Jew; died in Puebla. Judío and observer of Mosaic laws; relaxed in effigy in 1649 auto.
Abec.; AGN 405, No. 9; AGN 415, fol. 152; Medina, *México* 409.

Romero, "Fulano": former reconciliado; accused about 1604. Wearing silk and riding a horse.
AGN 368, fol. 321. [Fulano means name unknown.]

Rosa, Jose de la: great-great-grandson of Francisca de Carvajal; great-grandson of Catalina de Leon; 1706 petition for a certificate of "good health" so that he might be admitted to the clergy.
AGN 560, No. 3.

Roxas, Augustin de. *See* Augustin de Rojas.

Roxas, Geronimo de. *See* Jeronimo Nuñez.

Roxas, Juan de a. Juan de Rojas: b. Cubillan; son of Jorge de Arroja of Sabugal, Portugal, and Violante Rodriguez of Cubillan; m. Francisca Nuñez, relaxed in the 1649 auto. Judío and observer of Mosaic laws; bones disinterred; relaxed in effigy in auto of 1649.
Abec.; AGN 390, No. 1; AGN 405, fol. 531; AGN 415, No. 4; Medina, *México* 409.

Rozaval, Pedro la. *See* Pedro la Rocabal.

Ruipo: Portuguese; r. Manila; 1601 letters from the Holy Office about Ruipo and his sons. Suspicion of judaizante.
AGN 263, No. 1U.

Ruiz, Diego: r. Cholula; denounced in 1650. Descendant of Jews.
AGN 435, fol. 338.

Ruiz, Francisco Rosado Nuño: grandchild of Jews relaxed in Spain.
AGN 59, No. 7.

Ruiz, Jorge. *See* Jorge Rodriguez.

Ruiz, Juan: b. Jerez de la Frontera. Suspicion of judío.
AGN 1A, No. 22; AGN 22, No. 9; Toro, *Judíos* 102.

Ruiz, Miguel: 1594 proceso. Judaizante.
AGN 223, fol. 461.

Ruiz Esparza, Andres: Suspicion of Lutheranism.
AGN 126, No. 1; Toro, *Judíos* 1 cites heresy and suspicion of

judío [There is a variance between the Index, Toro, *Judíos* 1, and the proceso proper; Toro is correct.] AGN 223, No. 35.

Ruiz de Luna, Francisco: b. Cordoba, Spain; monk; defrocked for administering sacraments without being a priest; converted to Judaism while a cellmate of Luis de Carvajal, el Mozo; was penanced in the 1590 auto. Observer of Mosaic laws; reconciled March 25, 1601, sanbenito, 200 lashes, ten years in galleys.

Abec.; Liebman, *Enlightened* 67, 76; Liebman, *Guide* 1043, 1069; Medina, *México* 108, 109, 111 [where there is an addition by Julio Jiménez Rueda which states sent to Spain and six years in galleys].

Ruiz Marques, Antonio: testimony by Duarte Rodriguez. Judaizante. AGN 271, No. 1.

Ruiz Ortiz, Juan: r. Tlaxcala; commercial agent; 1575 proceso. Heresy and suspicion of judío.

AGN 59, No. 3; Toro, *Judíos* 10.

Salamanca, Juan de: barber; 1539 proceso. Judío and observer of Mosaic laws.

AGN 125, No. 1; Greenleaf, *Zumárraga* Medina, *México* 96; Toro, *Judíos* 10.

Salgado, Jeronimo: r. Granada, Nicaragua; arrested in 1623; died in prison. Judaizante; relaxed in effigy in 1626.

AGN 344, No. 1.

Salinas, Sebastian de: r. Zacatecas; 1693 proceso. Suspicion of judío. AGN 689, No. 5.

Salomon, Jose: r. Guatemala; doctor; 1768 proceso. Suspicion of judío.

AGN 1052, No. 20; Chinchilla Aquilar, 183 [which cites date as 1708].

Samaniego, Catalina de. *See* Tomé Gomez.

Saña, Antonio: English; arrested in Mexico in 1570. Judío, observer of Mosaic laws. Liebman, *Guide* 1026; Liebman, *Jews* 123; Medina, *México* 96; Jimenez Rueda 85; Toro, *Judíos* 9 gives name as Sañer and date as October 1521. *See also* Martin Asana.

Sanchez, Gonzalo: b. Extremadura, Spain; descendant of Jews; his wife also had Jewish parents; shoemaker. Judío and fraud in his application to Consejo de Suprema for license to come to New Spain; public auto, lashes, and 6 years in galleys.

Abec.; Medina, *México* 73 states he had also been before the Inquisition in Llerena.

Sanchez, Isabel. *See* Francisco Mellan.

Sanchez Manriquez, Pedro: mayor of Villa de Valles; 1724 proceso. Suspicion of judío.

AGN 792, No. 15.

Sanchez de Sosa, Francisco: 1644 proceso. Judaizante.

AGN 418, No. 41; AGN 425, fol. 553.

Sandoval, Luis: b. Seville; 1585 proceso. Judío or heresy.

AGN 126, No. 8 [which states heresy]; Medina, *México* 78 [which states Luis Sandoval was involved because of certain heretical statements and nothing concerning judaism]; Toro, *Judíos* 13 [states judío and cites vol. 161, No. 4].

San Ignacio, Joseph de a. Joseph or Jose Ignacio a. Juan Fernandez de Leon: age 30; b. Seville; a Bethlemite monk; 1706 proceso for judaizante, heresy, apostasy, and bigamy; defrocked; case reopened in 1712. Dogmatizer; relaxed alive.

AGN 465, fol. 580; AGN 712, No. 8; AGN 748, No. 6; Medina, *México* 283 [which states life imprisonment in 1712 auto], 416.

San Joseph, Marta de: 1654. Porging.

AGN 457, fol. 80.

San Lucar, Pedro: b. Seville; descendant of Jews. Suspicion of judío; absolved outside of an auto.

Abec.; AGN 223, No. 19; Liebman, *Jews* 139; Medina, *México* 74.

Santillan, Pedro. *See* Baltazar Diaz Santillan and Francisco Lopez Diaz.

Santoyo, Geronimo de: Catholic theologian. Denounced by the dean of the Cathedral of Guadalajara because he said in a sermon at the cathedral that "in Spain the rich were called Jews."

AGN 385, No. 18.

Segovia, Isabel de. *See* Isabel de Campos.

Segovia, Manuel de: 1642 testimony by Isabel de Silva. Judaizante.

AGN 393, No. 5; AGN 453, fol. 523.

Segueta, Fray Juan de: 1651. Information of his using Jewish ceremonies in order to prepare for death.

AGN 506, No. 11.

Segura, Gaspar de: 1642 proceso. Judaizante.

AGN 453, fol. 448.

Serrano, Francisco: 1539 declaration. Judío.

AGN 1A, No. 21.

Serrano, Gaspar: b. Spain; r. Puebla; 1713 proceso. Suspicion of judío.

AGN 753, fol. 527.

Serrano, Jorge. *See* Jorge Espinosa.
Serrano, Pedro Antonio: age 39; b. Villa de Peña, France; circumcised; known among the Jews as Isaac or Jacobo; merchant; single; came from Peru; 1690 proceso; previously sentenced by the Holy Office in Llerena for Judío. Suspicion of judaizante; sentenced June 24, 1692; abjuration de vehementi, confiscation of one-fourth of his property, spiritual penances, exile from the Indies and Madrid.
   Abec; AGN 511, No. 2.
Serrano, Rodrigo. Judaizante; absolved.
   AHN 1738.
Silba, Antonia de: b. Seville; r. Caracas; m. Duarte de Castaño. Judaizante.
   González Obregón, *Mexico* 701.
Silva, Catalina de. *See* Catalina de Silva Enriquez.
Silva, Clara de: b. Mexico; daughter of Antonio Rodriguez Arias and Blanca Enriquez; died prior to trial. Judaizante and observer of Mosaic laws; relaxed in effigy in 1649 auto, after her bones had been disinterred.
   Abec; Medina, *México* 408. The major part of her proceso is at the Gilcrease Institute.
Silva, Clara de: b. Seville; daughter of Juana Rodriguez de los Angeles; m. Diego Suarez de Figueroa; very observant Jewess; died prior to sentence. Judaizante and observer of Mosaic laws; relaxed in effigy in 1649 auto.
   Abec.; AGN 405, Nos. 6A, 7; AGN 414, fol. 243; AGN 415, fol. 247; AGN 453, fol. 141.
Silva, Elena de a. Elena Lopez a. Elena Silva Baez: b. Casteloblanco, Portugal; daughter of Gaspar Gonsalves Soburro, innkeeper, butcher, and hangman, and Leonor Vaez, both parents b. Casteloblanco and both reconciled for judaizante in Lisbon; full sister of Antonio Baez a. Captain Tirado and Simon Vaez Sevilla; sister of Maria Aeres, r. Pisa; m. Gomez de Silva; had a daughter, Isabel de Silva a. Isabel Correa; migrated to New Spain from Seville, "a common refuge for this rabble" (the Jews). Judío; reconciled in auto of 1649, confiscation of property, sanbenito, abjuration de vehementi, life imprisonment in Spain, her name among the other Jewish prisoners in jail was Naranja (orange) or Guacamaya (a type of parrot).
   AGN 381, No. 7; AGN 406, No. 1; AGN 413, fols. 105-111; AGN 414, Nos. 3, 7; AGN 417, fol. 536; AGN 419, No. 45; AGN 434, fol. 250; Boconegra (source of quotation) Medina, *México* 203.

Silva, Fernando de: r. Mexico.
> AHN 1738, no. 1.

Silva, Gomez de. *See* Elena de Silva.

Silva, Isabel de a. Isabel Correa: age 28; b. Casteloblanco; daughter of
Elena de Silva; m. Antonio Caravallo. Judío and observer of Mosaic
laws; reconciled in 1649, abjuration de vehementi, sanbenito, life
imprisonment, exile.
> AGN 406, fol. 354; AGN 419, No. 45; AGN 434, fol. 520; AGN
> 434, No. 7; AGN 453, fol. 452; AGN 503, No. 55; Medina,
> *México* 203, 205.

Silva, Isabel de a. la de Espinosa: age 52; b. Seville; daughter of Diego
Rodriguez de Silva, who was born in Murcia or Cordoba and died in
Angola, and Juana Rodriguez a. los de Angeles, b. Lisbon, reconciled
by the Inquisition in Granada and relaxed in effigy in Mexico; both
parents Hebrew New Christians; r. Mexico; m. Pedro Espinosa; died
in the cells. Judío and observer of Mosaic laws; relaxed in effigy in
the 1649 auto.
> AGN 393, No. 9; AGN 404, Nos. 1, 3; AGN 405, No. 69; AGN
> 406, fol. 46; AGN 415, fols. 380, 391, 465: Bocanegra; Medina,
> *México* 205.

Silva, Juan de: 1642 testimony by Luis Nuñez Perez. Judaizante.
> AGN 414, fol. 71.

Silva, Leonor de: arrested in 1635. Judaizante.
> AGN 405, fol. 460.

Silva, Nuño de: b. Oporto: pilot; sailed through the Straits of Magellan
with Sir Francis Drake. Suspicion of Lutheranism; convicted; public
auto in 1582; abjuration de vehementi, exile.
> Abec.; Medina, *México* 77; Novinsky 231, 237. Novinsky con-
> tends he was a Jew who had been imprisoned in Mexico in 1579,
> citing "Leite Filho Solidonio da Influencia do Elemento Judaico
> no Descombremento e Comercio do Brasil" in *Anais do 3 Con-
> greso de Historia Nacional* 4 (1938):696.

Silva, Nuño de a. Nuño Suarez a. Juarez de Figueroa: age 24, b. Patzcuaro, Mexico; son of Diego Suarez de Figueroa, reconciled in the
1648 auto, and Clara de Silva, b. Seville; single. Judaizante and
observer of Mosaic laws; confessed; reconciled in 1647 auto, sanbenito, abjuration de vehementi, jail for one year, exile from Indies,
Seville, and Madrid.
> Abec.; AGN 404, Nos. 1, 4; AGN 406, fols. 44, 143; AGN 408,
> No. 4 [mourning practices]; AGN 413, fols. 116-119; AGN 414,

fols. 231, 266; AHN 1738, no. 1; García 28:123; Medina, *México* 117, 194.

Silva, Rafael: arrested in 1635. Judaizante.

AGN 381, No. 7; AGN 417, fol. 545.

Silva, Simona de: 1642 testimony by Catalina Enriquez.

AGN 404, No. 1.

Silva Baez, Elena. *See* Elena de Silva.

Silva Enriquez, Catalina de a. Catalina de Silva a. Catalina Enriquez de Silva a. Catalina Tinoco Enriquez a. Catalina Tinoco Silva: age 35; b. Mexico; daughter of Blanca Enriquez and Antonio Rodriguez Arias; widow of Diego Tinoco; had 13 children, all except one born in Mexico City; mother of Juana Tinoco, Diego Tinoco, Miguel, Pedro, and Isabel who was b. in Zacatecas and m. Manuel de Acosta; her son Antonio died in Guatemala. Observer of Mosaic laws; relaxed alive in 1649 auto.

Abec.; AGN 404, No. 2; AGN 406, fol. 152; AGN 413, fols. 66-73, 298-303; AGN 414, fols. 247, 534; AGN 415, fols. 234, 338, 467; AGN 415, No. 6; AGN 419, No. 16; AGN 426, fol. 412; AGN 453, fol. 489; AGN 793, fol. 12; Liebman, *Guide* 1153, 1249; Medina, *México* 119, 203.

Silva Saucedo, Pedro: Portuguese; r. Chiquimula de la Sierra, Guatemala. Judaizante.

AGN 221, No. 3; AGN 337, No. 3.

Silvera, Alvaro: 1610 proceso. Being the son of a relaxed person and wearing silk.

AGN 478, No. 8.

Simon, Francisco: confectioner; denounced in 1736. Using Jewish rites.

AGN 859, fol. 429.

Sobremonte, Rafael de: age 17; b. Mexico; son of Thomas Treviño de Sobremonte and Maria Gomez; circumcised; single. Judaizante; reconciled in 1648 auto, abjuration de vehementi, first confined in a monastery where he was to be taught Christianity, then exile.

Abec.; García 28:255 [contains a very lengthy account]; Medina, *México* 119, 120, 195.

Sola, Juan de: b. Spain; accused with his brother-in-law in 1703. Suspicion of judío.

AGN 722, No. 10.

Sola, Pablo de: r. San Luis Potosi; 1646 proceso. Suspicion of judaizante.

AGN 425, No. 5.

Soria, Rodrigo de: 1539 declaration. Judío.

    AGN 1A, No. 20; Greenleaf, *Zumárraga* 98.

Sosa, Ana de a. Ana de Souza: no charge, but in 1597 she testified against others who were accused of judaizante.

    AGN 160, No. 2.

Sosa, Francisco: proceso. Saying that Indians had to have been punished with Tremino; relaxed secretly.

    AGN 435, fol. 5.

Sosa, Isabel de: arrested in 1599. Suspicion of judío.

    AGN 249, No. 13.

Sosa, Juana de. Judaizante; reconciled.

    AHN 1738.

Sosa y Prado, Manuel de: Portuguese; baker; 1694 proceso. Judío.

    AGN 520, No. 232; AGN 529, No. 11.

Sousa, Domingo de a. Domingo de Sosa: b. Lisbon; Franciscan monk; died in jail. Heretical judaizante; reconciled in effigy.

    Abec. [which states reconciled in 1620]; Toro, *Judíos* [states reconciled in 1626].

SUAREZ. *See also* JUAREZ and XUAREZ. All three spellings should be checked as these names were used almost interchangeably.

Suarez, Blanca. *See* Blanca Juarez.

Suarez, Gaspar. *See* Gaspar Juarez.

Suarez, Leonor. *See* Leonor Xuarez de Ocaña.

Suarez, Manuel a. Manuel Javares: b. Cubillan. Judaizante; reconciled in 1597.

    AGN 163, No. 3; Toro, *Judíos* 13.

Suarez, Nuño. *See* Nuño de Silva.

Suarez, Rafael de. *See* Diego Suarez de Figueroa.

Suarez, Violante a. Violante Juarez: age 36; b. Lima, Peru; natural daughter of Gaspar Suarez or Juarez; r. Guadalajara; m. Manuel de Mella. Judío and observer of Mosaic laws; reconciled in 1648 auto, confiscation of property, sanbenito, abjuration de vehementi, 100 lashes, life imprisonment.

    Abec.; AGN 405, No. 6A, AGN 414, fols. 254, 397; AGN 415, No. 6; fol 139; AGN 453, fol. 102; García 28:265; Medina, *México* 195.

Suarez de Aguilar, Francisco: r. Tepeaca; 1642 proceso.

    AGN 501, No. 22.

Suarez (Juarez) de Figueroa, Diego: age 52; b. Lisbon; son of Nuño Alvarez, b. Badajoz, Estremadura, and Ines Juarez de Figueroa, b. Lisbon; circumcised; r. Patzcuaro; merchant; m. first to Clara de Silva, b. and d. in Seville; had two children from his first marriage, Nuño de Silva and Rafael de Suarez; m. Teresa de Alarcon, b. Patzcuaro, not a Jewess; had two children from his second marriage, Josefa and Barnabe; arrested in Patzcuaro; observed kosher rules for meat while in jail. Judío and observer of Mosaic laws; reconciled in 1647, abjuration de vehementi, confiscation of property, sanbenito, jail for two years, exile from the Indies, Madrid, and Seville.

  Abec.; AGN 405, No. 2; García 28:99; Medina, *México* 116, 194. Proceso at the Huntington Library.

Suarez de Figueroa, Nuño. *See* Nuño de Silva.

Suarez de Figueroa, Pedro: testimony by Manuel Mella. Judaizante.

  AGN 405, No. 6A.

Suarez de Mezquita, Alejandro: 1710 proceso. Judaizante.

  His proceso is at the Huntington Library.

Suarez de Ocaña, Garcia. *See* García Xuarez.

Susnabar y Aguirre, Tomas de: accused in 1635; Judaizante.

  AGN 381, No. 5.

Tabera, Antonio de. *See* Nuño de Figueroa.

Taboada, Jose Gil: mayor of San Juan Teotihuacán; 1761 proceso against him and his brothers. Suspicion of judío.

  AGN 1033, No. 19.

Tabora, Leonor de: mother of Gonzalo de Mantilla. Judaizante.

  AHN 1738, no. 1.

Tal, Gonzalo de: Portuguese; servant of Alonso de Riviera. Judaizante.

  AGN 281, No. 16.

Tal, Pedro de: 1627 testimony. Judío.

  AGN 360, fol. 80.

Tavares, Manuel a. Manuel Tovares: b. Cubillan; father's name was Abraham. Judaizante; reconciled on March 25, 1601, 200 lashes, eight years in galleys, then life imprisonment.

  Abec.; AGN 252A, No. 1A; Medina, *México* 159. It appears that he escaped to Peru, where he used a number of aliases and was relaxed in 1625. *See* Diego de Andrada in Peru section.

Tavarez, Rodrigo: b. Villa de Purificacion; arrested in 1597. Judaizante and suspicion of being an observer of Mosaic laws; reconciled in

1601 auto, abjuration de vehementi, 100 lashes.

    Abec. [cites b. Fondon]; García 5:111 [contains a verbatim record of the sentence and proceedings in the torture chamber]; Medina, *México* 159.

Teborio, Barbara: 1642 testimony by Luis Nuñez Perez. Judaizante.

    AGN 414, fol. 62.

Tejera, Francisco: b. La Villa de Ande, Portugal; m. in Mexico; r. Toluca. Blasphemy and judío.

    AGN 18, No. 6; Greenleaf, *Zumárraga* 18; Toro, *Judíos* 191.

TEJOSO. *See also* TEXOSO.

Tejoso, Clara. *See* Clara Texoso.

Tejoso, Pedro. *See* Clara Texoso.

Testa, Alejandra: Heresy and judío.

    AGN 125, No. 4; Liebman, *Guide* 1030; Toro, *Judíos* 10.

Texoso, Beatriz a. Beatriz Enriquez Texoso: b. Lima; daughter of Pedro Gomez Texoso and Violante Rodriguez; r. Veracruz; died in cells. Observer of Mosaic laws.

    AGN 405, No. 4; AGN 415, fols. 163, 404; Medina, *México* 408.

Texoso (Tejoso), Clara: b. Lima; daughter of Pedro Tejoso and Clotilde Rodriguez; r. Veracruz; m. Duarte Rodriguez; had a son, Pedro; arrested in Puebla. Observer of Mosaic laws; reconciled on April 16, 1646, confiscation of property, sanbenito, 200 lashes, life imprisonment.

    Abec.; AGN 393, No. 3; AGN 404, No. 2; AGN 405, No. 4; AGN 414, fol. 302 and No. 1; AGN 415, fol. 177; AGN 415, No. 3, fol. 312; AGN 453, fol. 374; AGN 421, No. 11; García 28:46; Liebman, *Guide* 1133; Medina, *México* 113, 193.

Texoso, Francisca: age 54; b. Seville; daughter of Pedro Gomez Texoso and Violante Rodriguez; r. Veracruz; baker. Judío and observer of Mosaic laws; reconciled in 1646, sanbenito, confiscation of property, life imprisonment, abjuration de vehementi, public shaming.

    Medina, *México* 193. Her proceso is at the Huntington Library.

Texoso, Francisco. *See* Francisco Gomez Texoso.

Texoso, Isabel: age 60; b. Seville; daughter of Pedro Gomez Texoso and Violante Rodriguez; r. Veracruz; baker; a very learned Jewess; she adapted Catholic prayers for use by Jews. Observer of Mosaic laws; reconciled in 1646, sanbenito, confiscation of property, life imprisonment, abjuration de vehementi.

Abec.; AGN 393, No. 3; AGN 404, No. 2; AGN 414, No. 4; AGN
415, fol. 241; AGN 417, fol. 482; AGN 453, fol. 381; García
28:62; Medina, *México* 115, 193. The proceso is at the Huntington Library.
Texoso, Luis de: Judaizante; reconciled on April 16, 1646, confiscation
of property, sanbenito.
Medina, *México* 193.
Texoso, Pedro: *See* Pedro Gomez Texoso.
Texoso, Violante: b. Lima ca. 1623; natural daughter of Rafael Gomez
Texoso and Leonor de Flores; single. Judío and observer of Mosaic
laws; reconciled in 1646 auto, sanbenito, confiscation of property,
life imprisonment, exile.
Abec.; AGN 453, fol. 388; AGN (Riva Palacio) 57, No. 1; García
28:89; Medina, *México* 116, 194.
Tinoco, Antonio: Portuguese; son of Diego Tinoco and Catalina de
Silva Enriquez; descendant of Hebrew parents and grandparents on
both sides; died en route to Guatemala. Observer of Mosaic laws;
relaxed in effigy in 1649.
Abec.; AGN 312, No. 40; AGN 406, fol. 42; AGN 414, fol. 235.
Most of the proceso is at the Huntington Library.
Tinoco, Catalina de a. Catalina Enriquez: b. Mexico; accused in 1642.
Judío and observer of Mosaic laws.
AGN 404, No. 2; AGN 793, fol. 12. Very likely the same as
Catalina de Silva Enriquez.
Tinoco, Diego: b. Seville; merchant; circumcised; m. Catalina de Silva
Enriquez; had thirteen children, b. Mexico; practiced Judaism
openly. Judío and observer of Mosaic laws; died at sea en route to
Peru; relaxed in effigy in 1649 auto.
Abec.; AGN 405, No. 7; AGN 406, No. 1; AGN 410, No. 4; AGN
415, fols. 97, 544; AGN 453, fol. 10; AGN 793, fol. 12; Boca-
negra; Medina, *México* 408.
Tinoco, Diego. *See* Catalina de Silva Enriquez.
Tinoco, Francisca: testimony by Isabel Antuñez in 1642. Judaizante.
AGN 414, fol. 286.
Tinoco, Isabel: age 24; b. Zacatecas; daughter of Diego Tinoco and
Catalina de Silva Enriquez; granddaughter of Blanca Enriquez; m.
Manuel de Acosta a. Francisco de Torres; 1642 proceso; the *Rela-
ción* of the auto of 1649 states that "she observed Jewish rites in the

secret cells as if she had been living in the Jewish quarters of Amsterdam, Leghorn, or Pisa"; her nickname in the cells was "Music" because she had a good voice and sang a great deal. Judío and judaizante; reconciled in 1649 auto.

Abec.; AGN 333, No. 7; AGN 401, No. 7; AGN 453, fol. 528; Medina, *México* 203, 204.

Tinoco, Juan: proceso. Judaizante; exile [however as late as 1656 he was still in Mexico].

AGN 415, fol. 208; AGN 441, No. 4; AGN 499, fol. 517.

Tinoco, Juana: age 20; b. Mexico; daughter of Diego Tinoco, who died in Guatemala, and Catalina de Silva Enriquez; both parents Hebrew New Christians; m. Simon Juarez de Espinozo; wrote liturgical poems; confessed. Judío and observer of Mosaic laws; reconciled in 1646 auto, abjuration de vehementi, confiscation of property, sanbenito, life imprisonment.

Abec.; AGN 417, fol. 562; García 28:55; Liebman, *Guide* 1132; Medina, *México* 114, 193.

Tinoco, Micaela. *See* Manuel de Acosta a. Francisco de Torres.

Tinoco, Miguel; age 23; b. Mexico; son of Diego Tinoco and Catalina de Silva Enriquez; circumcised; apprentice to silversmith; single; served as sexton for Jews and distributed matzot before Passover. Judaizante and observer of Mosaic laws; reconciled on April 16, 1646, abjuration de vehementi, confiscation of property, sanbenito, jail for two years, exile from the Indies, Seville, and Madrid.

Abec.; AGN 404, No. 1; AGN 417, No. 16; AGN 504, No. 70; García 28:76; Medina, *México* 193.

Tinoco, Pedro: age 22; b. Mexico; son of Diego Tinoco and Catalina de Silva Enriquez; brother of Isabel Tinoco; doctor, with the title of bachiller. Observer of Mosaic laws; reconciled in 1649 auto, sanbenito, confiscation of property, abjuration de vehementi, 200 lashes, life imprisonment in Spain.

Abec.; AGN 396, No. 2; Medina, *México* 203, 204.

Tinoco Enriquez, Catalina. *See* Catalina de Silva Enriquez.

Tinoco Silva, Catalina. *See* Catalina de Silva Enriquez.

Tirada (Tirado), Antonio. *See* Antonio Baez.

Tobar y Torres, Luis de: r. San Luis de Paz; 1650 proceso; denounced for being of the Jewish race and irreverence in church. Suspicion of judaizante.

AGN 435, fols. 165, 182.

Torres, Duarte de: age 27; b. Casteloblanco; circumcised; merchant; m. Josefa Cruz, b. Patzcuaro, "mestiza, daughter of a Spaniard and a female Indian"; they had one daughter; he had several children in Spain by a previous marriage. Observer of Mosaic laws; reconciled in 1647 auto, confiscation of property, sanbenito, 200 lashes, life imprisonment, abjuration de vehementi, exile.

Abec.; García 28:105.

Torres, Francisco de. *See* Manuel de Acosta.

Torres, Jose de: r. Acapulco; soldier; denounced himself and others in 1671. Judaizante.

AGN 614, No. 8.

Torres, Pedro de: 1649 proceso. "Crime of judaismo."

AGN 433, fol. 538.

Torres, Simon Hernan de: 1642 testimony by Isabel de Silva. Judaizante.

AGN 404, No. 3.

Torres Mendoza, Juan de. *See* Juan de Mendoza.

Torres de Rivera, Juan de: b. Lisbon; broker of slaves; drowned off the isle of Borengo, the Philippines. Judaizante; relaxed in effigy in 1649 auto.

AGN 410, No. 3; [his name does not appear in Bocanegra].

Tovares, Manuel. *See* Manuel Tavares.

Treviño (Tremiño) de Sobremonte, Tomas: b. Medina del Rio Seco, Spain; son of Leonor Martinez de Villagomez, who was relaxed in Lisbon with another son ca. 1623; r. Antequera, Valley of Oaxaca, between 1619 and 1624; r. Mexico, Guadalajara, and again Mexico until 1649; m. Maria Gomez ca. 1630; father of Leonor Martinez, Rafael, Michael, Gabriel, and Salvador. Judaizante; imprisoned for one year in 1625; rearrested; relaxed in 1649 auto.

Abec. [twice]; AGN 365, Nos. 11, 33; AGN 373, No. 9; AGN 378, No. 2; AGN 381, No. 5; AGN 401, No. 3; AGN 405, No. 9; AGN 415, No. 5; AGN 426, No. 7; AGN 435, No. 1; AGN 684, fol. 476; AGN (Riva Palacio) 20, No. 5; Liebman, *Jews* chap. 11; Medina, *México* 119, 175, 200, 204, 206.

Tristan, Ana a. Ana Enriquez: b. either Jena or Seville; daughter of Simon Lopez and Clara Tristan, b. Seville; full sister of Isabel Tristan; single; died prior to arrest and was buried according to Jewish ritual. Observer of Mosaic laws; bones disinterred; relaxed in effigy in 1649 auto.

Abec.; AGN 415, fol. 157; AGN 453, fol. 76; Bocanegra [which states "Mamó en la leche el Judaismo" (she had been suckled in the milk of Judaism)]; Medina, *México* 408.

Tristan, Clara. *See* Isabel Tristan, Ana Tristan, and Luis Fernandez Tristan.

Tristan, Isabel: age 50; b. Seville; daughter of Clara Tristan, b. Seville, and Simon Lopez; sister of Manuel Lopez Nuñez, b. Seville, and Pedro Lopez Nuñez, b. Seville, r. Manila, and relaxed in effigy in 1649; m. her uncle Luis Fernandez Tristan who was relaxed in effigy in 1649 as "judaizante dogmatista"; her home was noted for adherence to Jewish ritual; assisted in preparing the dead for burial in accordance with Jewish law; arrested in 1642. Judío and observer of Mosaic laws; tortured; confessed; died in prison; relaxed in effigy in 1649.

AGN 311, No. 2; Medina, *México* 205.

Ubago, Baltazar de a. Baltazar del Brago: denounced in 1630 for saying that Jewish familiars paid for the house of the Inquisitor in Tacubaya; a criminal case was instituted against him in 1631. Judío.

AGN 372, No. 3.

Ullis de Luna, Francisca: b. Cordoba. Heretical judaizante; reconciled in 1591.

González Obregón, *México* 681.

Uruzel, Jose: French; first musician of the Royal Regiment; circumcised; 1785 proceso. Suspicion of judío.

AGN 1032, No. 7.

VAEZ. *See also* BAEZ and VAZ.

Vaez, Anton. *See* Juana Enriquez.

Vaez, Diego: 1642 testimony. Observer of Mosaic laws.

AGN 391, No. 10.

Vaez, Francisco: r. Manila; letter signed by the bishop of Japan advising the Holy Office that Francisco Vaez could be expected in Mexico, since he had fled from Manila and been relaxed in effigy there for judaizante.

AGN 293, No. 8.

Vaez, Francisco: b. San Vicente Davera; r. Pachuca; servant of Manuel de Lucena. Judaizante; fugitive; relaxed in effigy.

Abec.; AGN 152, No. 3; Medina, *México* 133.

Vaez, Gaspar. *See* Gaspar Vaez Sevilla.

Vaez, Gonzalo: b. Casteloblanco; son of Francisco Lopez Sevilla a. Simon Rodriguez, reconciled in Lisbon, and Maria Aeres, r. Pisa with her daughters where they observed Judaism openly; related to many who were in the cells of the Holy Office; his Jewish name was Samuel; circumcised; r. Coyoacan; peddler in the interior of the country; arrested in 1630 for having opened the dossiers of the Holy Office; tortured but confessed nothing; freed; rearrested in 1642; examined for sanity. Judaizante; relaxed in 1649 auto.

    Abec.; AGN 391, No. 10; AGN 509, No. 6; Medina, *México* 204.

Vaez, Hernan: name mentioned in the proceso of Catalina Enriquez.

    Proceso of Catalina Enriquez in the Huntington Library.

Vaez, Jorge. *See* George Baez a. Jorge Lais.

Vaez, Leonor. *See* Leonor de Rojas.

Vaez, Leonor. *See* Simon Vaez Sevilla and Pedro Fernandez Castro.

Vaez Alcaceria, Jorge. *See* Thomas Nuñez de Peralta.

Vaez de Azevedo, Sebastian a. Captain Sebastian Vaz de Azevedo: age 58; b. Lisbon; son of Felipe Vaz a. Baez and Leonor de Azevedo, both of Lisbon and Hebrew New Christians; first cousin of Manuel Mendez de Miranda; encomendero; ship chandler and protector of fleet; married to an Old Christian related to one of the ministers of the Holy Office, both unnamed in Bocanegra's *Relación.* Judaizante; tortured, reconciled, sanbenito, fined 2,000 ducats.

    Abec.; AGN 393, No. 7; AGN 430, No. 7; AGN 435, fol. 404; AHN 1738 [contains his will]; Bocanegra;.Medina, *México* 219, 227.

Vaez Casteloblanco, Antonio. *See* Antonio Baez.

Vaez Casteloblanco, Francisco. Suspicion of judaizante; reconciled in the 1648 auto.

    Medina, *México* 194.

Vaez de Lemus, Jorge: accused in 1604. Porging.

    AGN 368, No. 93.

Vaez Mendez, Francisco. *See* Gonzalo Flores.

Vaez Mendez, Gonzalo. *See* Gonzalo Flores.

Vaez Mesignana, Juan. *See* Francisco de Acosta.

Vaez Pereira, Rodrigo. *See* Melchor Rodriguez and Duarte Rodriguez a.

    Duarte Rodriguez Tejoso. *See also* Rodrigo Vaez Pereira in Lima.

Vaez de Rojas, Leonor. *See* Leonor de Rojas.

Vaez Sevilla, Gaspar a. Gaspar Vaez (Baez): b. Mexico ca. 1624; son of

Juana Enriquez and Simon Vaez Sevilla; it was hoped that he would be the Messiah predicted by the Kabbalists; tortured. Judío and observer of Mosaic laws; reconciled in 1646, abjuration de vehementi, life imprisonment in Spain.

AGN 390, No. 11; AGN 407, No. 5; AGN 411, No. 1; García 28:52; Medina, *México* 114, 193.

Vaez Sevilla, Leonor: b. Mexico; daughter of Simon Vaez Sevilla and Juana Enriquez; sister of Gaspar Vaez Sevilla; her father created a confusion by naming two daughters Leonor, which was his mother's name. Judaizante and observer of Mosaic laws.

Bocanegra; González Obregón, *Mexico* 701; Liebman, *Guide* 1156; Medina, *México* 409.

Vaez Sevilla, Simon: age 51; b. Casteloblanco; son of Leonor Vaez, b. Casteloblanco, and Gaspar Gonzales a. Gonzalves Soburro, b. Casteloblanco, innkeeper, butcher, and municipal hangman who had been reconciled for judaizante by the Inquisition in Lisbon; younger brother of Antonio Baez; circumcised; m. Juana Enriquez; father of Gaspar Vaez Sevilla and two daughters named Leonor Vaez; the older daughter m. Pedro Fernandez de Castro and r. Pisa with her children and her father's sister Maria Aeres; the younger Leonor was a child in Mexico residing with her parents at the time her father was accused; he was likely the wealthiest man in New Spain and acted as banker for the church, several monasteries, and contingents of the Spanish army; he controlled many ocean-going ships. Judío and observer of Mosaic laws; reconciled in 1649 auto, confiscation of property, sanbenito, abjuration de vehementi, life imprisonment in Spain.

Abec.; AGN 396, No. 3; AGN 398, No. 1; AGN 414, No. 6; AGN 416, Nos. 2, 24; AGN 417, No. 16; AGN 419, No. 33; AGN 421, No. 10; AGN 488, No. 5; AGN 492, No. 6; AGN 503, No. 54; Guijo 46-47; Medina, *México* 116, 203, 218. AGN 396, No. 4, and AGN 399, No. 2, contain much information about the slaves of Simon Vaez Sevilla, Thomas Nuñez Peralta, and Luis de Mesquita, who showed devotion to their masters as they risked their lives carrying messages among the prisoners and in and out of the secret cells.

Vaez Torres, Fernando: 1642 testimony. Judaizante.

AGN 391, No. 10.

Valencia, Josef or Jose de: r. Tetelan; m. Juana Magdalena; confessed. Judío.

Gonzalez Obregon, *México* 690.

Valle, Ana: niece of Marcos del Valle; r. Toluca. Judaizante.
AGN 435, No. 35; AGN 477, No. 13.
Valle, Baltasar del a. Baltasar Diaz: b. Zamora ca. 1591; r. Pachuca; m.
Isabel Lopez Cardado. Suspicion of judío; tortured; case suspended
on March 3, 1626; imprisoned again in 1634 as an observer of Mosaic laws; reconciled in auto of April 2, 1635, confiscation of property, sanbenito; 200 lashes, life imprisonment.
AGN 380, No. 1. Most of the proceso is at the Huntington Library.
Valle, Francisco de: Portuguese; 1662 proceso. Judaizante.
AGN 579, No. 4.
Valle, Isabel: niece of Marcos del Valle; r. Toluca; denounced in 1650;
1661 testimony. Judaizante.
AGN 435, No. 36; AGN 477, No. 13.
Valle, Jeronimo: r. Toluca; student; denounced in 1650 for jumping
over and spitting on a cross that was on the floor. Judaizante; reconciled.
AGN 435, fol. 96.
Valle, Marcos del a. Simon Lopez: b. Quintala, Portugal; m. Violante
Mendez. Judío; a criminal case was opened in 1624; tortured; case
suspended in 1626; rearrested; confessed; reconciled.
Abec.; AGN 349, No. 4; AGN 381, Nos. 5, 7; AGN 404, No. 1;
AGN 414, No. 2; AGN 415, No. 5; AGN 582, No. 7 [states that
Marcos del Valle was accused of judaizante in 1662, but I believe
this information refers to another individual, perhaps his son];
AGN 632, No. 36: Medina, *México* 184.
Vara, Antonio: b. Casteloblanco; testimony by Maria de Rivera in
1642. Judaizante.
AGN 415, fol. 229.
Vargas, Pedro de: Portuguese; r. San Miguel, Guatemala; 1677 proceso.
Judaizante.
AGN 633, No. 6.
Vasquez, Ana de: 1642 testimony by Catalina de Silva Enriquez. Judaizante.
AGN 415, fol. 484.
Vasquez, Jose: 1642 proceso. Judaizante.
AGN 453, fol. 491.
Vasquez, Leonor: r. Celaya; 1614 testimony.
AGN 278, No. 12.
Vasquez, Manuel: mayor of Panuco and Tampico; 1783 proceso. Suspi-

cion of judaizante, reading and possessing books by Voltaire and other prohibited authors.

AGN 1283, Nos. 3, 5.

Vasquez, Maria de: 1642 testimony by Catalina de Silva Enriquez. Judaizante.

AGN 415, fol. 482.

VAZ. *See also* BAEZ and VAEZ.

Vaz, Felipe. *See* Sebastian Vaez.

Vaz, Leonor. *See* Elena de Silva.

Vaz de Azevedo, Sebastian. *See* Vaez de Azevedo, Sebastian.

Vega, Pedro de la. *See* Pedro Carretero.

Vera, Juan de: b. Spain or Canary Isles; merchant; 1731 proceso. Judío.

AGN 824, No. 16.

Vergara, Silvao: testimony from Peru; 1630 proceso. Judaizante.

AGN 366, No. 4.

Victoria, Francisco de a. Francisco Victoria Barahona: b. Madrid; 1715 proceso; denounced himself and others in Spain and Mexico. Observer of Mosaic laws.

AGN 761, No. 40.

Villalta, Nicolas: 1734 letter from the Suprema directing him to serve the balance of a five-year sentence imposed at Seville at the prison of San Juan de Ulloa, Veracruz.

AGN 854, fol. 180.

Villardes, Miguel de: 1698 proceso against him and others. Suspicion of judaizante.

AGN 540, No. 25.

Villareal, Pedro de: r. Leon, Guatemala, and Grenada, Nicaragua; 1623. Judío.

AGN 356, fols. 29-30; Chinchilla Aquillar 184.

Villauriti, Jose de a. Diego Rodriguez Garcia: r. Tlaxcala; meat supplier; 1733 proceso. Suspicion of judío.

AGN 873, No. 14.

Villegas, Francisco de: r. Zacatecas; 1628 proceso and a letter from the comisario in Zacatecas. Suspicion of judaizante.

AGN 365, No. 24.

Villegas, Fray Juan de: r. Puebla; teacher of the novices at San Agustin de la Puebla. Suspicion of being an observer of Mosaic laws.

AGN 471, No. 125.

Villena, Marques de: viceroy of New Spain from 1640 to 1642; mentioned in the letters included in the proceso of Diego Ximenez de la Camara. Judaizante.

> AGN 416, fol. 438; González Obregón, *Rebeliones* 207-241. [I doubt he was a Jew.]

Viveros, Gaspar de: 1650 proceso. Judaizante.

> AGN 436, fols. 42, 52, 58.

Voz Medrano, Joseph: mestizo. Judaizante; reconciled.

> AHN 1738.

Ximenez de la Camara, Diego: 1643 proceso. Judaizante.

> AGN 416, fol. 430. [In his proceso are letters concerning him and Marques de Villena, Don Guillen de Lamport a. Guillermo de Lombard, Francisco de Royas Ayara, and Antonio de Peralta.]

Ximon, Juan: b. Spain; surgeon at Sosa; r. Cuautla. Suspicion of judaizante.

> AGN 296, No. 11A.

Xuarez. *See also* Suarez and Juarez.

Xuarez (Juarez), Blanca: 1642 proceso. Judaizante.

> AGN 453, fol. 363.

Xuarez, Garcia a. Garcia Suarez de Ocaña: son of Diego de Ocaña, reconciled in 1528. Condemned to wear sanbenito for a short time.

> Medina, *México* 95.

Xuarez, Gaspar. *See* Gaspar Juarez.

Xuarez, Lope: 1642 testimony by Thomas Nuñez de Peralta. Judaizante.

> AGN 415, fols. 299, 400.

Xuarez (Juarez), Manuel: Portuguese; r. Veracruz; m. Ana Fernandez, his first cousin; denounced from Cartagena in 1625; he and his wife died prior to sentence. Suspicion of judío or judaizante; relaxed in effigy in 1635.

> Abec.; AGN 353, No. 23; AGN 381, No. 5; Medina, *México* 185.

Xuarez de Ocaña, Leonor: daughter of Diego de Ocaña, reconciled in 1528; mother of a son also named Diego de Ocaña. Condemned to wear sanbenito for a short time.

> Medina, *México* 95.

Zaldiva, Maria: r. Manila; 1641 testimony. Judaizante.

> AGN 293, No. 29.

Zarate, Maria de: b. Mexico; r. Tacubaya; m. Francisco Botello; on torture bed for over one hour; the doctors found that although no bones were broken, she had been physically maltreated. Judío and observer of Mosaic laws; reconciled in 1659 auto; compelled to watch her husband go to the stake; they were not permitted to speak to each other; fined 100 pesos for extraordinary expenses of the Holy Office, confiscation of property, sanbenito, abjuration de vehementi; had to spend four years in hospital to recover from the effects of the torture bed.

 Abec.; AGN (Riva Palacio) 25, No. 2; Jiménez Rueda 275.

Zerda, Manuel de la: r. Maracaibo. Judío.

 AGN 1738, No. 1.

Zerecedo, Esteban: Spanish; r. Tlacolula (sic) in Oaxaca; m. Tomasa Olivares. Suspicion of judaizante and superstitious acts.

 AGN 1108, fol. 137.

Zuarez, Manuel: 1632-1635 proceso. Judaizante.

 AGN 381, No. 5 [which spells the name Zuarez; this case could be another reference for Manuel Juarez].

TWO

New Granada (Cartagena)

Alcobaya Quatin, Luis: arrested in June, 1623. Judaizante; case suspended so that he could go to New Spain, to Mexico City, while the
inquisitors were awaiting his defenses to the accusation which had
been lost.

AHN lib. 1012, fols. 66-68; AHN lib. 1020, fol. 278; Medina,
Cartagena 195 [refers to a Luis Alcobia who had been arrested in
Yaguana, but Medina never found the proceso and it is not
known if Luis Alcobia is a pseudonym of Luis Alcobaya Quatin.]

Alvarez, Felipe: Portuguese; arrested on January 11, 1641, on charges
that had been instigated from Lima. Judío and observer of Mosaic
laws; reconciled, confiscation of property, sanbenito.

AHN lib. 1021, fols. 50r, 73r-76; Medina, *Cartagena* 245.

Alvarez Prieto, Manuel: Portuguese; arrested on August 12, 1642, in
Cuba; tortured on November 29, 1646; died in prison on August 25,
1651. Judío; bones disinterred and relaxed in effigy on April 25,
1653.

AHN leg. 1620, No. 15: Medina, *Cartagena* 272 [Medina con-
siders him one of the most notable Jews of the era].

Aranjo (Araujo), Juan: died in Caracas. *See* Juan de Aranjo of Mexico.

Araujo Coronel, Baltasar de: b. Bayone, Galicia, Spain; r. Santa Antioquia; circumcised; merchant; had been in five or six synagogues.
Heretic and judaizante; reconciled in auto of June 17, 1626, sanbenito for six months.

Medina, *Cartagena* 188.

Arias del Valle, Miguel: Portuguese. Judaizante; reconciled in auto particular on January 15, 1668.

AHN leg. 1621, No. 11.

Baez, Daniel: Portuguese; denounced himself to the Holy Office; first audience on April 14, 1682. Judío; absolved thereafter *ad cautelam* (for his own benefit and protection).

AHN lib. 1023, fol. 279r.

Campo, Juan del: Portuguese; r. Cartagena; he was very poor and received charity food in jail. Judío; reconciled, confiscation of property, sanbenito.

AHN lib. 1020, fols. 482r-484r; AHN lib. 1021, fols 16r-18r.

Chavez, Luis de a. Luis Mendez Chavez: Portuguese; arrested in July 1649. Judaizante; reconciled on April 25, 1653.

AHN leg. 1620, No. 20; AHN lib. 1021, fols. 239r-243r, 317, 369.

Costa, Domingo de: b. Picanzos, near Coimbra; shoemaker; was in the auto of 1626. Judío, abjuration de levi, fined 100 pesos, five years exile.

Medina, *Cartagena* 191.

Cutiño, Sebastian: Portuguese; arrested on January 17, 1641. Observer of Mosaic laws; reconciled, confiscation of property.

AHN lib. 1021, fols. 51r-69-71r; Medina, *Cartagena* 246 [where a letter of the Visitador Pedro de Medina Rico is cited in the footnote stating that the confiscated property of Cutiño was valued at more than 70,000 pesos].

Diaz, Manuel Francisco: Portuguese; arrested on July 29, 1636. Judaizante; the prosecution of his case was suspended in 1638 while awaiting the arrival of two procesos that had been instituted against him in Seville.

AHN lib. 1020, fols. 518-519; AHN lib. 1021, fols. 36r-37r.

Diaz de Lucena, Luis. *See* Luis Diaz de Lucena in Peru.

Diaz Pimienta, Jose: b. Remedios, Cuba; friar, circumcised in Caracas when he was converted to Judaism; arrested in Rio de la Hacha in 1720. Judío.

Adler, E., 172-180 [which has a lengthy account of this case and of how he was burned at the stake after reembracing Christianity]; Medina, Cartagena 356 [cites life imprisonment]; PAJHS, vol. 9 [contains an account similar to the one given by Adler]. *See also* Jose Pimentel in New Spain.

Duarte, Pedro: Portuguese; arrested in September 1641; tortured; confessed to being a Jew. Judío; reconciled outside of an auto, confiscation of property, sanbenito.

AHN lib. 1021, fols. 53, 76-79; Medina, *Cartagena* 246.

Enriquez (Henriquez), Benito: Portuguese; r. Caracas; arrested on July 1, 1653. Judío; reconciled on August 22, 1654, with "other penalties."

> AHN lib. 1021, fols. 374r-375, 394r; AHN leg. 1738, No. 1; Medina, *Cartagena* 274.

Fernandez de Acosta, Antonio: Portuguese; arrested in 1642; denounced himself voluntarily. Judío; reconciled on May 28, 1644.

> AHN lib. 1021, fols. 85r-86; Medina, *Cartagena* 246.

Fernández Suarez, Luis: Portuguese; arrested on July 22, 1636; tortured five turns. Judío; reconciled, confiscation of property, sanbenito.

> AHN lib. 1020, fols. 515-515r; and AHN lib. 1021, fols. 33r-35.

Fonseca, Manuel de: Portuguese; r. Tolu; arrested on January 27, 1606; had been in five or six synagogues in Italy; came from Rome with a "traveling priest" (sacerdote peregrino); accused by his friend, a doctor; imprisoned in public jail in Cartagena. Judaizante; reconciled, confiscation of property either in 1609 or in 1610, abjuration de levi.

> AHN lib. 1029, fols. 438-446r; Medina, *Cartagena* 33.

Fonseca Henriquez, Manuel de: Portuguese; arrested on August 22, 1636, in Cartagena; confessed on the second turn of the wheel that he had been a judío and judaizante for the previous three years. Judío; reconciled, confiscation of property, sanbenito.

> AHN lib. 1020, fols. 511r-512r; AHN lib. 1021, fols. 26r-29; Medina, *Cartagena* 226.

Franco, Luis a. Luis Franco Diaz: b. Lisbon; r. Cartagena; arrested on October 8, 1624, when he was about to leave for "other kingdoms"; heretic; confessed to being a Jew; was in auto of June 17, 1626. Judaizante; observer of Mosaic laws; abjuration de vehementi, confiscation of one third of his property, reconciled, exiled from Zaragoza and Cartagena.

> AHN leg. 1620, No. 5; AHN lib. 1020, fol. 529; AHN leg. 1620, No. 6, fols. 9, 10 [contains the proceso of Pedro Lopez which refers to Luis Franco]; Medina, *Cartagena* 189; Revah, p. 60.

Gomez Barreto, Luis: Portuguese; arrested in 1636 and absolved on February 2, 1638; rearrested on July 24, 1650. Judío; reconciled on April 25, 1653, confiscation of one half of property, exile from the Indies.

> AHN leg. 1620, Nos. 15 and 18; Medina, *Cartagena* 272.

Gomez Coello, Vicente: arrested on April 10, 1689. Judaizante; reconciled in auto particular on December 11, 1689.

> AHN lib. 1023, fols. 423-430.

Gomez de Leon, Francisco: Portuguese. Arrested in August, 1613; had struck a crucifix in Havana; confessed that he was a Jew and wished to die in the Mosaic law; sentenced to be relaxed alive, but because of the scruples of the inquisitor Salcedo, his case was sent to the consejo in Spain; reconciled, sanbenito, eight years in the galleys, then life imprisonment.

AHN lib. 1020, fols. 149-152r; Lea, *Spanish Dependencies* 501; Medina, *Cartagena* 109.

Henriquez, Juan Jose: arrested in 1710. Suspicion of judío; reconciled in 1710.

Medina, *Cartagena* 355.

Heredia, Francisco de: Portuguese; arrested on March 25, 1638, in Cartagena; confessed after four turns of the wheel. Judaizante; reconciled, confiscation of property, sanbenito.

AHN lib. 1020, fols. 507-509; Medina, *Cartagena* 225.

Herrera, Juan de: an old man; b. Extremadura; r. Tunja in 1592; had been in Flanders and Rome, arrested in Popayan. Suspicion of judío and observer of Mosaic laws; absolved from torture by majority vote; sentence outside of auto of December 17, 1595.

Lea, *Spanish Dependencies* 455; Medina, *Cartagena* 29; Medina, *Lima* 1:286.

Juarez, Antonio a. Antonio Xuarez: Portuguese; delated against himself. Judío; reconciled in 1632.

AHN lib. 1020, fol. 308; Medina, *Cartagena* 209.

Lopez, Domingo. *See* Domingo Lopez of Peru.

Lopez, Pedro: Portuguese; r. Zarogoza, New Granada; arrested in April 1625. Judío; reconciled; died prior to the filing of a second accusation.

Medina, *Cartagena* 175.

Lopez de Acosta, Fernando: Portuguese; arrested on July 22, 1636, in Cartagena. Judaizante.

AHN lib. 1020, fols. 516-516r.

Lopez Mesa, Alvaro: Portuguese; arrested on January 17, 1641. Observer of Mosaic laws and judaizante; abjuration de vehementi, confiscation of property, sanbenito.

AHN lib. 1021, fols. 52r, 58-64r; Medina, *Cartagena* 246. *See* Alvaro Lopez Mesa in Mexico.

Lopez Mesa, Duarte: arrested on April 7, 1636, in Cartagena. Judaizante; reconciled.

AHN lib. 1020, fols. 480-482; AHN lib. 1021, fols. 14-16r.

Lopez de Nacal, Pedro a. Pedro Lopez de Vaccal: Portuguese; arrested in June, 1625; observed the Sabbath; died in prison and was buried in the prison yard. Judío; reconciled in effigy in the auto of June 17, 1626.
AHN lib. 1020; AHN leg. 1620, No. 6; Medina, *Cartagena* 196.

Lopez de Noroña, Manuel: Portuguese; r. Cartagena; arrested on July 29, 1636; after seven turns, the wheel and cords broke. Judaizante; absolved.
AHN lib. 1020, fols. 509-510; AHN lib. 1021, fol. 41r; Medina, *Cartagena* 227.

Luca, Francisco de: b. Castillo David, Portugal; "beat a Christ" and other nefarious acts; died in prison. Heretic and judaizante; reconciled in effigy in the auto of June 17, 1626.
Medina, *Cartagena* 192.

Martinez Leon, Antonio: Portuguese; arrested on February 2, 1690. Judaizante; reconciled in auto particular on April 29, 1691.
AHN lib. 1023, fols. 485r-490r.

Mendez, Antonio: Portuguese; arrested in Mompox. Judío; reconciled in 1627, confiscation of property.
AHN lib. 1020, fols. 273-274; Medina, *Cartagena* 194.

Mendez Hernández, Salvador: b. Portugal. Observer of Mosaic laws; relaxed in effigy in Seville; escaped; arrested in Nombre de Dios on San Juan Day; tried by Servan de Cerezuela, first inquisitor of the Holy Office in Peru; no record of his sentence in Lima. As appears from the correspondence, the inquisitor was more concerned with the ease with which the escapees from Spain entered into the New World by fraudulent means, and with the connivance of ship captains and masters who went unpunished.
Medina, *Cartagena* 13 [where he is called a Portuguese Jew].

Montesinos, Antonio: Portuguese; arrested in 1641. Judaizante; case suspended for lack of sufficient proof.
AHN lib. 1012, fols. 158-159. [In September 1644 he appeared in Amsterdam and contacted the famous rabbi, publisher, diplomat, and author Menasseh Ben Israel, among whose works is the *Hope of Israel*, which repeats the stories told by Montesinos. Montesino's name among the Jews was Aaron Levi de Montesinos; his father, Luis Montesinos, was a member of the Amsterdam Jewish community. Aaron said that he had found the Lost Ten Tribes of Israel in the Andes Cordilleros inland in New Granada and that although they were Indians they spoke some Hebrew and knew of their ancestry.]

Mota, David de la: age, over 50; b. Velez, Malaga, Spain; r. Santa Cruz de Dinamarca; silversmith; m. a Jewess; circumcised in "San Eusta-quio" [Saint Eustatius]; his parents had been penanced by the In-quisition in Spain and his grandfather relaxed; had no hesitancy in divulging that he was a Jew, 1789; Judío; claimed Danish citizenship and was freed, as Spain feared reprisals from the Danish consul.

    Lea, *Spanish Dependencies* 469; Medina, *Cartagena* 359.

Nuñez Lopez, Jacob: denounced in Cuba. Judío; reconciled in 1712.

    Medina, *Cartagena* 356.

O., Maria de la: arrested in 1616; had been previously punished for judaizante in Toledo. Wearing silk and gold; confined to this city limits of Granada; [the trip from Tunja to Cartagena was considered sufficient punishment.].

    AHN lib. 1020, fols. 116-118; Medina, *Cartagena* 108.

Paz, Luis de: Negro; arrested in 1655; died in cells. Judaizante; case suspended.

    Medina, *Cartagena* 292.

Paz Pinto, Blas de: b. Evora, Portugal; r. Cartagena; leader, if not a rabbi, of the Jewish community and much beloved by all the towns-folk; arrested on July 22, 1636; tortured; confessed to being a Jew on the third turn of the wheel; died eight days after torture. Judío; reconciled in effigy, confiscation of property.

    AHN lib. 1020, fols. 20r-25r; AHN lib. 1021, fols. 503-507r; AHN leg. 1601, No. 32; AHN leg. 1603, No. 2, fols. 205, 206; and AHN leg. 1603, No. 4, fols. 365, 366, and 645v-650v; AHN leg. 1608, Nos. 17, 18, 31; AHN leg. 1609 No. 19; Lea, *Spanish Dependencies* 466; Medina, *Cartagena* 224.

Pereira, Duarte a. Andres de Saldaña: Portuguese; arrested on January 11, 1641. Observer of Mosaic laws; reconciled, confiscation of prop-erty.

    AHN lib. 1021, fols. 50r, 71r-73r; Medina, *Cartagena* 246.

Piñero, Francisco: Portuguese; arrested on April 6, 1636. Judaizante; reconciled, confiscation of property, sanbenito.

    AHN lib. 1020, fols. 484r-486r; AHN lib. 1021, fols. 18r-20r.

Reyes, Baltasar de los: Portuguese; r. Cartagena; surgeon; arrested April 17, 1616; one of his parents had been relaxed alive in Evora. Wearing silk and gold, reconciled, fined in 1616.

    AHN lib. 1020, fols. 114-116; Medina, *Cartagena* 108.

Reyes, Gaspar de los a. Rafael de los Reyes: Portuguese. Judío; reconciled in auto particular in the Convent of Santo Domingo on June 6, 1655, 200 lashes in public streets.

AHN lib. 1021, fols. 396-396r; Medina, *Cartagena* 293.

Rodríguez, Antonio: b. Moncorbo, Portugal; r. Guatemala; New Christian; first imprisoned in Cartagena; rearrested in Guatemala in 1624. Judaizante and concealer of heretics; reconciled; sanbenito for one year; served at a hospital which was to be his prison.

AGN 354, fol. 97; Chinchilla Aquilar, 184; Medina, *Cartagena* 190; Revah 60.

Rodriguez, Luis: brother of Luis a. Juan Rodríguez Pardo; tortured; confessed to being an observer of Mosaic laws. Judío; reconciled in 1627, confiscation of property, sanbenito, 100 lashes in public streets, life imprisonment.

AHN lib. 1020, fols. 275-276; Medina, Cartagena 195.

Rodríguez, Sebastian: Portuguese. Judaizante; reconciled in 1632, confiscation of property, sanbenito.

AHN lib. 1020, fols. 274r-275.

Rodríguez, Sebastian: b. Lisbon; had been in Angola, Jamaica, Mexico, Peru, and Panama before coming to New Granada; could speak Nahautl, the language of the Aztec Indians; arrested on January 23, 1642. Observer of Mosaic laws and "beating a crucifix"; reconciled in auto of May 24, 1644, in the church of Santo Domingo.

AHN leg. 1620, No. 12; AHN lib. 1021, fols. 99-108r, 122; Medina, *Cartagena* 267.

Rodriguez Cabral, Francisco: was in the auto-da-fé of February 2, 1614, for having adulterated a book of the Creed, which was thought sufficient proof that he was a Jew. Judío.

Porras Troconis, *Historia de la Cultura en el Nuevo Reino de Granada* (Seville, 1952) 465.

Rodríguez Mesa, Juan: b. Estremoz, Portugal; r. Cartagena; arrested on March 15, 1636; member of the Jewish community, observed the Sabbath, clean clothing and clean linens for table and beds on Friday afternoons, broke fasts on fish, eggs, and vegetables, and ate no pork or fish without scales; charged "por judío, judaizante, observante de la ley de Moisen ... fautor, encubridor de herejias"; his house is referred to as a "synagogue"; he is named in the proceso of Luis Gomez Barreto. Judío; reconciled, confiscation of property, exile from the Indies, life imprisonment.

AHN lib. 1020, fols. 476-480; 482r-484r; AHN lib. 1021, fols.

9-14, 16r-18r; AHN leg. 1061, No. 18; AHN leg. 1608, Nos. 4, 5, 6, 9, 10; AHN leg. 1610, No. 17; Medina, *Cartagena* 222, 226.

Rodriguez Mexia, Juan: presbyter of Badajoz; stated openly that he was a Jew as was his father, and that they both were observers of Mosaic laws; arrested in 1783 in Cartagena; on the verge of his being freed became insane and was hospitalized. Judío; case suspended.

Medina, *Cartagena* 358.

Rodríguez Nuñez, Diego: b. Viseu, Portugal; r. Jamaica; reconciled in Coimbra and sentenced to exile in Angola for six years, but had not complied. Judaizante; banished perpetually from the Indies and ordered to go to Angola.

Medina, *Cartagena* 190.

Rodriguez Pardo, Luis a. Juan Rodriguez Pardo: r. Pamplona. Judío; reconciled in 1627, confiscation of property.

AHN lib. 1020, fols. 274-274r; Medina, *Cartagena* 194.

Rodriguez de Solis, Francisco: Portuguese; arrested on July 22, 1636, in Cartagena. Judaizante; reconciled, confiscation of property, sanbenito.

AHN lib. 1020, fol. 522; AHN lib. 1021, fols. 29-33.

Silva Castillo, Francisco de: Portuguese. Judío and judaizante; reconciled in auto of October 1, 1656.

AHN lib. 1020, fols. 519-519r; AHN lib. 1021, fols. 37r-38, 397r; Medina, Cartagena 293. [One report states case suspended and property returned.]

Vaez, Duarte: Portuguese; r. Pamplona. Observer of Mosaic laws and judaizante; case suspended in March, 1658.

AHN lib. 1021, fols. 439-441; AHN lib. 1022, fol. 13; Medina, *Cartagena* 203 [where the sentence is not stated].

Vicente, Juan: b. Campo Mayor, Portugal; shoemaker; previously reconciled for judaizante in Coimbra and Lima. Judío; relaxed.

Lea, *Spanish Dependencies* 466; Medina, *Cartagena* 193.

Villalobos, Jorge: Portuguese; r. Bogota; doctor; arrested because he did not want to contribute for a statue of San Roque. Judaizante; reconciled on July 22, 1653, fine, exile for two years.

Medina, *Cartagena* 274.

THREE

Peru

Acevedo, Jeronimo de: age 40; b. Pontevedra, Galicia; merchant; widower. Judaizante and observer of Mosaic laws; confessed; reconciled but sentenced to galleys for life because he tried to revoke his confession, sanbenito, 100 lashes.

> AHN 1031, fol. 154; AHN 1041, fol. 58r; Friedlander 79; Medina, *Lima* 2:64, 122.

Acevedo, Juan de: b. Lisbon; money-keeper for Antonio Gomez de Acosta; friend of Manuel Henriquez; learned about Judaism in Guinea; arrested in February 1636; his revelations involved people in Spain, Portugal, Guinea, Cartagena, and other places in the Indies and explanations about the observances of Mosaic rites. Judaizante; relaxed in 1639.

> AHN lib. 1031, fol. 22v; AHN lib. 1041, fol. 55; Friedlander 79; Medina, *Lima* 2:55, 56, 133.

Acosta, Juan de: age 22; b. Pernambuco, Brazil; son of Luis de Valencia, Portuguese; single. Judaizante; reconciled, confiscation of property, sanbenito; abjuration de vehementi, life imprisonment in Seville.

> AHN 1031, fol. 17r (cites as merchant, confessed to judaismo); Medina, *Lima* 2:125.

Acuña, Antonio de: b. Seville in 1615; son of Portuguese parents; merchant; came to Peru with Diego Lopez de Fonseca, who was relaxed in 1639; confessed; implicated other Jews in Cartagena. Judío and judaizante; reconciled, abjuration de vehementi, sanbenito, two years prison in Seville.

> AHN lib. 1031, fol. 16r; AHN lib. 1041, fol. 52; Medina, *Lima* 116; Palma 1219.

Aguilar, Antonio: Portuguese; tried in absentia as fugitive. Judío; relaxed in effigy.
>AHN lib. 1029, fols. 324r-326r; Friedlander 81; Medina, *Lima* 1:311.

Almayda, Alejandro de: b. Lamego; goldsmith. Judío.
>AHN lib. 1030, fol. 189.

Alvarez, Alonso: brother-in-law of Juan Alvarez; arrested in 1570. Observer of Mosaic laws; tortured.
>Bohm 20; Kayserling 133 [states relaxed alive]; Medina, *Lima* 1:139.

Alvarez, Doña: wife of Juan Alvarez; arrested in 1570. Observer of Mosaic laws.
>Kayserling 133 [states relaxed alive]; Medina, *Lima* 1:139.

Alvarez, Juan: b. Zafra; licenciado and doctor of medicine; arrested in 1570. Observer of Mosaic laws.
>Kayserling 133 [states that he was the uncle of Alonso Alvarez and that he was relaxed alive with his wife and children]; Medina, *Lima* 1:139.

Alvarez, Manuel: b. Rioseco, Portugal; had a store in the passage in Lima; fled to Guailas province but was apprehended; confessed ser judío, tortured. Judaizante; reconciled, confiscation of property, sanbenito, abjuration de vehementi, 100 lashes, galleys for four years, then life imprisonment.
>AHN 1031, fol. 59v; AHN lib. 1041, fol. 58v.; Medina, *Lima* 63, 126; Palma 1219.

Alvarez, Martin, *See* Mateo Antuñez.

Alvarez de Espinosa, Manuel: age 44; b. Valladolid, Portugal; reared in Madrid; merchant. Judaizante; reconciled, sanbenito, life imprisonment.
>AHN lib. 1030, fol. 288; Lea, *Spanish Dependencies* 422; Medina, *Lima* 2:29.

Andrada, Diego de a. Manuel de Fonseca y Andrada a. Diego de Guzman a. Manuel de Tavares (in Mexico): b. Cubillan, Portugal; his father's name was Abraham; reconciled in Mexico in 1601 for being an observer of Mosaic laws; denied having ever been baptized in order to avoid punishment; told inquisitors that his Hebrew name was David Ruth [more likely Baruch].
>Abec.; Friedlander 113; Lea, *Spanish Dependencies* 422; Medina, *Lima* 2:31. *See also* under Mexico.

Andrade, Leonor de: wife of Rodrigo Henriquez de Fonseca, who committed suicide in the cells by opening his veins with a bone; the family was located in Santiago de Chile. Observer of Mosaic laws; relaxed in effigy January 23, 1664.

> AHN leg. 1648, Nos. 18, 19b; AHN lib. 1031, fols. 415-415r, 431r, 483r. Friedlander 171, 172; Medina, *Chile* 459 et seq.

Anriquez, Manuel: Portuguese; merchant; tortured three turns on thigh; confessed. Judaizante; reconciled in 1595, sanbenito, life imprisonment.

> Friedlander 84; Medina, *Lima* 1:280; Palma 1224.

Anriquez de Fonseca, Diego: Portuguese; miner; arrested in September 1601. Judío and observer of Mosaic laws; reconciled.

> AHN lib. 1029, fols. 302r-305r; Friedlander 83 [where his name is spelled Anrique]; Medina, *Lima* 1:310 [also Anrique].

Antonio, Isabel: age 18; b. Seville; daughter of Antonio Moron and Maior de Luna; m. Rodrigo Vaez Pereira; exchanged coded notes in jail. Judío, judaizante, and observer of Mosaic laws; reconciled, confiscation of property, sanbenito, 100 lashes for the notes, life imprisonment.

> AHN lib. 1031, fol. 21r; Friedlander 84: Medina, *Lima* 2:55, 119; Palma 1219.

Antuñez, Mateo a. Martin Alvarez: Portuguese; r. Potosi; very poor and in debt. Judaizante; died in the cells; reconciled in effigy.

> AHN lib. 1029, fols. 309r-311r; Friedlander 84; Medina, *Lima* 1:311.

Araujo, Manuel de: Portuguese. Judío; reconciled between 1625 and 1631.

> Lea, *Spanish Dependencies* 422; Medina, *Lima* 2:32.

Argote, Rosa. Judaizante.

> Medina, *Lima* 2:330.

Arias, Francisco: arrested in 1635. Judaizante; case later suspended.

> Friedlander 85; Medina, *Lima* 2:150.

Avila, Rodrigo de, the younger: b. Lisbon; worked for his uncle of same name who was merchant in the Street of Merchants. Judío and judaizante; reconciled in auto of 1639, abjuration de vehementi, sanbenito, confiscation of property, 100 peso fine for extraordinary costs of the Holy Office, exile from Indies and Spain.

> AHN lib. 1031, fol. 12v.

Baez Machado, Francisco. *See* Francisco Vaez Machado. *See* Rodrigo Vaez Pereira.

Barahona, Francisco de Victoria, a. Francisco de la Peña a. Francisco

Serrano: b. Pazos, Galicia, Buron Valley; descendant of New Christians; merchant; m. in France in a Jewish ceremony; then lived with another woman as a Catholic in Puebla de los Angeles. Judaizante; observer of Mosaic laws, and concealer of heretics; reconciled in auto of 1625; rearrested between 1631 and 1639 for wearing silk clothes, carrying a dagger and a gold sword, and riding a horse; fined ca. 1631; exiled.

> AHN lib. 1030, fol. 289v; Friedlander 191; Lea, *Spanish Dependencies* 422; Medina, *Lima* 2:26.

Bel, Manuel: b. Lisbon, 1604; a peddler; jailed March 1, 1635; denied charge. Judaizante; case suspended in auto of August 17, 1635.

> Medina, *Lima* 2:61, 62.

Bermejero, Francisco. *See* Pedro de Contreros.

Blanco, Francisco: Judaizante.

> Medina, *Lima* 2:330.

Bravo, Maria. Judaizante.

> Medina, *Lima* 2:330.

Busugnet, Juan Bautista: b. Paris, 1688; silversmith; r. Lima; had lived in Amsterdam; testimony against him, March 1711. Stated that Jewish law was better than that of Christians; tortured; tried to hang himself; reconciled, confiscation of property, sanbenito, abjuration de vehementi, three years jail at Valdivia.

> Medina, *Lima* 2:210.

Caceres, Francisco de. *See* Simon Osorio.

Cardoso, Esteban. *See* Alvaro Dordero de Silva.

Castro, Maria Francisca Ane de: b. Toledo; r. Lima; married; famous as a great beauty; the last person in Peru to go to the stake, though the Suprema had ordered that she not be relaxed. Judaizante, observer of Mosaic laws; confiscation of property (from which the Holy Office profited); her children and grandchildren were forbidden to hold titles of public office or nobility; relaxed alive in 1736.

> Friedlander 89-91; Medina, *Lima* 2:265 [2:269 has an additional account in the record of Nicolas Flores, a priest who tried to aid her]; Palma 1243, 1244. [Evidence indicates she was a courtesan.]

Cava, Antonio. Judaizante.

> Medina, *Lima* 2:330.

Cintron, Esteban: circumcised; arrested on December 7, 1603. Judaizante; freed.

> AHN lib. 1029, fols. 123r-125; Medina, *Lima* 1:308.

Coello, Manuel: age 62. b. near Lisbon; a presbyter; Suspicion of judaizante; defrocked, suspended from priestly orders for life.

Medina, *Lima* 2:61, 92.

Contreras, Pedro de: son of Bachiller Francisco Bermejero, ex-mayor of Oropesa, who had been accused of judaizante and burned in effigy in Albuquerque; spent many years in the cells of the Inquisition; tortured. Judío; relaxed in 1595.

Friedlander 92 and 117 [which states that the father, penanced under the name of Francisco Gonzalez Bermeja, was accused of judío, escaped and lived in Oropesa under another name, and was relaxed in effigy]; Medina, *Lima* 1:285; Palma 1224.

Cordero, Antonio: age 24; b. Arronches, bishopric of Portalegre, Portugal; merchant; m. Isabel Brandon of Seville in Seville; arrested on April 2, 1635. Judío and judaizante; reconciled, confiscation of property, abjuration de vehementi, tortured, exile.

AHN lib. 1031, fol. 14; Friedlander 93; Medina, *Lima* 2:80, 116; Palma 1219.

Cordero de Silva, Alvaro a. Esteban Cardosa: b. Quintena, near Vergaza, Portugal; r. Potosi; Jewish ancestry; constable or mayor; converted from Catholicism. Observer of Mosaic laws and judaizante, reconciled, sanbenito, confiscation of property, six years in galleys, 100 lashes, life imprisonment.

Lea, *Spanish Dependencies* 422; Medina, *Lima* 2:29, 32.

Coronado, Luis. *See* Manuel Lopez.

Coronel, Amaro Dionis: age 43; b. Tomar; a merchant; came to Lima from Cartagena. Judío and observer of Mosaic laws; reconciled, confiscation of property, sanbenito, abjuration de vehementi, life imprisonment.

AHN lib. 1031, fol. 18v; Friedlander 113; Medina, *Lima* 2:56, 117.

Coronel, Jeronimo: New Christian. False testimony.

Medina, *Lima* 1:307.

Correa, Antonio: b. Zelorico (sic); r. Potosi; grocer. Observer of Mosaic laws; confessed; took the cross at audience; reconciled, sanbenito, jail for three years in the convent of La Merced, exiled to Spain [died as a friar at Osuna in 1622; much has been written about him].

AHN lib. 1029, fols. 292r-294r; Friedlander 173; Lea, *Spanish Dependencies* 421; Medina, *Lima* 1:311; Palma 312.

Correa, Antonio. Judaizante.

Friedlander 96; Medina, *Lima* 2:330.

Correa, Simon: b. Villamayor, Portugal; owned a store in partnership with Cristobal de la Torre; jailed March 3, 1636; tortured; confessed on the fourth turn. Judaizante and observer of Mosaic laws; reconciled November 17, 1641.

> AHN lib. 1040. fol. 1, AHN lib. 1041, fol. 57; Medina, *Lima* 2:61, 156.

Cruz, Matheo de la: b. Torre de Moncorbo, Portugal, 1610; brother of Enrique Lorenzo; a merchant involved with Rodrigo Fernandez. Judaizante; confessed under torture. Judío; reconciled, 100 lashes, 6 years in galleys, confiscation of property, sanbenito, life imprisonment.

> AHN lib. 1031, fol. 13v; AHN lib. 1041, fol. 59v.; Medina, *Lima* 2:65, 119, 127; Palma 1219.

Cuaresma (Quaresma), Tome: b. Serpa, Portugal; surgeon; m. Maria Moran, who was b. Granada, in Lima; "healed all those of the Hebrew Nation." Judío, observer of Mosaic laws, and dogmatizer; relaxed alive in auto of January 23, 1639.

> AHN lib. 1031, fols. 22r, 206-212; AHN lib. 1041, fol. 54r; Medina, *Lima* 2:54, 137; Palma 1218, 1219, 1274.

Delgado, Cristobal: arrested January 2, 1640; Observer of Mosaic laws; reconciled, confiscation of property, sanbenito, jail for one year, auto of November 17, 1641.

> AHN lib. 1031, fol. 137r; Friedlander 99; Medina, *Lima* 2:156.

Delgado, Sebastian: b. Concello (sic), Portugal; was awaiting appointment as a familiar of the Holy Office; jailed April 20, 1636. Judaizante; case suspended.

> Medina, *Lima* 2:64, 92.

Diaz, Esteban: arrested relative to "complicidad grande," the Jewish Conspiracy; many Jews testified.

> Friedlander 100; Medina, *Lima* 2:67.

Diaz, Fernando: Portuguese; seller of objects of witchcraft; arrested in October 1604. Observer of Mosaic laws; reconciled.

> AHN lib. 1029, fols. 306-308; Friedlander 100; Medina, *Lima* 1:310.

Diaz, Francisco: b. Cazella, Portugal; barber; knew about the history of the Jews; denounced by the comisario at Cartagena in 1592. Suspicion of judío; ten years in jail.

> Friedlander 100; Medina, *Lima* 1:232, 273.

Diaz, Pascual: b. 1596 in Miranda; related to Manuel Luis Matos; r. Lima; box merchant; spoke about "Hebreos" living in Guinea and practicing Judaism openly and freely; arrested March 10, 1635. Judío and observer of Mosaic laws; reconciled in 1639, confiscation of property, sanbenito, abjuration de vehementi, 200 lashes, life imprisonment.

AHN lib. 1031, fol. 60r; AHN lib. 1041, fol. 55r; Friedlander 101, Medina, *Lima* 2:56, 88, 128.

Diaz, Philipe (Felipe): r. Cuzco; involved with Rodrigo Fernandez, Matheo de la Cruz, and Matheo Enrique. Judaizante; reconciled, confiscation of property, sanbenito, life imprisonment.

Medina, *Lima* 2:65, 127.

Diaz de Lucena, Luis: Portuguese; r. Cartagena; merchant; arrested in Cartagena on January 25, 1604. Observer of Mosaic laws; reconciled in auto of March 13, 1605, confiscation of property, sanbenito, jail for three years, exile to Spain.

AHN lib. 1029, fols. 294r-296; Friedlander 101; Medina, *Cartagena* 32; Medina, *Lima* 1:310.

Diaz Tavares, Gregorio: b. 1560 in Portugal; market broker; miner; bankrupt; swore only by the God of Abraham and Israel; tried to convince the theologian who tried to convert him. Judío; relaxed alive.

AHN lib. 1029, fols. 322-324r; Friedlander 101; Medina, *Lima* 1:311.

Diego, Luis: a fugitive. Judío, relaxed in effigy in auto of 1639.

Friedlander 102.

Dios, Hernando de. *See* Hernando Najera Aranz.

Dorado, Juan. Judaizante.

Medina, *Lima* 2:330.

Duarte, Luis. *See* Luis Noble.

Duarte, Manuel: Portuguese; r. Huancavelica; arrested in September 1603. Observer of Mosaic laws; reconciled.

AHN lib. 1029, fols. 291r-292r; Friedlander 103; Medina, *Lima* 1:310.

Duarte, Sebastian: b. Montemayor the New; son of Duarte Rodriguez, who had been imprisoned by the Holy Office in Evora and relaxed in effigy as judaizante and judío, having died in the cells; brother of Ana Lopez, who with her husband Gaspar Fernandez and their sons and his own sons, Vicente and Simon Rodriguez, had been imprisoned in Evora; his sister Guiomar Lopez and her husband Francisco Vaez, a silk weaver, and their children Antonio Rodriguez Orta and Marta Lopez were penanced by the Holy Office in Lisbon; merchant; m. Isabel Enriquez; brother-in-law of Manuel Bautista Perez in whose house he lived; arrested on August 11, 1635; wrote in secret code while in prison; confessed. Judío and observer of Mosaic laws; relaxed in auto of January 23, 1639, after exchanging "osculo de paz al modo judaica," a kiss of peace in the Judaic manner.

Medina, *Lima* 2:51, 60, 135, 136, 143.

Enrique, Matheo: age 34; b. Moncorbo, Portugal; r. mining area of Guamanaga; single; involved with Rodrigo Fernandez and Matheo de la Cruz. Judío, judaizante, and observer of Mosaic laws; confessed; reconciled; confiscation of property, sanbenito, life imprisonment in Seville.

AHN 1031, fol. 14r; Friedlander 105; Medina, *Lima* 2:65, 127.

Enriquez, Duarte: b. about 1580; Portuguese; r. Lima; taught Judaism by Gaspar Lopez Aguerto; said that he would pay anything for a copy of *Espejo de Consolación*, a book much beloved by the Jews of New Spain: tortured but did not reveal the names of other Jews. Judío; relaxed alive.

AHN lib. 1029, fols. 311r-318r; Friedlander 104; Medina, *Lima* 1:310. For information on the *Espejo de Consolación*, see Liebman, *Jews*.

Enriquez, Manuel: b. Lamego, Portugal; peddler; arrested on December 6, 1635; previously reconciled by the Inquisition in Coimbra; tried to escape; tortured; thought to be insane, but finally sentenced. Judaizante; relaxed in 1647.

Medina, *Lima* 2:55, 56, 157 [which states that due to his insanity, he never went to the stake]; Palma 1274 [states relaxed in the auto of January 23, 1664].

Enriquez Cuello, Pedro. *See* Pedro de Valcazar.

Enriquez de Rivero, Felix: previously reconciled. Judaizante and observer of Mosaic laws; reconciled even though a relapso, confiscation of property, sanbenito removed at the tablado on November 17, 1641.

Friedlander 104; Medina, *Lima* 2:156.

Espinosa, Antonio: b. Almagro; brother of Manuel and Jorge Espinosa; arrested in Potosi. Judaizante; his name is missing from the *Relación* of the auto of 1639.

AHN lib. 1031, fols. 111-116; AHN lib. 1041, fol. 53; Medina, *Lima* 52, 124, 131.

Espinosa, Fernando de: b. 1602 in Moncorbo, Portugal; arrested April

1636; confessed. Judío; reconciled in 1639 auto, confiscation of property, sanbenito, abjuration de vehementi, jail for three years in Seville, exile from the Indies.

AHN lib. 1031, fol. 59v; AHN 1041, fol. 58v; Friedlander 106; Medina, *Lima* 2:63, 121.

Espinosa, Jorge de: age 28; b. Almagro; brother of Manuel and Antonio Espinosa, who had brought him from Panama; merchant; confessed to judaizante in jail. Judío; reconciled in 1639 auto, sanbenito, confiscation of property, ten years in galleys, then life imprisonment in Seville.

AHN lib. 1031, fol. 19v; Medina, *Lima* 2:52, 124; Palma 1219.

Espinosa, Manuel de a. Manuel Mendez: age 26; b. Villaflor; miner; tortured; confessed. Judío and judaizante.

AHN lib. 1031, fol. 20v.

Espinosa (Spinosa), Manuel de: b. in 1603 in Almagro, La Mancha; brother of Antonio Espinosa and Jorge de Espinosa; had traveled extensively; single; tortured; confessed and testified against many others; tried to revoke confession; reconfessed. Judaizante; reconciled, confiscation of property, sanbenito, 400 lashes for lying, ten years in galleys, life imprisonment.

AHN lib. 1031, fol. 21r; Friedlander 108; Medina, *Lima* 2:52 [which states that his first sentence was to be relaxed alive], 124, 130.

Espinosa Estebez, Fernando de: b. Guarda, Portugal; single; had traveled extensively throughout the viceroyalty; cousin of others by same name in 1639 auto; brought from Conchucos where he was in hiding from Inquisition; confessed. Judio, judaizante, and observer of Mosaic laws; reconciled, confiscation of property, sanbenito, life imprisonment.

AHN 1031, fol. 16r [name cited as Fernandez de Espinosa] Friedlander 107; Medina, *Lima* 2:121, 127.

Estacio, Antonio de: Heresy; fine of 2,400 pesos.

Friedlander 108 [states "apparently a French Jew"]; Medina, *Peru* 1:110, 188.

Farias, Pedro: age 40; b. Guimaras, Portugal; traded with Diego de Ovalle. Judío and judaizante; reconciled in auto of 1639, abjuration de vehementi, 200 pesos of royal pieces of eight as fine, exile from Indies and Spain for life.

Friedlander 109; Medina, *Lima* 2:63, 115.

Fernandez, Antonio a. Francisco Fernandez: b. Almendra (sic) bish-

opric of Lamego; r. Potosi; m. Blanca Lopez; denounced by Felipa
Lopez "caste and generation of Jews." Judío; reconciled, confiscation of property, sanbenito, five years in galleys.

    AHN lib. 1029, fols. 57-59; Medina, *Lima* 1:296; Palma 2:25.

Fernandez, Antonio a. Antonio de la Palma a. Antonio de Victoria (in
Mexico) a. Antonio Sanchez (in Lima and Cuzco) a. Anonimo de
Salazar; b. Valladolid or Almendra; parents were New Christians;
merchant; admitted "soy judío." Judaizante and observer of Mosaic
law; reconciled, sanbenito, confiscation of property.

    AHN lib. 1030, fols. 188, 278; Friendlander 109; Lea, *Spanish
Dependencies* 422, Medina, *Lima* 2:29.

Fernandez, Catalina: daughter of Martin Fernandez de Enciso and
Juana de Rebolledo; sister of Rodrigo de Rebolledo and Juan Fer-
nandez de Rebolledo; m. Baltasar Diaz de Avila; widowed; married
Fabricio de Godoy. Judaizante.

    Castillero, Alfredo, personal communication, May 11, 1970.

Fernandez, Francisco: b. La Guarda, Portugal, 1602; a peddler; arrested
December 10, 1635. Judaizante; reconciled, confiscation of property, sanbenito, jail for one year; exile from the Indies.

    AHN 1031, fol. 60r; AHN 1041, fol. 55r; Medina, *Lima* 2:56.

Fernandez, Francisco. *See* Antonio Fernandez.

Fernandez, Geronimo a. Geronimo Hernandez: age 22; b. Seville; Portuguese parents; commission peddler; r. Lima with nephew Antonio
Acuña; under torture gave the names of many Jews in Lima and "all
the rest of Peru"; confessed "ser judío"; denied and then reconfessed. Judío and judaizante; reconciled in 1639, confiscation of
property, sanbenito, 200 lashes, 5 years in galleys, then life imprisonment.

    AHN 1031, fols. 19r, 62v; AHN 1041, fol. 53v; Friedlander 111;
Medina, *Lima* 2:51, 122; Palma 1219.

Fernandez, Jose. Judaizante.

    Medina, *Lima* 2:300.

Fernandez, Rodrigo: Portuguese; a merchant; left or fled from Cuzco
when hearing of Inquisition arrests; arrested in 1636 10 days from
Lima in Guanuco, with Matheo de la Cruz, Matheo Enrique, and
Philipe Diaz, all Jews; they had 20 or more mules carrying gold,
silver, and clothing. Judío and judaizante; reconciled November 17,
1641, sanbenito, confiscation of property, life imprisonment.

    AHN lib. 1031, fol. 2; AHN lib. 1042, fol. 373; Friedlander 112;
Medina, *Lima* 2:65, 156.

Fernandez, Tomas. Judaizante; case suspended 1637.

Medina, *Lima* 2:330.

Fernandez de Brito, Antonio: Portuguese; "lost man and gambler;" arrested in July 1603. Observer of Mosaic laws; reconciled.

AHN lib. 1029, fols. 300-301; Friedlander 110; Medina, *Lima* 1:310.

Fernandez Cutiño, Gaspar: age 26; b. Villaflor, Portugal; r. Lima; box merchant; jailed on January 11, 1636; confessed; died in the cells. Judaizante; reconciled in effigy.

AHN lib. 1031, fol. 21r; AHN 1041, fol. 56v [gives name as Gaspar Hernandez, b. Seville]; Medina, *Lima* 2:57, 58, 123.

Fernandez de Enciso, Martin: m. Juana de Rebolledo; father of Juan Fernandez de Rebolledo, Rodrigo de Rebolledo, and Catalina Fernandez; with son Juan was first of their group of Jews to arrive in Panama in 1530; others came in 1536. Observer of Mosaic laws.

Castillero, Alfredo, personal communication, May 11, 1970.

Fernandez de las Heras, Juan: porging and observing the Jewish Sabbath; possibly "slightly crazy"; a letter of the Consejo to the Tribunal in Lima cautions that greater care should be taken of similar cases in the future. Judaizante; relaxed alive in 1595.

Medina, *Lima* 1:285; Palma 1224.

Fernandez de Rebolledo, Juan: son of Martin Fernandez de Enciso and Juana de Rebolledo; brother of Rodrigo de Rebolledo and Catalina Fernandez; influential in naming of high officials for Panama; contributed financially to the conquest of the province of Panama. Observer of Mosaic laws.

Castillero, Alfredo, personal communication, May 11, 1970.

Fernandez de Vega, Antonio a. Antonio de Santiago: age 50; b. La Torre de Moncorbo, Portugal; r. Huancavelica, Peru; peddler; denounced himself. Judío; reconciled, confiscation of property, sanbenito, abjuration de vehementi, exile to Spain.

AHN lib. 1031, fol. 16r; AHN lib. 1041, fols. 243-243r; Friedlander 110; Medina, *Lima* 2:56, 117.

Fernandez Viana, Francisco: Portuguese; arrested in March 1604. Observer of Mosaic laws; reconciled.

AHN lib. 1029, fols. 288r-289r; Friedlander 111; Medina, *Lima* 1:310.

Fernandez Viana, Pedro: age 37; b. Villareal, Portugal; dealer or broker of Negroes; arrested on April 5, 1604. Observer of Mosaic laws; reconciled.

AHN lib. 1029, fol. 281r; Friedlander 112; Medina, *Lima* 1:310.

Fonseca, Duarte: b. Toledo; made holes in jail walls. Judío; reconciled in auto of 1639, confiscation of property, sanbenito, 100 lashes, five years in galleys, then life imprisonment.

AHN lib. 1031, fol. 259r; Friedlander 113; Medina, *Lima* 2:151.

Fonseca, Fernando de. Judaizante.

Medina, *Lima* 2:150.

Fonseca, Manuel de: b. Cubillan, bishopric of La Guarda; Jewish ancestry; surgeon; arrested in Cartagena; it was claimed that he knew all the Davidic Psalms in the vernacular and could recite them from memory; he copied a book while incarcerated but never on Saturdays. Judaizante; abjuration de levi ca. 1610, exile.

AHN lib. 1030, fols. 306v, 327; Medina, *Lima* 1:318.

Garcia de Caceres, Diego: b. 1577; son of Francisco Garcia; a soldier in the Spanish army; praised by Valdivia; an encomendero in Santiago de Chile; held several municipal offices in Santiago between 1550 and 1583; d. 1586; his Jewish origin not learned until 1621.

Bohm 19.

Gomez, Duarte a. Antonio de Salazar: b. Lisbon; parents were New Christians; scribe. Judaizante and observer of Mosaic laws; reconciled, sanbenito, confiscation of property, abjuration de vehementi; rearrested in 1631 for wearing silk clothing, carrying a sword and dagger, and riding a horse; fined, exiled.

Friedlander 181; Lea, *Spanish Dependencies* 422; Medina, *Lima* 2:29.

Gomez, Roque: b. Saldaña, Castile Vieja; Portuguese parents. Judaizante; case suspended due to his insanity.

Friedlander 117; Medina, *Lima* 2:52.

Gomez Aceituno, Gonzalo: brother had been relaxed by the Holy Office; constable of the Royal Audencia of La Plata; arrested May 1636. Suspicion of judío; case suspended 1639.

Friedlander 116; Medina, *Lima* 2:66.

Gomez de Acosta, Antonio: b. Braganza ca 1591; merchant; arrested on August 11, 1635; confessed to being an observer of Mosaic laws and judaizante. Judío and judaizante; reconciled, confiscation of property, sanbenito, life imprisonment in Seville.

AHN lib. 1031, fol. 19r; Friedlander 115; Medina, *Lima* 2:52, 117.

Gomez de Acosta, Baltazar: b. Valladolid; Portuguese parents; nephew of Gomez de Acosta, a reconcoliado; r. in Lima but traveled to Cartagena. Judaizante; confessed; reconciled, confiscation of property, sanbenito, abjuration de vehementi, life imprisonment.

AHN lib. 1031, fol. 19r; Friedlander 116; Medina, *Lima* 2:118.

Gomez de Oliva, Leon a. Leonel Gomez Pereira: r. Santiago de Chile; m. Josefa Machado, the daughter of Lucoa Gomez de Oliva; brother-in-law of Dr. Juan Gomez, b. Viana, Portugal, presbyter of the Cathedral; accused in 1679. Judaizante; reconciled December 12, 1679.

AHN leg. 1647, No. 14; Friedlander 117.

Gomez Piñero, Pedro: age 40; b. Lisbon; married in Cuzco; arrested in La Plata. Judío; reconciled, two years in jail, confiscation of property, abjuration de vehementi.

AHN lib. 1029, fols. 52v-53v; Medina, *Lima* 1:296; Palma 1225 [which gives name as Pedro Gomez].

Gomez Portaces, Antonio. Judaizante.

Medina, *Peru* 2:150.

Gomez de Salazar, Diego a. Diego de Oliva: age 25; b. Seville; son of Gonzalo Gomez and Isabel Mendez; both parents Portuguese and New Christians; merchant. Observer of Mosaic laws.

AHN lib. 1030, fols. 188v, 284; Friedlander 116; Lea, *Spanish Dependencies* 422; Medina, *Lima* 2:28.

Gonzales Bermeja, Francisco. *See* Pedro de Contreras.

Gonzalez, Manuel: b. Moncharaz, near Villaviciosa; married. Judaizante and judío; abjuration de vehementi, exile.

AHN lib. 1031, fol. 12r; Friedlander 118; Medina, *Lima* 2:116.

Gonzalez, Matias. Judaizante.

Medina, *Lima* 2:68.

Gonzalez Maduro, Santos. *See* Antonio de los Santos.

Gonzalez de Miranda, Alvaro: fugitive. Judío; relaxed in effigy.

Friedlander 117; Medina, *Lima* 1:311.

Gribaldo, Antonio. Judaizante.

Medina, *Lima* 2:330.

Gudiel, Francisco de: b. Seville, 1518; son of Diego Fernandez and Catalina de Salas; father of Luisa de Salas; carne to New Spain in 1535 and left for Chile in 1543; one of the founders of Concepción; held many royal posts in Chile.

Bohm 19, 20.

Gutierrez, Pedro: b. Toledo; r. Trujillo; a New Christian; testimony against him and his mother given at Valladolid. Judío and observer of Mosaic laws; tortured June 25, 1703; confessed; reconciled October 29, 1703, abjuration de vehementi, confiscation of property, life imprisonment. Retried in 1705; sent to Seville to serve sentence; when ship stopped at Panama and he was found not wearing his sanbenito, a third trial took place; he was taken to Portobelo from where he escaped to Jamaica.

    Friedlander 118; Medina, *Lima* 2:196.

Henriquez, Manuel: Portuguese; a New Christian; formerly reconciled in Coimbra; arrested December 8, 1635. Suspicion of judaizante; confessed to judío under torture; regarded as insane for a time; condemned in 1647 to be relaxed but execution delayed until 1656.

    AHN leg. 1648, No. 18; AHN lib. 1031, fols. 352-359; AHN lib. 1041, fol. 55; Friedlander 120; Palma 1274.

Henriquez de Fonseca, Rodrigo a. Diego Sotelo: a doctor; circumcised; m. Leonor Andrade; brother-in-law of Luis Rivero; entire family devoted to Judaism; came to Lima through Buenos Aires, Cordoba, Tucuman; m. Francisca Rivero; a relative, Juan Mateos, gave testimony in Malaga implicating him; arrested August 30, 1656. Judaizante; relaxed January 23, 1664.

    AHN lib. 1031, fols. 398, 414-414r, 482r, AHN leg. 1648, fols. 16-18 [the word *trefes*, "not kosher," appears in the proceso]; Medina, *Chile* 459 et seq.

Heredia, Fernando de: Portuguese; r. Cuzco; New Christian. Judío; reconciled, confiscation of property, sanbenito removed on the platform at auto of November 17, 1641.

    AHN lib. 1031, fol. 135; Friedlander 122; Medina, *Lima* 2:156.

Hernandez, Francisco: age. 35; b. Guarda; r. Lima; peddler. Judaizante; reconciled, confiscation of property, sanbenito, abjuration de vehementi, jail for one year, exile to Spain.

    AHN lib. 1031, fol. 18r; Medina, *Lima* 2:56, 57, 121.

Hernandez, Geronimo. *See* Geronimo Fernandez.

Hernandez, Nuño: age 40; b. San Vicente de Davera (sic), bishopric of La Guarda; brother or cousin of Manuel Ramos; r. Lima; operator of mule teams; a tall, husky man; withstood most unspeakable torture on potro twice and water in his throat; never said a word. Judaizante; fined 300 pesos for extraordinary costs of the Tribunal; exiled from the Indies.

    AHN lib. 1029, fol. 119.

Herrera, Juan de. *See* Juan de Herrera of Cartagena.

Hoces, Agustin de: r. Trujillo, Peru; a lay brother or lay friar of the Augustinians; denounced himself. Observer of Mosaic laws; reconciled, 200 lashes, term in galleys.

AHN lib. 1029, fols. 119-123r; Friedlander 123; Medina, *Lima* 1:308.

Jorge, Hernan: age 32; Portuguese; r. Potosi; shoemaker; died in prison hospital. Judío and judaizante; relaxed in effigy in 1595.

Medina, *Lima* 1:285; Palma 1224.

Leal, Antonio: candy manufacturer; when others said "loado sea Jesucristo"—praised be Jesus Christ—he said instead "loado sea Dios"—praised be God. Suspicion of judío; reconciled between 1618 and 1622, sanbenito, confiscation of property, jail for one year.

AHN lib. 1031, fols. 124-158; Friedlander 126; Medina, *Lima* 2:12.

Leon, Bartolome de: age 21; b. Badajoz; Portuguese ancestry; a relative of Diego Lopez de Fonseca, Jorge de Silva, and Juan Rodriguez de Silva; partner or comrade of Antonio de Acuña, Manuel de Rosa, Antonio Cordero, and Geronimo Fernandez; merchant; confessed ser judío then revoked the confession and feigned insanity. Judío and judaizante; observer of Mosaic laws; reconciled, sanbenito, 200 lashes, ten years in galleys.

Medina, *Lima* 2:51, 117; Palma 1219.

Leon Cisneros, Juan de: arrested February 11, 1655, because he did not send his children to school on Saturdays and bought only fish with scales. Judaizante; reconciled February 16, 1666, confiscation of property, sanbenito.

AHN lib. 1031, fols. 510-513r; Medina, *Lima* 2:168.

Leon Pinelo, Diego: [one of the most notable literary figures in Peru; honored by the University of San Marcos.]. Judío.

Medina, *Lima* 2:155.

Lima, Gonzalo de: b. 1556 in Portugal; son of New Christians; r. Potosi; married. Judaizante; reconciled between 1601 and 1603.

Friedlander 173; Medina, *Lima* 1:306.

Lima, Juan de: b. Moncorbo, Portugal ca. 1609; brother of Luis de Lima; servant of "la de Ossuna"; made trips to silver mines at Potosi; single; arrested in Huancavelica; confessed. Judaizante; reconciled in auto of 1639, sanbenito, confiscation of property, jail for six months, exile for life from Spain and Indies.

Friedlander 128; Medina, *Lima* 2:124.

Lima, Luis de: age over 40; b. Moncorba, Portugal; brother of Juan and Thomas de Lima, who were in the same auto with him; merchant; denounced himself on February 12, 1636; made holes in the walls while in the cells in order to communicate with others on the outside. Judío; relaxed in auto of January 23, 1639.

> AHN lib. 1031, fols. 213-225; AHN lib. 1041, fol. 56v; Friedlander 128; Medina, *Lima* 2:58, 133, 134.

Lima, Thomas de: age 30; b. Moncorbo, Portugal; r. Lima; brother of Luis de Lima; merchant; "judaized in the cells of the Holy Office;" confessed. Judaizante; reconciled, sanbenito, confiscation of property, 400 lashes, life in the galleys.

> AHN 1031, fol. 14r; AHN 1041, fol. 57v; Friedlander 130; Medina, *Lima* 2:60, 129; Palma 1219.

Lopes Matos, Juan: Judaizante; reconciled in auto of 1639, sanbenito, confiscation of property, exile from Indies and Spain.

> Friedlander 134; Medina, *Lima* 2:151.

Lopez, Antonio: Portuguese; r. Lima; m. Antonia Malgareja; escaped the Inquisition. Judío.

> Friedlander 130.

Lopez, Domingo: Portuguese; r. Cartagena; merchant; arrested in 1604; tortured 12 turns to the wrists and 15 turns while in potro; had 12 pitchers of water poured down his throat; while in potro cried out, "Lord God Israel." Judaizante; absolved in auto of March 13, 1605, goods returned.

> AHN lib. 1029, fols. 349r-353r; Friedlander 133; Lea, *Spanish Dependencies* 421; Medina, *Cartagena* 32; Medina, *Lima* 1:313.

Lopez, Felipa: age 31; Portuguese; married; while in the cells she revealed the names of many other Jews. Judío and judaizante; abjuration de vehementi, confiscation of property, irremissable life imprisonment.

> AHN lib. 1029, fols. 39r-43; Friedlander 133; Medina, *Lima* 1:295; Palma 1225.

Lopez, Gaspar: Portuguese; peddler; denounced himself; said that his parents had fasted according to Mosaic laws which he had also followed; desired to convert to Christianity; Judaizante; absolved *"ad cautellam."*

> Friedlander 133; Medina, *Lima* 2:9.

Lopez, Gaspar: a. Gaspar Lopez de Aguerto: Portuguese; merchant;

poor and bankrupt; taught Judaism to Duarte Enríquez; was considered a very learned Jew; arrested in April 1601. Judío and observer of Mosaic laws; reconciled.

AHN lib. 1029, fols. 298-299r; Friedlander 133; Medina, *Lima* 1:310.

Lopez, Juan: either came from a good family or was a squire. Judaizante; reconciled in 1595, sanbenito, life imprisonment.

Friedlander 134; Medina, *Lima* 1:280; Palma 1224; he is mentioned in the proceso of Juan Rodriguez Mesa of Cartagena.

Lopez, Manuel: Judío; auto of 1581.

Palma 1213. [It is possible that this is the same person as Manuel Lopez a. Luis Coronado.]

Lopez, Manuel: Portuguese; brother of Antonio Nuñez; fugitive. Judío; relaxed in effigy.

Friedlander 135; Medina, *Lima* 1:311.

Lopez, Manuel. *See* Manuel Rodriguez.

Lopez, Manuel a. Luis Coronado: b. Yalves; sailor; had gathered with other Jews in Seville. Judío and observer of Mosaic laws; sentenced outside of auto sometime between 1581 and 1585; reconciled in auto of October 29, 1581, sanbenito, confiscation of property, life imprisonment at the Hospital for Sailors, was to use only the name Luis Coronado.

Kayserling [states Lopez confessed that he was a Jew and that religious services were held at his house]; Medina, *Lima* 1:150, 180; Palma 1213.

Lopez, Pedro: Portuguese; r. Cuzco; arrested in November 1603. Judío and observer of Mosaic laws; reconciled.

AHN lib. 1029, fols. 296-297; Friedlander 135; Medina, *Lima* 1:310.

Lopez de Fonseca, Diego: age 42; b. Badajoz; merchant; partner of Antonio de Acuña; m. Leonor de Andrada, b. Seville; tortured to compel revelation of other Jews. Observer of Mosaic laws; relaxed alive on January 23, 1639.

AHN lib. 1031, fols. 89-98; AHN lib. 1041, fol. 52; Medina, *Lima* 2:48, 49, 51, 93, 116, 117, 131.

Lopez de Lisboa, Diego: father of Diego Leon Pinelo and Antonio de Leon, famous literary figures, and Juan Rodriguez Leon, canon of Cathedral in Puebla, New Spain; his father and uncle had been re-

laxed in Lisbon; a mayordomo, priest, and confessor for Archbishop
Fernando Arias de Ugarte; arrested in archbishop's palace. Beating a
figure of Jesus; returned to Spain.

> AHN lib. 1041, fols. 257-263v (note letter of Inquisitors of May
> 15, 1637, concerning this family); Friedlander 127; Medina, *Lima*
> 2:154, 155.

Lopez Matos, Manuel. Judaizante; auto of 1639.

> AHN lib. 1031, fol. 60v, AHN lib. 1041, fol. 55r.

Lopez Serrano, Bernardo de: b. Villaflor, Portugal; m. in Bordeaux,
France. Judaizante and observer of Mosaic laws, spiritual penance,
abjuration de vehementi.

> AHN lib. 1030, fol. 188v; Friedlander 130; Lea, *Spanish Depen-*
> *dencies* 422; Medina, *Lima* 2:29.

Lopez Suarez, Gaspar: arrested in Potosi, 1642; tortured and confessed,
1648. Judío; reconciled May 9, 1648, sanbenito, confiscation of
property, 100 lashes.

> AHN lib. 1031, fols. 343-344r; Friedlander 133; Medina, *Lima*
> 2:157.

Lopez de Vargas, Diego: age about 33; b. Braga, Portugal; arrested in
October 1603; tried for reading *Republicans del Mundo* which had a
chapter about Jews; tortured; confessed to being an observer of
Mosaic laws, but later revoked the confession; tortured a second
time; said nothing. Judío; relaxed alive.

> AHN lib. 1029, fols. 318r-321r; Friedlander 132, 133; Medina,
> *Lima* 1:310.

Lorenzo, Enrique: age 32; b. Moncorbo, Portugal; brother of Matheo de
la Cruz, who was also in the 1639 auto; used to travel to Portobelo
with encomenderos; had been in Panama, and told of the Jews there;
jailed on January 14, 1636; arrested in Panama, which was under the
jurisdiction of Cartagena, but the Holy Office in Peru retained its
jurisdiction because the prisoners might have been punished too
lightly or escape there; tortured. Judío and observer of Mosaic laws;
reconciled, abjuration de vehementi, sanbenito, confiscation of property, 100 lashes, ten years in galleys.

> AHN lib. 1031, fol. 18v; AHN lib. 1041, fol. 56v; Medina, *Lima*
> 2:58.

Lucena, Baltasar de: b. Vicente de la Vera (Davera) in 1580; arrested
1599; Jewish parents; brother of Gaspar de Lucena of Lima and
Manuel de Lucena of Mexico; r. Potosi; young; single; bankrupt;

arrested in 1599; tortured in *caput alienum;* never confessed or delated against others; Judío and judaizante; relaxed alive on December 10, 1600.

> AHN lib. 1029, fols. 61-65; Friedlander 153; Medina, *Lima* 1:297; Palma 1225.

Lucena, Gaspar de a. Gaspar de Silva: Portuguese; brother of Manuel de Lucena of Mexico. Judío; reconciled, confiscation of property, sanbenito, life imprisonment.

> AHN lib. 1029, fols. 55v-57r; Friedlander 136; Medina, *Lima* 1:296.

Luis, Diego: fugitive. Observer of Mosaic laws; relaxed in effigy.

> Medina, *Lima* 1:311.

Luna, Gonzalo de: he and Juan Vicente were the only ones in the Holy Office cells when Pope Clement's Bull of Pardon arrived "which prohibited the Inquisition from proceeding to Judgment against the Jews." Judío.

> Friedlander 136; Medina, *Lima* 1:303.

Luna, Maior de: b. Seville of Portuguese parents; m. Antonio Moron; well esteemed by the important people in Lima. Judaizante; reconciled in 1639, confiscation of property, sanbenito, 100 lashes because she communicated secretly in the Holy Office cells, life imprisonment.

> AHN lib. 1031, fol. 20v; AHN lib. 1041, fol. 54r; Friedlander 106; Medina, *Lima* 2:55.

Luna, Mencia de: age 46 (though she claimed to be 26); b. Seville; daughter of Portuguese parents; m. Enrique Nuñez de Espinosa; arrested on November 22, 1635; tortured; died in the cells during torture. Observer of Mosaic laws; no final sentence until 1664.

> AHN leg. 1647, Nos. 10, 18; AHN lib. 1031, fol. 18v; Friedlander 137; Palma 1221, 1229, 1274.

Luque, Hernando de: possibly related to a man of the same name who was associated with Pizarro and Almagro; closely bound to the Rebolledos and their group. Judaizante.

> Castillero, Alfredo, personal communication, May 11, 1970.

Luque, Hernando de: said to be a Jew; agent of Gaspar de Espinosa; associated with Pizarro and Almagro. Judaizante.

> Castillero, Alfredo, personal communication, May 11, 1970.

Maldonado, Aldonsa. *See* Diego Nuñez de Silva.

Maldonado de Silva, Francisco a. Bernardo Francisco Maldonado de

Silva: b. San Miguel del Tucuman (New World); son of Diego Nuñez de Silva, a surgeon reconciled in 1604; had two sisters; a bachelor and surgeon; became involved when he tried to convert a sister to Judaism; circumcised himself in jail; changed his name to Eli Nazarine while in prison. Judío and observer of Mosaic laws from age 18; jailed 1626; relaxed alive in auto of January 23, 1639.

>AHN 1031, fols. 119-126; Friedlander 159 et seq; Medina, *Lima* 2:131, 132. [Maldonado de Silva was one of the most illustrious Jewish figures in the colonial period and much has been written about him in Spanish.]

Marques Montesinos, Manuel: Judaizante; reconciled in 1639 auto, confiscation of property, sanbenito, exile.

>AHN lib. 1031, fol. 259r; Friedlander 144; Medina, *Lima* 2:151. Mentioned in the proceso of Juana Enriquez of Mexico.

Marquez Montesionos, Francisco: age 40; b. Torre de Moncorbo, bishopric of Braga, Portugal; brother of Marques Montesinos, who escaped the attempt of the Holy Office to apprehend him; traveled much, had been to New Spain. Judaizante; reconciled, abjuration de vehementi, 200 lashes, confiscation of property, sanbenito, ten years in galleys, then life imprisonment.

>AHN lib. 1031, fol. 18v; AHN lib. 1041, fol. 55r; Friedlander 143; Medina, *Lima* 2:56, 121. Mentioned in the proceso of Juana Enriquez of Mexico.

Matos, Manuel Luis: age 36; b. Trejo (Fresno), Portugal; related to Pascual Diaz, who was in the same auto with him; had a store in the Callejon (a passageway near the Calle de los Judíos); confessed. Judío and observer of Mosaic laws; reconciled, sanbenito, confiscation of property, abjuration de vehementi, jail for three years, 200 lashes.

>AHN lib. 1031, fol. 17v; AHN lib. 1041, fol. 53r; Friedlander 144; Medina, *Lima* 2:57, 126, 127.

Mendez, Alvaro: Portuguese. Celebrated "pascuas de los bollos cencellos," Passover, in France; sent money to relatives in Amsterdam where his own family resided; possessed knowledge of the Scriptures; tortured and confessed. Judaizante; reconciled, confiscation of property, sanbenito, six years in galleys, life imprisonment.

>AHN lib. 1030, fols. 190, 367-369; Friedlander 145; Medina, *Lima* 2:41.

Mendez, Duarte. *See* Juan Duarte Mendez.

Mendez, Francisco a. Francisco Meneses: age 25, b. Lamego, Portugal; r. in mining site in Guananago; denounced himself. Judaizante; reconciled, abjuration de vehementi, confiscation of property, sanbenito for only one day, exile from Spain and the Indies.

    AHN lib. 1031, fol. 20r; Medina, *Lima* 2:120 [cites age as 30].

Mendez, Francisco de. *See* Francisco de Montoya.

Mendez, Juan Duarte a. Duarte Mendez: b. 1568; Portuguese; merchant. Judaizante or suspicion of judaizante; reconciled; on December 17, 1595, he was ordered to report to the Tribunal in Seville; nine years later he was again ordered to report to the Suprema.

    Friedlander 146 [cites charge as judaizante]; Medina, *Lima* 1:280; Palma 1224.

Mendez, Manuel. *See* Manuel de Quiros.

Mendez de Dueñas, Garci: age 58; b. Olivera, Portugal; son of Alvaro Gil and Isabel Lopez; merchant; his wife, Leonor de Herrera, and his children escaped to France; hanged himself. Observer of Mosaic laws and concealer of judaizantes and heretics; bones disinterred; relaxed in effigy.

    AHN leg. 1648, No. 16; AHN lib. 1030, fol. 189; Friedlander 158; Lea, *Spanish Dependencies* 422; Medina, *Lima* 2:28.

Meneses, Francisco. *See* Francisco Mendez.

Montecid, Domingo: b. Santarem, Portugal, in 1587; wax and candy maker in Portugal; peddler in Peru; small farmer for Manuel Bautista Perez; jailed on August 11, 1635. Judío and observer of Mosaic laws; reconciled in auto of 1639, confiscation of property, sanbenito, exile for life.

    AHN lib. 1031, fol. 55v; AHN lib. 1041, fol. 54v; Friedlander 147; Medina, *Lima* 53, 114.

Montoya, Francisco de a. Francisco Mendez: b. 1605; a candy maker; New Christian. Judaizante; reconciled, confiscation of property, sanbenito, jail for two years, exile.

    AHN lib. 1031, fol. 134; Friedlander 148; Medina, *Lima* 2:156.

Morata Osorio, Martin. Judaizante.

    Friedlander 148; Medina, *Lima* 2:68, 92.

Morin, Nicholas: French. Suspicion of judío and judaizante; reconciled in auto of April 5, 1592.

    Friedlander 149 [cites charge as judío and judaizante]; Palma 1224 [cites charge as suspicion of Judaism].

Moron, Antonio: b. Fondon, Portugal, ca. 1589; brother of Mencia de

Luna; captain; gambler; m. Maior de Luna, b. Seville; father of Isabel
Antonia, whose husband was jailed; tried to flee Panama when his
son-in-law was arrested. Judaizante.

AHN leg. 1647, No. 18; AHN lib. 1041, fol. 54r; Friedlander 149.
[Sources disagree about his sentence.]

Najera Arauz, Herando a. Hernando de Dios: royal scribe at Ecija. Had
been arrested at Cuzco on September 9, 1609; accused of "seeing his
own dead son" and washing his hands before and after dinner. Judaizante; reconciled, sanbenito, life imprisonment.

Friedlander 151; Medina, *Lima* 2:9.

Nicolao the Greek, Benito: arrested for porging and for saying that
fornication between two unmarried people was not a sin; punishment unknown but possibly reconciled in April 1604.

Friedlander 151 [which gives the name as Benito Nicola]; Medina,
Lima 1:275, 308.

Noble, Luis a. Luis Duarte: b. Evora, Portugal; served as a soldier for six
years in Chile; arrested in Callao as a result of an investigation about
a stolen cross; confessed to a Jesuit prior to coming to the Holy
Office. Observer of Mosaic laws; reconciled in private, spiritual penance, lashes, term in galleys.

Friedlander 151; Medina, *Chile* 327; Medina, *Lima* 2:11.

Nombela, Gregorio. Judaizante.

Medina, *Lima* 2:330.

Nuñez, Alvaro a. Manuel Nuñez Alvaro de Almeyra; b. Braganza, Portugal; r. La Plata; bachiller, doctor of medicine. Judío and observer of
Mosaic laws; reconciled in auto of March 13, 1605.

AHN lib. 1029, fol. 281; Friedlander 152; Kayserling 134; Medina, *Cartagena* 143; Medina, *Lima* 1:310. *See also* Alvaro Nuñez
of Rio de La Plata.

Nuñez, Antonio: brother of Manuel Lopez. Relaxed in effigy.

Friedlander 152; Medina, *Lima* 1:311.

Nuñez, Antonio: b. 1567; retail merchant. Judaizante; reconciled on
December 17, 1595, life imprisonment, sanbenito.

Friedlander 152; Medina, *Lima* 1:280.

Nuñez, Jorge: Portuguese; did not want to buy mules on Saturday;
porged and observed the Sabbath; tortured; attempted suicide.
Judío; relaxed alive on December 17, 1595.

Friedlander 156; Lea, *Spanish Dependencies* 420; Medina, *Lima*
1:283; Palma 1224.

Nuñez, Luis: b. Coimbra, ca. 1569; had Jewish parents; was circumcised (but stated this was not on account of Judaism); a bachelor and presbyter; jailed May 8, 1635. Observer of Mosaic laws.

> Friedlander 150. Medina, *Lima* 2:61.

Nuñez, Pascual: age 22; b. Verganza (Braganza), Portugal; single; a peddler. Judaizante and judío, jailed April 14, 1636; confessed, reconciled, 200 lashes for lying about his property, galleys for life.

> AHN lib. 1031, fol. 13r; AHN lib. 1041, fol. 58; Friedlander 157; Medina, *Lima* 2:63, 128.

Nuñez Alvaro de Almeyra, Manuel. *See* Alvaro Nuñez.

Nuñez de Cea, Duarte: age 45; Portuguese; dealer in Negro slaves; m. in Lisbon to Simona Nuñez; admitted that he had always observed fasts, et cetera; was unrepentant; at the stake he said that he was a Jew and that he was dying as an observer of the law of Moses as had his parents and ancestors. Judaizante; relaxed alive in 1600.

> AHN leg. 1648, No. 7; AHN lib. 1029, fols. 65-67r; Friedlander 153; Keyserling 133; Lea, *Spanish Dependencies* 420; Medina, *Lima* 1:297; Palma 1225 [states age as 40 years].

Nuñez Duarte, Francisco: age 44; b. La Guarda or Santarem; all of his family were New Christians; brother of Gaspar Nuñez Duarte; had been a second lieutenant in a company of soldiers; merchant; had a store on Calle de los Judíos; arrested on August 11, 1635. Judaizante; confessed; reconciled, confiscation of property, sanbenito, 100 lashes, six years in galleys, then life imprisonment in Seville. [The Holy Office found his confession to be "late and incomplete."]

> AHN lib. 1031, fols. 18r, 62v; AHN lib. 1041, fol. 53r; Friedlander 154; Medina, *Lima* 2:52; Palma 1219.

Nuñez Duarte, Gaspar: b. La Guarda in 1603; brother of Francisco Nuñez Duarte; traveler; arrested in 1635. Judaizante; reconciled, confiscation of property, sanbenito, 200 lashes, perpetual service as oarsman in galleys [though the rules of the Holy Office limited this punishment to ten years] because he revoked his confession.

> AHN lib. 1041, fol. 42r; AHN lib. 1031, fol. 19v; Inq. lib. states that his service in the galleys was to last six years; Friedlander 155; Medina, *Lima* 2:52, 121, 123; Palma 1219.

Nuñez de Espinosa, Enrique: b. Lisbon; son of Antonio de Brito and Beatriz Espinosa, both of Bordeaux; reared in France; had been in Mexico and Panama; m. Mencia de Luña; arrested in 1623. Judío; tortured, but failed to break down; case suspended; rearrested on

August 11, 1635; judaizante; testified against others after confessing; reconciled on January 23, 1639, 200 lashes, ten years in galleys, sanbenito, confiscation of property, life imprisonment.

> AHN lib. 1030, fols. 174-179; AHN lib. 1031, fol. 18r; AHN lib. 1041, fol. 54v; Friedlander 154 [which states that he was reared in Seville]; Medina, *Lima* 2:53, 119, Palma 1219.

Nuñez de la Haba, Diego a. Pedro Nuñez de la Haba: b. Trujillo, Peru, 1710; denounced but escaped from jail. Beating a cross; sentenced in absentia December 23, 1738, to five years in jail, 200 lashes when apprehended.

> Friedlander 152; Lea, *Spanish Dependencies* 436; Medina, *Lima* 2:265.

Nuñez Juarez, Andres: b. Mogodouro, Portugal; had Jewish parents, denounced himself. Judío and judaizante; abjuration de vehementi, confiscation of property; was permitted to remove the sanbenito at the reading of the sentence at the auto because of his contrition and repentance.

> AHN lib. 1029, fols. 53v-55v; Friedlander 152; Medina, *Lima* 1:296; Palma 1225.

Nuñez Magro de Almeyda, Manuel: b. Condeja, close to Coimbra; Jewish ancestry; presbyter in church; starved himself to death. Heretic and judaizante; relaxed in effigy.

> Friedlander 156, 157; Lea, *Spanish Dependencies* 422; Medina, *Lima* 2:30.

Nuñez de Oliviera, Francisco: b. Braganza, Portugal; young; single; merchant; arrested in November 1598; attempted suicide twice. Judío; reconciled, confiscation of property, sanbenito, jail for six years.

> AHN lib. 1029, fol. 45v-49v; Friedlander 155; Medina, *Lima* 1:295; Palma 1225.

Nuñez de Silva, Diego: b. Braganza; Portuguese; m. Aldonsa Maldonado; father of Francisco Maldonado de Silva, one of the most illustrious Jewish figures in the colonial period; practiced medicine in Cordoba del Tucuman, in the viceroyalty of Peru; arrested in May 1601. Judío and judaizante; reconciled; moved to Callao.

> AHN lib. 1029, fols. 140 and 284r-286r; Friedlander 13; Medina, *Lima* 1:310.

Nuñez de Silva, Diego: son of Diego Nuñez de Silva and Aldonsa Maldonado; arrested in May 1602. Judío; reconciled.

> AHN lib. 1029, fols. 139r, 286r-288r; Friedlander 152; Medina, *Lima* 1:310.

Oliva, Diego de. *See* Diego Gomez de Salazar.

Olivos, Friar Javier. Judaizante.

Medina, *Lima* 2:330.

Omepezoa, Pedro de: b. 1510; Portuguese; an encomendero on Concepcion; m. Luisa de Salas, daughter of Francisco de Gudiel. Judaizante.

Bohm 20.

Orgoños, Rodrigo de : b. Oropesa, diocese of Toledo, 1505; son of Alonso Jimenez and Beatriz Dueñas; served in the expedition of Almagro, an associate of Pizarro in the conquest of Peru. Judaizante.

Bohm 17.

Ortega, Juan: age 22; b. Bordeaux; parents were Portuguese; peddler; sanbenito removed while he was in jail because he was a model prisoner. Judaizante.

AHN lib. 1030, fol. 276v; Friedlander 158; Lea, *Spanish Dependencies* 422; Medina, *Mexico* 2:28.

Ortiz, Agustin. Judaizante.

Medina, *Lima* 2:330.

Osorio, Simon a. Simon Rodriguez a. Francisco de Caceres: b. San Combadan, Portugal; administered the obrajes, shops where slaves and prisoners wove cloth and made wearing apparel for the Duchess of Lerma; arrested on December 22, 1635; testimony in his proceso that he and two of his brothers had invested in the Compañia de Olandeses contra Su Majestad, the Dutch Company against the Spanish Crown; he wore curls and perfume; there were two paintings of him, one as a woman. Reconciled, confiscation of property, sanbenito, abjuration de vehementi, six years in the galleys, 100 lashes, exile.

AHN lib. 1031, fol. 12v; AHN lib. 1041, fol. 55r; Medina, *Lima* 2:57, 114, 115. [His proceso reveals great confusion about the identity of his parents (three different sets are named) as well as about his place of birth.]

Osorio, Martin Morata. *See* Martin Morata Osario.

Ovalle, Diego de: age 53; b. Emont, near Evora, Portugal; merchant; had children; his daughter m. Francisco de Vergara, who was arrested on May 15, 1636, but who was freed and whose property was returned to him on January 18, 1640. Judaizante; reconciled on September 15, 1642.

AHN leg. 1647, No. 4; AHN leg. 1648, No. 2.

Palma, Antonio de la. *See* Antonio Fernandez.

Parra, Francisco de la: b. Peru; celebrated Passover; arrested January 3, 1640. Judaizante; reconciled in auto of November 17, 1641.

AHN lib. 1031, fol. 140r; Friedlander 160; Medina, *Lima* 2:156.

Parra, Juan de la: b. Peru; celebrated the Festival of Unleavened Bread or the Lamb; celebrated Passover for seven days; arrested January 3, 1640. Observer of Mosaic laws; reconciled November 17, 1641, confiscation of property, sanbenito, exile.

AHN lib. 1031, fol. 139r; Medina, *Lima* 2:156.

Paz, Enrique de: age. 35; b. Guarda; owned a store in partnership with Francisco Gutierrez de Coca, a familiar of the Holy Office; confessed to judío and judaizante. Judío and observer of Mosaic laws; reconciled in auto of 1639, confiscation of property, sanbenito, 200 lashes, four years in galleys, abjuration de vehementi, exile.

AHN lib. 1031, fol. 21r; AHN lib. 1041, fol. 55v; Friedlander 161; Medina, *Lima* 54, 129, 130.

Paz, Manuel de: age 40; b. Pedrira, Portugal; owned a Bible; arrested August 12, 1636; hanged himself in cells. Judaizante; relaxed in effigy in 1639 auto.

Friedlander 162; Medina, *Lima* 2:137; Palma 1218, 1220, 1274.

Pena, Francisco de la. *See* Francisco de Victoria Barahona.

Pereira, Diego: Portuguese; arrested in Chuciuto province. Suspicion of judío.

Medina, *Lima* 2:66.

Periera Diamante, Diego: b. Sancel, near Evora, Portugal; jailed in Cuzco; not in 1639 auto or any other public auto. Judaizante; five years in prison for being in communication with other prisoners, though "he does not seem to be part of the conspiracy."

Medina, *Lima* 2:6, 150.

Pereyra, Juan Antonio: Portuguese. Judaizante; sentenced in private auto November 11, 1736, abjuration de vehementi, 200 lashes, reconciled, 10 years at presidio at Valdivia, confiscation of half of property.

Lea, *Spanish Dependencies* 436.

Perez, Domingo: age 50; b. Angora, Isla Tercera, Portugal; r. Huancavelica; shoemaker; m. Ana Garcia de la Vega. Suspicion of judaizante; reconciled, confessed and repented.

AHN lib. 1030, fols. 189, 274-276; Friedlander 163; Lea, *Spanish Dependencies* 422; Medina, *Lima* 2:27.

Perez, Manuel Bautista: b. Anzan, Coimbra, Portugal; New Christian; m. Guimor Enriquez, his cousin, also a New Christian, b. Seville; had several children; was extremely wealthy, owned an extensive library, and was a benefactor of the University of San Marcos; arrested on August 11, 1635; attempted suicide in the cells by knifing his stomach; wrote coded messages while in the cells to his two brothers-in-law; the *Relación* states that he heard his sentence at the auto of January 23, 1639 with "great severity and majesty." Judío; relaxed alive.

> AHN lib. 1031, fol. 22v; Lewin, *Mártires y Conquistadores Judíos en la América y Hispana* (Buenos Aires: Editorial Candeladro, 1954), 209-210 [states b. in Seville and taken to Portugal where he was reared]; Medina, *Mexico* 2:134.

Perez de Acosta, Diego: escaped to Italy. Judío; relaxed in effigy.

> Friedlander 163; Medina, *Lima* 1:311. *See also* Diego Perez de Acosta in Rio de La Plata.

Perez de Freitas, Rafael: died in cells in 1630 awaiting trial. Judaizante.

> Medina, *Lima* 2:40, 330.

Piña, Manuel de. Judaizante.

> Friedlander 168.

Quaresma, Tome. *See* Tome Cuaresma.

Quiros, Manuel de: a. Manuel Mendez: b. Villaflor, Portugal; r. in mining site of Huamanaca; single. Judaizante; reconciled, confiscation of property, abjuration de vehementi, sanbenito for one year, exile for life from Indies.

> AHN lib. 1031, fol. 20r; Friedlander 169; Medina, *Lima* 2:127.

Ramirez Cartagena, Licenciado: high municipal official of the Holy Office; not a Jew but involved with them.

> Friedlander 88; Palma 216.

Ramos, Manuel: Portuguese; New Christian; had been in Mexico; had been relaxed in effigy in 1605; rearrested ca. 1610. Suspicion of judío; tortured; absolved in 1611.

> AHN lib. 1029 fol. 116 (1603-1604) [refers to a Manuel Ramos who was to be arrested "por judío" but who fled and who was a cousin of Nuño Hernandez].

Ramos, Samuel: Portuguese; New Christian. Suspicion of judío; tortured; died; relaxed in effigy 1605; later absolved.

> Medina, *Lima* 1:319.

Ramos de Rojas, Juan: r. Lima; rented out mules. Judaizante; confessed only to being a Moor and having "judaized."

> Medina, *Lima* 2:60.

Rebolledo, Juana de: m. Martin Fernandez de Enciso; mother of Juan

Fernandez de Rebolledo, Rodrigo de Rebolledo, and Catalina Fernandez. Observer of Mosaic laws.

Castillero, Alfredo, personal communication, May 11, 1970.

Rebolledo, Rodrigo de: son of Martin Fernandez de Enciso and Juana de Rebolledo; brother of Juan Fernandez de Rebolledo and Catalina Fernandez; very influential in Panama 1530-1540. Observer of Mosaic laws.

Castillero, Alfredo, personal communication, May 11, 1970.

Reyes, Melchor de los: age 30; b. Lisbon; reared in Madrid; r. Lima and San Luis Potosi; box merchant; jailed on January 10, 1636; he had concealed the jewels and clothing of Enrique de Paz, and had placed four ingots of silver in boxes which he left for safekeeping with Dionisio Manrique, consultant for the Holy Office, an officer with the longest period of service as an officer of the court of Audiencia. Judío and judaizante; reconciled, confiscation of property, sanbenito, abjuration de vehementi, 200 lashes, ten years in galleys, life imprisonment.

AGN 425, fol. 474; AHN lib. 1031, fol. 14v; AHN lib. 1041, fols. 55r-56v; Medina, *Lima* 2:57, 126.

Riberos, Pedro de: Portuguese; a fugitive. Observer of Mosaic laws; relaxed in effigy.

Medina, *Lima* 1:311.

Rivero, Luis a. Juan Sotelo: b. Peru, 1620; son of Felipe Rivero and Guiomar Rodriguez de Andrade, who was a niece of Maria Andrade and cousin of Violante Rodriguez, Duarte Fernandez Valencia, and Simon Nuñez, all of Malaga; brother of Leonor de Andrade, who m. Rodrigo Henriquez de Fonseca. Judío; relaxed in effigy January 23, 1664.

AHN leg. 1648, No. 18; AHN lib. 1031, fols. 415-415r, 431r, 483r; Friedlander 171, 172; Medina, *Chile* 459 et seq.

Rodriguez, Alvaro: arrested in 1635. Judaizante.

AHN lib. 1031, fol. 142r (cites arrest as 1640); Friedlander 173 (states case suspended); Medina, *Lima* 2:156 (states reconciled in the 1641 auto; confiscation of property, sanbenito, life imprisonment).

Rodriguez, Alvaro: b. Portalegre; had no relatives in Peru; his confiscated property was valued at $14,000; died in cells ca. 1698. Judaizante.

Friedlander 173; Lea, *Spanish Dependencies* 434; Medina, *Lima* 2:243.

Rodriguez, Alvaro: r. Lima; arrested in April 1601 for refusing to show a parchment to the comisario of Tarija; tortured. Judaizante; reconciled about the beginning of 1602.

> AHN lib. 1029, fols. 234-236r; Medina, *Lima* 1:307.

Rodriguez, Andres: a. Andres de Sosa: b. Fondon in 1562; brother of Francisco Rodriguez Duarte; single. Judío; confessed; reconciled, loss of all property, abjuration de vehementi, six years in galleys.

> AHN lib. 1029, fol. 32v; Friedlander 173; Medina, *Lima* 1:295; Palma 1225.

Rodriguez, Francisco: b. Villaflor, Portugal; operator of mule team between Lima and Callao; charge made against him by other Portuguese because he would not make deliveries on Saturdays; tortured twice and badly wounded. Judaizante; relaxed alive on December 17, 1595.

> Friedlander 175; Medina, *Lima* 1:283-285; Palma 1224.

Rodriguez, Francisco: age 26; Jewish parents; confessed to being a Jew, then revoked the confession; had been before the Tribunal in Mexico, where he had been sentenced to two years' exile from Mexico City but not from the Indies, which was the common exile. Judío; reconciled, confiscation of property, life imprisonment.

> Abec. [which lists a Francisco Rodriguez, an accomplice of Felipa Lopez, in the Mexican auto of December 8, 1596]; AHN lib. 1029, fols. 35r-39v; Friedlander 176; Medina, *Lima* 1:295; Palma 1225.

Rodriguez, Gaspar: Portuguese; denounced by Felipa Lopez. Judaizante; reconciled in 1600 auto, sanbenito, jail for four years.

> Friedlander 177; Medina, *Lima* 1:296.

Rodriguez, Isabel: age 15; b. Lima; daughter of Felipa Lopez. Judío and judaizante; reconciled, abjuration de vehementi, two years in jail.

> AHN lib. 1029, fols. 50v-52v; Friedlander 178; Medina, *Lima* 1:295; Palma 1225.

Rodriguez, Manuel a. Manuel Lopez: Portuguese. Judío; tried to escape; "appeared crazy"; no confession under torture; absolved; goods confiscated; sentenced sometime between 1600 and 1601.

> AHN lib. 1029, fols. 68-70.

Rodriguez, Pablo a. Pablo Rodriguez Duarte: age 36; b. Montemayor, Portugal; half-brother of Sebastian Duarte; merchant; an agent of Manuel Bautista Perez; single. Judaizante; reconciled, abjuration de vehementi, life imprisonment.

AHN lib. 1031, fol. 15r; Friedlander 180; Medina, *Lima* 2:128; Palma 1219.

Rodriguez, Simon. *See* Simon Osorio.

Rodriguez, Thomas: b. Venta de Arrola, Portugal ca. 1605; majordomo for the Archibishop and agent of Diego Lopez of Lisbon; jailed March 7, 1636.

  Friedlander 180; Medina, *Lima* 2:61 (notes not in 1639 auto).

Rodriguez de Acevedo, Nuño: Portuguese; arrested on December 2, 1599; was not tortured because he was lame and had a broken leg. Judaizante; reconciled early in 1602.

  AHN 1029, fols. 236r-241r; Friedlander 179; Medina, *Lima* 1:307. *See also* Alvaro Rodriguez de Acevedo of Rio de la Plata.

Rodriguez Arias, Francisco. *See* Francisco Ruiz Arias.

Rodriguez Arias, Juan. Judaizante; reconciled in auto of 1639, confiscation of property, sanbenito.

  AHN lib. 1031, fol. 258; Friedlander 178; Medina, *Lima* 2:150.

Rodriguez Delgado, Matias: arrested January 2, 1640. Observer of Mosaic laws; reconciled in auto of November 17, 1641, sanbenito, confiscation of property, jail for one year.

  AHN lib. 1031, fol. 138r; Friedlander 99; Medina, *Lima* 2:156.

Rodriguez Duarte, Juan: b. 1605 in Montemayor; a merchant; lived with uncle Sebastian Duarte, who was relaxed in 1639; jailed February 25, 1636. Judaizante and observer of Mosaic laws; reconciled, abjuration de vehementi, life imprisonment, sanbenito, confiscation of property, galleys for four years.

  AHN lib. 1031, fol. 15; AHN lib. 1041, fol. 57v; Friedlander 178; Medina, *Lima* 2:60, 125; Palma 1219.

Rodriguez Guerrero, Manuel: arrested in Tucuman in a church. Judaizante; reconciled in auto of 1595.

  Friedlander 179.

Rodriguez de Leon, Antonio: Portuguese; b. Bayonne, r. Potosi; merchant; bankrupt; arrested in October 1603. Judío and observer of Mosaic laws.

  AHN lib. 1029, fols. 302r-305r; Friedlander 174 [states that he was a miner in Potosi]; Medina, *Lima* 1:310.

Rodriguez de Lucena, Gaspar: denounced by Felipa Lopez. Judío and judaizante; reconciled, confiscation of property, sanbenito, four years in galleys.

  AHN lib. 1029, fol. 1; Friedlander 177; Medina, *Lima* 1:296.

Rodriguez Muñoz, Domingo: Portuguese; arrested on July 29, 1636; died in the cells ca. 1637. Judío.

AHN lib. 1031, fol. 67r; Friedlander 174.

Rodriguez Pereira, Gaspar: age 43; b. Villa Real; single; merchant; confessed. Judío and judaizante; reconciled in auto of 1639, sanbenito, confiscation of property, abjuration de vehementi, jail for three years, 200 lashes, five years in galleys for attempting to recant confessions.

AHN lib. 1031, fol. 19v [states b. Madrid]; Friedlander 177; Medina, *Lima* 2:58, 122.

Rodriguez de Silva, Juan: age 39; b. Estremoz, Portugal; brother of Jorge de Silva; came to Peru from Panama to aid brother; convinced brother to denounce himself on February 18, 1636, as "ser judío"; feigned insanity. Judaizante and observer of Mosaic laws; confessed "ser judío"; relaxed.

AHN lib. 1031, fol. 24; Friedlander 178; Palma 1218, 1219, 1274; Medina, *Lima* 2:59, 60, 132, 133; Garcia de Proodian 174 [states reconciled].

Rodriguez de Silvera, Diego: Portuguese; r. Huamanga. Judío and observer of Mosaic laws; reconciled.

AHN lib. 1029, fols. 289r-291r; Friedlander 174; Keyserling 134; Medina, *Lima* 1:310.

Rodriguez Tabares, Henrique a. Jorge Henrique Tabares: age 19 or 20; brother of Jorge Rodriguez Tabares; jailed August 11, 1635; testified against others; transferred to a hospital for the insane in 1648; did not appear in any auto until 1666 for that reason. Judaizante.

AHN leg. 1648, No. 15; AHN lib. 1031, fols. 339-341r; AHN lib. 1041, fol. 54; Friedlander 185; Medina, *Lima* 2:53, 157.

Rodriguez Tabares, Jorge: b. Seville, ca. 1600; m. in Lima to Geronima Marmolejo, b. Frejnal, Portugal; jailed on August 11, 1635. Judío and judaizante; reconciled, confiscation of property, sanbenito, abjuration de vehementi, life imprisonment in Seville.

AHN lib. 1031, fol. 17v; AHN lib. 1041, fol. 54v; Friedlander 186; Medina, *Lima* 2:53, 124; Palma 1219.

Rodriguez Tavares, Jorge: b. Utrera, Portugal; arrested in August 1603; his brother who had been arrested by the Holy Office testified against him. Judío and judaizante; absolved in April 1604.

AHN lib. 1029, fols. 114-115; Friedlander 178; Medina, *Lima* 1:308.

Rosa, Diego de la: b. and r. Quito; embroiderer. Judío, abjuration de
   levi; six years exile from Quito and four years from Trujillo, confined to Lima and five leagues around it, to confess and have com-
   munion on the three festivals of each year for two years.
      Friedlander 180; Medina, *Lima* 1:150; Palma 1213.

Rosa (Rossa), Manuel de: age 25; b. Portalegre; single; silk weaver;
   servant of Diego Lopez; suspicion that the Congregation of the
   Young of which he was the sacristan might have been a synagogue,
   tortured; confessed. Judío and judaizante; reconciled, sanbenito,
   confiscation of property, life imprisonment in Seville.
      AHN lib. 1031, fol. 14r; Friedlander 180; Medina, *Lima* 49, 125;
      Palma 1219.

Ruiz Arias, Francisco: age 23; b. Alcaiz, near Casteloblanco, Portugal;
   traveled to mining areas of Alto Plano; denounced himself; confessed
   ser judío. Judaizante and observer of Mosaic laws; reconciled, confiscation of property, abjuration de vehementi, sanbenito could be
   removed after auto.
      AHN 1031, fol. 15r [cites name as Francisco Rodrigues Arias];
      Friedlander 181; Medina, *Lima* 2:127.

Ruiz de Marchen, Martin: left Panama in 1560 for Lima, where he
   established himself permanently. Observer of Mosaic laws.
      Castillero, Alfredo, personal communication, May 11, 1970.

Salazar, Anonimo de. *See* Antonio Fernandez.

Salazar, Antonio de. *See* Duarte Gomez.

Sanchez, Antonio. *See* Antonio Fernandez.

Santiago, Antonio de. *See* Antonio Fernandez de Vega.

Santos, Antonio de los a. Santos Gonzalez Maduro: b. Capeludos, bishopric of Braga, Portugal; son of Antonio Gonzalez Maduro and Maria
   Alvarez; merchant; a familiar of the Holy Office; jailed April 17,
   1636. Judaizante; freed in 1637.
      Medina, *Lima* 2:63, 90, 92, 109, 138, 148.

Serrano, Francisco. *See* Francisco de Victoria Barahona.

Silva, Alvaro de: b. Tierra de Verganza (Braganza), Portugal; r. Potosi;
   bailiff or constable. Judaizante; case pending in 1625.
      AHN lib. 1030, fol. 188v.

Silva, Bartolome de. Observer of Mosaic laws; reconciled in auto of
   January 23, 1639, confiscation of property, sanbenito, jail for one
   year.

AHN 1031, fol. 136r; Friedlander 183; Medina, *Lima* 2:156.

Silva, Bernardo de. Judaizante.

Medina, *Lima* 2:330.

Silva, Gaspar de. *See* Gaspar de Lucena.

Silva, Jorge de: b. Estremoz, Portugal, ca. 1602; r. Lima; had come from Panama; dealer in Negroes; taught Judaism to Mencia de Luna; arrested on August 11, 1635; confessed ser judío. Judío; reconciled in auto of 1639, confiscation of property, sanbenito, abjuration de vehementi, 200 lashes, galleys for life.

AHN lib. 1031, fol. 16r; AHN lib. 1041, fol. 53r; Friedlander 183; Medina, *Lima* 53, 59, 117, 123; Palma 1219.

Silvera, Gaspar de: Portuguese; r. Huancavelica; arrested in 1603. Judío; reconciled.

AHN lib. 1029, fols. 297-298; Friedlander 184; Medina, *Lima* 1:310.

Silvera, Juan de: Portuguese; operator of mule teams. Observer of Mosaic laws; reconciled.

AHN lib. 1029, fols. 308-309r; Friedlander 184; Medina, *Lima* 1:310.

Sosa, Amaro de. Judaizante.

Medina, *Lima* 2:330.

Sosa, Andres de. *See* Andres Rodriguez.

Sosa, Antonio de a. Antonio de Sosa Hurtado: b. Villamean, near Viseu, Portugal; m. in Lima. Judaizante; reconciled on May 7, 1643.

AHN lib. 1031, fols. 281-284r; AHN lib. 1041, fols. 53r; and Medina, *Lima* 2:52. Mentioned in proceso of Juan Rodriguez Mesa.

Sotelo, Diego. *See* Rodrigo Henriquez de Fonseco.

Sotelo, Juan. *See* Luis Rivero.

Tabares, Francisco Jorge: brother of Jorge Rodriguez Tabares and Henrique Rodriguez Tabares. Judaizante; case suspended three years after his arrest.

Friedlander 185 [charge cited as judío]; Medina, *Lima* 2:66, 150.

Tabares, Henrique Jorge. *See* Henrique Rodriguez Tabares.

Tabares, Manuel de. *See* Diego de Andrada.

Trillo (Truxillo), Juan de: b. Priego, Andalucia; parents were New Christians; peddler. Observer of Mosaic laws; reconciled, sanbenito, confiscation of property, life imprisonment.

AHN lib. 1030, fol. 286; Friedlander 186; Lea, *Spanish Dependencies* 422; Medina, *Lima* 2:29.

Truxillo, Juan de. *See* Juan de Trillo.

Vaez Enriquez, Garcia: b. Seville ca. 1599; Portuguese ancestry; brother of Guiomar Enriquez and Isabel Enriquez; brother-in-law of Manuel Bautista Perez; circumcised; r. Lima; merchant; confessed to judaismo. Judaizante; reconciled, confiscation of property, sanbenito, abjuration de vehementi, life imprisonment.

AHN 1031, fol. 17r; Friedlander 187; Medina, *Lima* 2:123, 143.

Vaez Machado, Francisco. Judaizante; reconciled in 1595, sanbenito, nine years imprisonment.

Friedlander 187; Lea, *Spanish Dependencies* [name spelled as Baez]; Medina, *Lima* 1:281; Palma 1224.

Vaez (Baez) Pereira, Rodrigo: b. Monsanto, near La Guarda, ca. 1600; merchant; m. Isabel Antonio de Moron in Lima; arrested on August 11, 1635; tortured. Judaizante; relaxed after garrote on January 23, 1639.

AHN lib. 1031, fols. 198-205; AHN lib. 1041, fol. 53r; Friedlander 187; Medina, *Lima* 2:52, 135; Palma 1219.

Valcazar, Gonzalo de: merchant; arrested May 9, 1640. Observer of Mosaic laws, reconciled in auto of November 17, 1641, confiscation of property, sanbenito, exile.

AHN lib. 1031, fol. 141; Friedlander 188; Medina, *Lima* 2:156.

Valcazar, Pedro de a. Pedro Enriquez Cuello: merchant; arrested September 7, 1640; tortured; confessed after the first turn. Observer of Mosaic laws; reconciled in auto of November 17, 1641, confiscation of property.

AHN lib. 1031, fol. 142; Medina, *Lima* 2:156.

Valencia, Feliciano de: age 37; b. Braganza, Portugal; brother of Francisco Nuñez de Olivera; lawyer; m. Maria de Fonseca in Lisbon. Judío; reconciled in 1600 auto, confiscation of property, sanbenito.

AHN lib. 1029, fols. 59r-61r; Friedlander 189; Medina, *Lima* 1:296; Palma 1225.

Valencia, Luis de: age 60; b. Lisbon; brought from Panama by Holy Office; had been in New Spain; "appeared to be circumcised."Judaizante and observer of Mosaic laws; reconciled, confiscation of property, sanbenito, fine of 300 pesos; convicted only of suspicion.

AHN lib. 1031, fol. 14v; AHN leg. 1647, No. 12; Friedlander 189.

Vasquez, Francisco: b. Mondi, Portugal, ca. 1589; "a loafer"; married; r. Lima; feigned insanity. Judaizante and observer of Mosaic laws; reconciled, confiscation of property, sanbenito, charged 200 pesos for expenses of Holy Office, abjuration de vehementi, life imprisonment, exile.

AHN lib. 1031, fol. 12v; Friedlander 189; Medina, *Lima* 2:60, 115; Palma 1219.

Vasquez de Acuña, Diego: age 72. Suspicion of judaizante and other heretical propositions; fined 1,000 pesos between May 26, 1635, and August 17, 1638.

Friedlander 189; Medina, *Lima* 2:98.

Vega, Antonio de: b. Villa de la Frontera, Portugal, 1600; r. Lima; traveling merchant; confessed, then revoked confession. Judío and observer of Mosaic laws; relaxed in auto of 1639.

AHN lib. 1031, fol. 22v; AHN lib. 1041, fol. 55r; Friedlander 190; Medina, *Lima* 2:130.

Vega, Luis de: age 40; b. Lisbon; silversmith; m. Isabel Bautista Perez in Seville, sister of Manuel Bautista Perez; tortured; confessed to judío and judaizante. Judaizante; reconciled, confiscation of property, sanbenito, jail for two years, exile.

AHN lib. 1031, fol. 15r; AHN lib. 1041, fols. 55r-56v; Medina, *Lima* 2:56, 125.

Vergara, Francisco de: m. daughter of Diego de Ovalle; arrested on May 15, 1636; freed and property returned to him on January 18, 1640.

AHN leg. 1648, No. 2.

Vicente, Juan: b. 1569 in Campomayor, Portugal; shoemaker; arrested on December 10, 1601. Judío and observer of Mosaic laws; reconciled in auto of June 17, 1612, confiscation of property, sanbenito, life imprisonment, exile.

Friedlander 190; García de Proodian 498. *See also* Juan Vicente of Mexico.

FOUR

Rio de la Plata

Rio de la Plata was the southeast province of the viceroyalty of Peru (originally named Nueva Castile). La Plata covered approximately the area occupied now by Argentina, Uruguay, and Paraguay. The distance from Buenos Aires to the capital of the viceroyalty, Lima, was more than 800 leagues (approximately 3,000 miles) over difficult terrain and past unfriendly Indian tribes, a journey that required three months. Although the conquest of the territory was ostensibly completed by 1535, more than a semblance of ordered life did not set in until the arrival of Viceroy Antonio de Mendoza in 1551.

The Tribunal of the Holy Office of the Inquisition was established in Lima in 1570. By 1575, it requested the Consejo in Spain to separate the province of Rio de la Plata from Peru and have the Consejo itself assume jurisdiction over matters of faith arising in the hinterlands of the largest viceroyalty in the Spanish colonial empire. Despite the almost innumerable and continuous appeals for a separate tribunal or tribunals for Buenos Aires, Asunción, and Córdoba, neither the king nor the Consejo yielded to the importunities. Comisarios, appointed by the Lima Tribunal, were fairly active in Santiago de Chile and Buenos Aires. Local bishops served in the place of the comisarios, as they had the right to do under their episcopal powers, in such places as Santiago del Estero and Tucumán. Episcopal records of autos-da-fé are not available for most areas, and other records have been lost or destroyed by fire or vandalism. Most of the material in this section has been drawn from Medina's *La Inquisición en el Rio de la Plata.* With rare exception the cases he cited in this book are duplicated in his other works covering South America.

It is for these reasons that this section has few names and is presented in narrative form. The absence of names is not indicative of the absence of secret Jews. My article "The Great Conspiracy in Peru" belies any presumption of their absence as does the additional evidence adduced herein. In the book *Francisco Moyen or the Inquisition as it Was in South America* (London: Henry Sotheran & Co., 1869, p. 189), Benjamin Vicuña Mackenna wrote of 200,000 ducats paid in 1630 as a bribe to the Viceroy Conde de Chinchon "for permission of residence of 6,000 Portuguese (also judaizing because they were rich) and whom, for the purpose of robbing them, he threatened with expulsion."

Jerónimo de Loaisa, archbishop of Peru, celebrated an auto-da-fé in 1549. Juan Miller, a Lutheran from Flanders, was the hapless victim. Ricardo Palma and Tano Lorente agree with Calancha that the bishop celebrated autos also in 1560 and 1566, but Medina disagrees with that because the autos were held in Cuzco and La Plata (Medina, *Rio de la Plata,* p. 17). The bishop went to these places because they were parts of his diocese.

The inquisitorial activities in the La Plata area were more often than not motivated by political considerations (Medina, *Rio de la Plata,* p. 110), but the Jews played no part in the political tug-of-war that was waged for over a century between the secular and clerical powers and between the secular powers and the monastic orders. In fact, as will be shown, some Jews were benefited by the animus between the various powers. In 1581 the Peruvian bishops dared to write that they *"desairsen,"* disrespected, the Inquisition, meaning the Holy Office.

Licenciado Serván de Cerezuela was the first inquisitor to serve the Lima tribunal (1569-1582). He wanted to appoint comisarios for the most important cities and ports of the vast area under his control, but he discovered that there was a scarcity of capable and qualified personnel. This condition continued for many decades. Another great problem that beset the area was the venality of the clergy. The orderly processes of administering the faith—including the search for heretics—was not of the first priority. Francisco de Toledo, the viceroy in 1567, stated that many clergymen and friars were enriching themselves in his vast jurisdiction. On December 23, 1567, the Vicar General of the provinces of Tucumán, D. Juries y Diaguitas, advised Cardinal Espinosa of Spain that there was much vice and sin in existence in these places.

One of the first cases commenced by an appointee of Serván de Cerezuela was that of Diego de Padilla of Córdoba in 1579. He was accused of being a Jew because he said that "he believed in God, our Holy Lady, and in Abraham and Moses" and that he observed some fast days. He was imprisoned and his property sequestered.

The next Jew involved was the Portuguese Duarte Mendez of Tucumán, who is discussed under Lima (Medina, *Rio de la Plata,* 129; Medina, *Lima* 1:280). He had been wearing the Jesuit habit when he was apprehended. The most notable descendant of Jews in Tucumán was Bishop Francisco de Victoria (Medina, *Rio de la Plata* 138, name spelled also as Vitorio. For the genealogy of the bishop see I. S. Revah, "Fundo de manuscritos pour l'histoire des nouveaux chretiens portugais," *Boletin International de Bibliografia Luso-Brasilera,* 2 [April-June 1961] p. 293). The bishop's brother, Diego Peréz de Acosta (Medina, *Lima* 1:311;) was burned in effigy in the auto-da-fé of March 13, 1605. He had escaped to Italy, and there is the suspicion that his escape was facilitated by the family connection. He had resided in Venice and "Saona" (sic) prior to coming to the New World. The bishop and his brother were related to Martin Hernandez, who was relaxed alive by the Granada Inquisition, and to Piedra Sanctas de Granada, of another noted Jewish family of Granada, many of whom had worn sanbenitos.

By 1605 the number of Jews involved in inquisitional hearings increased considerably and their presence was more evident. Alvaro Nuñez, a Portuguese doctor in Tucumán, was jailed in La Plata. He admitted that he had observed the Mosaic laws, (Medina, *Rio de la Plata* 143). Two other Jews, Diego Nuñez de Silva, a doctor residing in Cordoba, and his son Diégo de Silva had been arrested earlier and they had implicated Alvaro Nuñez. Alvaro was brought from La Plata to the secret cells in Lima (Medina, *Rio de la Plata* 143). He and the two who had delated against him were in the auto of March 13, 1605.

A letter from Lima dated August 31, 1607, mentioned the finding of a medal with a figure representing Moses and the Twelve Tribes (Medina, *Rio de la Plata* 155). Jorge de Paz, a Portuguese merchant in Córdoba, was penanced in 1615 because he refused to attend mass and said, "You go to your mass and I will go to the devil's mass." Juan Acuña de Noronha was arrested in Santiago del Estero (Medina, *Lima* 2:31). He had Jewish parents and stated, "Praise God, the Lord of the heaven be blessed; how grand is the God of Israel, Abraham, Isaac, and Jacob." He was familiar with the Old Testament. He went to the stake on December 22, 1622 (Medina, *Rio de la Plata* 151, 152).

Just as New Spain was flooded by incoming secret Jews in the first two decades of the seventeenth century, so they came also to Rio de la Plata from Brazil as well as from the Iberian Peninsula (Medina, *Chile* 360). The following is a translation of excerpts of a letter written by the comisario at Buenos Aires and follows the portion of the letter referring to the arrival of Jews, some of whom were escapees from the Holy Offices in Spain. Others were fleeing the new inquisitors in Brazil.

> . . . at dawn the parish crosses would appear adorned with horns. Furthermore, two Jews walked through the streets with a crucifix under their capes. Whenever they met another of their nation, they would uncover the crucifix and say "Give a donation for this *bebodo*," which in Portuguese means drunk. And we have never known of such wickedness ever being punished.

The flow of Portuguese fugitives (read Jews) did not cease. In mid-April 1619, eight ships had entered the port of Buenos Aires. The Portuguese, wrote Medina, had paid the Spanish passengers to take them among their servants since the Castillians had the requisite license to immigrate. They succeeded in entering the country despite the efforts of the governor. As noted in the introduction, the friars came to the help of the Jews. Fray Juan de Vergara, a Dominican, and his friars defied the authorities and aided the illegal immigrants (Medina, *Rio de la Plata* 162).

Another letter from Licenciado Francisco de Trijo of La Plata to the Consejo requested "the uncovering of judaismo" in the area. In April of 1619 an Italian doctor, Diego Manuel, was apprehended while trying to land at the port. He was one of the very few who failed. The arrival in Brazil of the inquisitors from Lisbon who came to imprison "judíos and judaizantes" spurred the flight to La Plata (Medina, *Rio de la Plata* 158.) In 1631, the area under the jurisdiction of the Porteño comisario extended more than 1,200 leagues and included Paraguay, Chile, and as far north as Popayan.

Of the Jews who fled from Brazil, the largest number established themselves in Tucumán. The *fiscal* of the Charcas audiencía, Don Sebastian Alarcón, wrote to the king of March 1, 1636, that "a countless number of Jews had arrived and continued to arrive" (Medina, *Rio de la Plata* 170). Medina devotes a complete chapter to the proceso of Francisco Maldonado de Silva, who was arrested in Santiago de Chile in July 1626, sent to Lima, and burned alive in the auto of January 23, 1639.

Medina supplies *in extenso* a most informative letter sent by Manuel de Frías, attorney-general for the viceroyalty in the seventeenth century, to the king pleading for the establishment of a tribunal in Buenos Aires. He notes that many of the Portuguese Jews entering and leaving the La Plata region were "rich, powerful and intelligent" and engaged successfully in dealing with all classes and merchandise and Negroes, and that they correspond with other Jews in all parts of the "kingdom of Peru." The fiscal, Sebastian Alarcón, informed the king that the cost of maintaining a tribunal at Tucumán would be self-liquidating because the proceeds from confiscations would exceed the cost (Medina, *Rio de la Plata* 213, 214). There are a few other cases that originated from Rio de la Plata. Rodrigo Lopez, a Portuguese merchant, was arrested in 1640 and freed in 1641. Juan Rodríguez Estela, over 60 years of age, was arrested in Tucumán in February 1673 and arrived in Lima January 30, 1674. He had previously reconciled in Lisbon, fled to Brazil, then to Buenos Aires, where he married and reared a family. He confessed to being a Jew. Alvaro Rodríguez de Acevedo was also arrested in 1673, and he is reported in Lima (Medina, *Lima* 2:307). Manuel de Coyto, a sculptor in Buenos Aires, had been born in San Miguel de Barrero, near Oporto. He was 35 when arrested June 30, 1673; he was charged with heresy and suspicion of being a Jew. He was later tortured and then reconciled on August 21, 1678. He abjured de levi, received 200 lashes, and was exiled to the presidio at Valdivia for four years.

In *Los Portugueses en Buenos Aires* by R. de Lafuente Machain of the Royal Academy of History (Madrid, 1931), the author lists (pp. 116-174) the names of many who came to Buenos Aires in the seventeenth century. Many who came from Brazil in 1603 without a license were deported by Governor Frias on July 15, 1603. It is probable that many who remained were Jews. An example would be Francisco Alvarez (possibly Alvarez de Acosta, who was born in Viana de Camiña and who married Ana Gomez in 1635. She was the daughter of Miguel Geronimo and Guillerma Mendez). There are many names of Portuguese men who married daughters of Portuguese in Buenos Aires.

I mention the book and list of names to allay any thought that the inquisitors apprehended all the Jews in the New World. Lafuente Machain states that many Jews fled Recife in 1654 when Portugal recaptured Brazil. The Jews went to the Antilles, New Granada, Portobelo, Cartagena, and "Antioquia, a center of a great agglomeration of *hebreas*" (p. 52).

The deterioration of the power of Spain in South America, the growth of smuggling, and the continued presence of English and Dutch warships offshore all combined to lessen the influence of the inquisition of the Holy Office and the zeal of the local bishops to weed out heretics. The arrival of many Dutch, Huguenots, and Jews in Chile in 1725 was noted (Medina, *Chile* 254).

The Bull of Pope Clement VIII, which gave a conditional pardon in 1605 to all Portuguese Jews, made a lasting impression on the entire southern portion of the viceroyalty. The benign tolerance of the Inquisitor Francisco Verdugo (1601-1623), who dismissed over 100 denunciations against Portuguese Jews in the seventeenth century, established a pattern that was followed by many of his successors except for Manozca (1624-1638) and his colleagues in the middle 1630s. However, general suspicions of the motives of the officials of the Holy Office and later disclosures of pilferage by inquisition officials cooled the ardor of subsequent inquisitors.

Appendix A

Autos-da-fé celebrated in America

Mexico

1523 (?)	1572	1602
1528	Feb. 28, 1574	Apr. 20, 1603
1532	Mar. 6, 1575	Mar. 25, 1605
1536	Feb. 19, 1576	1606
1537	Dec. 15, 1577	1608
1538	1578	Mar. 22, 1609
1539	Oct. 11, 1579	Nov. 25, 1611
1540	1580	Mar. 18, 1612
1549	1581	Apr. 3, 1620
1552	1582	Oct. 5, 1621
1555	1583	June 15, 1625
1556	1585	1626
1558	1589	Mar. 17, 1630
1560	Feb. 24, 1590	1632
1561	Apr. 24, 1590	Apr. 2, 1635
1562	July 4, 1590	1636
1563	July 24, 1590	Jan. 23, 1639
1564	1591	1645
1565	1592	Apr. 16, 1646
1566	1593	Jan. 23, 1647
1567	1594	Mar. 30, 1648
1568	1595	Apr. 11, 1649
1569	Dec. 8, 1596	July 10, 1650
1570	1597	Mar. 21, 1651
1571	Mar. 25, 1601	Jan. 6, 1652

Dec. 12, 1654	Feb. 8, 1688	1733
Oct. 29, 1656	Mar. 5, 1690	1735
Nov. 19, 1658	(Oaxaca)	1736
Nov. 19, 1659	Jan. 15, 1696	1739
Sept. 30, 1662	June 14, 1699	1740
Jan. 21, 1663	Feb. 28, 1700	1741
Dec. 7, 1664	Sept. 27, 1700	1754
Dec. 18, 1665	Mar. 2, 1701	1757
June 1, 1666	May 17, 1703	Sept. 6, 1767
Dec. 7, 1667	Feb. 28, 1704	Mar. 13, 1768
Feb. 3, 1668	1707	1778
Feb. 10, 1669	1708	1781
Dec. 7, 1670	1712	1783
Nov. 25, 1671	1715	1789
Feb. 25, 1674	1721	1790
Mar. 22, 1675	1722	Aug. 9, 1795
Mar. 22, 1676	1728	1814
Mar. 20, 1678	1730	Nov. 26, 1815
Mar. 20, 1679		

Cartagena de las Indias

Feb. 2, 1614	June 6, 1655	May 30, 1688
June, 1618	Oct. 1, 1656	Dec. 11, 1689
Mar. 13, 1622	Sept. 16, 1657	Apr. 29, 1691
June 17, 1626	Jan. 15, 1668	March, 1695
Aug. 6, 1627	May, 1669	Apr. 27, 1697
June 25, 1628	Mar. 2, 1670	Apr. 29, 1699
Mar. 7, 1632	Aug. 24, 1671	Jan. 10, 1700
Mar. 26, 1634	Sept. 4, 1671	June 20, 1700
June 1, 1636	Sept. 4, 1672	Feb. 24, 1707
Mar. 25, 1638	Feb. 17, 1675	Mar. 18, 1708
July 22, 1642	Apr. 4, 1677	May 21, 1708
May 24, 1648	Oct. 23, 1678	May 26, 1711
Sept., 1648	Nov. 12, 1679	July 9, 1713
Nov. 28, 1649	Dec. 21, 1681	July 29, 1714
Dec. 21, 1650	Oct. 28, 1682	June 11, 1715
Apr. 25, 1653	July 29, 1683	Nov. 30, 1715
July 22, 1653	Aug. 29, 1683	June 20, 1717
Apr. 28, 1654	Feb. 11, 1685	Feb. 5, 1782
May 8, 1655	Sept. 9, 1685	

Lima

Nov. 15, 1573	Aug. 11, 1635	Nov. 28, 1719
Apr. 13, 1578	Aug. 17, 1635	Dec. 21, 1720
Oct. 29, 1581	June 1, 1636	1728
Nov. 30, 1587	Mar. 25, 1638	July 12, 1733
Apr. 5, 1592	Jan. 23, 1639	Dec. 23, 1736
Dec. 17, 1595	Nov. 17, 1641	Nov. 11, 1737
Dec. 10, 1600	May 9, 1648	Oct. 19, 1749
Mar. 13, 1605	Jan. 23, 1664	Apr. 6, 1761
June 1, 1608	Feb. 16, 1666	Sept. 1, 1773
June 17, 1612	June 28, 1667	1776
Dec. 22, 1622	Oct. 8, 1667	Feb. 18, 1800
Dec. 21, 1625	Mar. 16, 1693	Aug. 27, 1803
Feb. 27, 1631	Oct. 8, 1694	Sept. 10, 1805
Mar. 26, 1634	Oct. 29, 1703	July 17, 1806

Appendix B

Itemization of documents
with special Jewish interest

1. AGN 87 has a list of *familiars*, 1572-1627, and a second list for 1660-1701.
2. AGN 89, No. 37, has information about persons who were in the New World illegally because their ancestors were penanced or burned at the stake in Spain.
3. AGN 1560, No. 3A, is the report of the public autos-da-fé in Seville on September 24, 1559; December 22, 1560; April 26, 1562; October 23, 1563; October 30, 1563; and May 13, 1566.
4. AGN 213, No. 44, has information concerning the autos-da-fé in New Spain in 1590 and December 3, 1592.
5. AGN 216, No. 10, has information and denunciations against the Jews who were absent on St. Peter's Day.
6. AGN 216, No. 20, is the publication of the 1596 auto-da-fé in the Great Plaza.
7. AGN 223, fols. 158, 170, contains the letters from Madrid about Jews, part of the fleet burned in Cadiz, and about Simon Rodriguez.
8. AGN 239 to AGN 248 contain testimony and declarations, pertaining to Jews.
9. AGN 254 contains resumés of procesos, affairs, instructions, et cetera, about people in the secret cells.
10. AGN 275, No. 5, is the report of cases disposed of in the auto-da-fé of March 28, 1605, Easter Sunday, in the Convent of Santo Domingo.
11. AGN 335, No. 86, is the draft of a letter denouncing the existence of a synagogue on Calle Santo Domingo.

12. AGN 341, No. 7, is the draft of a letter to the Suprema referring to Jews, Dutch, and Filipinos.
13. AGN 345 has a letter from the tribunal at Valladolid, Spain, giving many genealogies and the result of the case of Gonzalo Enriquez de Lineo at Llerena.
14. AGN 347, fols. 344-497, contains letters to and from the inquisitors and the Consejo in Spain from 1571-1624.
15. AGN 382, Nos. 5 and 7, contains additional information regarding Jews.
16. AGN 389, No. 8, has testimony about criminals who had gone or been ordered to Spain.
17. AGN 407, Nos. 3 and 17, has some peripheral matter concerning a relationship of the constable of the secret cells and about a book, *Virtues of Moses*.
18. AGN 416, No. 7, has the list of witnesses, not prisoners, and of people absent or dead in Mexico.
19. AGN 416, No. 37, has the Inquisition edict that all those holding property of Jews must denounce the Jews and surrender the property.
20. AGN 416, No. 38, consists of drafts of letters sent to the Consejo, 1643-1656.
21. AGN 419, fols. 3-19, is the treasury report on sequestered property of prisoners.
22. AGN 416, No. 42, is a letter dated May 24, 1649, to the Consejo naming those who were to wear sanbenitos, the autos-da-fé, and Juan Pacheco de León.
23. AGN 416, No. 43, is the memorandum of prisoners exiled to Spain and "Signs of Jews."
24. AGN 426, fols. 491-499, has the votes of the inquisitors concerning the 1646 auto-da-fé.
25. AGN 426, fols. 500-506, concerns autos-da-fé of April 16, 1646 and January 23, 1647.
26. AGN 432, No. 7, relates the acts against some *reconciliados* who pretended to go to Veracruz to embark for Spain but remained in Puebla.
27. AGN 435, fol. 339, has procesos against Jewish penitents in Puebla for being on the streets at night, the men and women being in full dress and the women wearing mantillas.

28. AGN 454, No. 15, is an alphabetical list of witnesses sent in 1650 to the Santo Oficio in Cartagena that also contains data on votes and prisoners, some of whom were accomplices of Jewish religious practitioners.
29. AGN 454, No. 28, contains the documents exchanged between the Viceroy, Count of Alba, and the Santo Oficio about the exiled prisoners.
30. AGN 454, No. 29, is the 1650 receipt by the naval commander for prisoners to be transported to Spain.
31. AGN 485, No. 8, is a prophecy in Hebrew found in a little marble box sent by the papal envoy to France to Cardinal Burgence.
32. AGN 502, No. 18, contains acts and the 1663 order for the publication of the Edict of Faith in Mixteca because of the presumption that Portuguese Jews resided there.
33. AGN 503, No. 54, pertains to action on the petition of the Santo Oficio regarding the expenses of 316 pesos incurred in the repair of Simon Vaez's houses.
34. AGN 504, No. 5, is the proceso by the Royal Treasurer to recover 5,103.3 reales from Doña María de León, widow of Jacinto Torres.
35. AGN 584, No. 12, is an order of embargo or sequestration of goods made in Xalapa, Tabasco, belonging to persons penanced.
36. AGN 673, No. 51, (see also AGN [Riva Palacio] 43, No. 3) has sample questions to be put to witnesses for examination and proof of absence of heresy and of Jewish ancestry.
37. AGN 780, No. 12 is a 1719 report and summary of cases against the faith with sentences since the auto-da-fé of June 16, 1715.
38. AGN 818, No. 8, is the index of all pending cases, 1660-1728.
39. AGN 848, fol. 275, concerns an auto-da-fé particular held Sunday November 15, 1753, in the Church of the Convent of Santo Domingo.
40. AGN 976, No. 61, has the order for sending the four-volume *History of the Jews* in French by Samuel Basnage to the calificador for expurgation. AGN 979 No. 12 has the denunciation of the history.
41. AGN 1017, No. 4, has the denunciation of three small volumes, *Secret Memoirs of the Republic of Letters,* in French, by the author of "Jewish letters."
42. AGN 1408, No. 1, is the edict of September 16, 1802, prohibiting the entry of Jews into New Spain.

43. AGN 1408, No. 13, concerns the book *Bello Judaico* by Flavius Josephus, 2 volumes, addressed to a monk whose vicar applied for permission for the entry of the books.
44. AGN 1408, No. 23, indexes all cases and papers, 1771-1803, with the status of all.
45. AGN 1422, No. 15, is an index of all cases and papers, 1780-1803, by another secretary.
46. AGN 1429, fol. 59, is a request for the entry into the country of two cases of books, among which were *Customs of the Israelites and Christians*.
47. AGN (Riva Palacio) 3, No. 2, has instructions to comisarios on matters of faith.
48. AGN (Riva Palacio) 7, No. 2, is a letter to Spain with an alphabetical index, 1600-1616.
49. AGN (Riva Palacio), 35, Nos. 5, 6, 7, and 16 is a report of the auto of March 25, 1601.
50. AGN (Riva Palacio) 35, No. 17, is the 1667 report of sanbenitos hung in the Cathedral.
51. AGN (Riva Palacio) 49, general index of cases 1571-1719.

Notes to the introduction

1. Alexandre Herculano, *Historia da origem e Estabelecimento da Inquisicâe em Portugal*, ch. 1 and passim.
2. Richard E. Greenleaf, *The Mexican Inquisition of the Sixteenth Century*, p. 74 and passim.
3. Herculano, *Historia*, vol. 3, pp. 281, 283.
4. Silvio Zavala, *The Colonial Period in the History of the New World*, abridged in English by Max Savelle. Mexico: Panamerican, de geographice Historia, 1962, p. 230.
5. Irving A. Leonard, "Montalban's El Valor Perseguido and the Mexican Inquisition 1682," *Hispanic American Historical Review* 11 (1953):47; and Henry C. Lea, *History of the Inquisition in the Spanish Dependencies*, ch. 6.
6. Hubert Herring, *A History of Latin America*, p. 179.
7. Clarence Haring, *The Spanish Empire in America*, p. 189.
8. Greenleaf, *Mexican Inquisition*, p. 18.
9. Greenleaf, *Zumárraga and the Mexican Inquisition*, p. 19.
10. Haim Beinart, "The Judaizing Movement in the Order of San Jeronimo in Castile."
11. José Toribio Medina, *La Inquisición en el Rio de la Plata*, p. 17. Medina notes that Calaucha wrote that Archibishop Loaisa celebrated three autos-da-fé "before the coming of the Tribunal"— 1548, 1560, and 1565. Palma and Llorente are in accord with this statement, but Medina disagrees and believes that Caucha is including Cuzco and autos from La Plata. See also pp. 161, 162.
12. Riva Palacio, *México à través de los Siglos*, vol. 2, p. 703.

13. José del Olma, *Relación histórico del auto general de fé que se celebra en Madrid,* (Madrid, 1690), pt. 1, pp. 23-26.

14. Charles Gibson, *American Historical Review,* vol. 75, June 1970, no. 5, p. 1553, a review of Richard E. Greenleaf's *The Mexican Inquisition of the Sixteenth Century.*

15. *Hispanic American Historical Review,* vol. 43, no. 4, November 1963, pp. 551, 552.

16. Greenleaf, *Mexican Inquisition* p. 26.

17. José Toribio Medina, *Historía del Tribunal del Santa Oficio de la Inquisición en México,* p. 7.

18. Antonine Tibesar, O.F.M., "The Peruvian Church at the Time of Independence," *The Americas,* vol. 26, April 1970, no. 4, p. 349, 373-Appendix II, The Lima Inquisition Papers.

19. Seymour B. Liebman, *Guide to Jewish References in the Mexican Colonial Era, 1521-1821,* p. 110.

20. Seymour B. Liebman, "The Abecedario and a Check-List of Mexican Inquisition Documents at the Henry E. Huntington Library," p. 554.

21. J. Horace Nunemaker, "Inquisition Papers of Mexico," p. 3; and Josephine Yocum McClaskey, "Inquisition Papers of Mexico, II, The Trial of Luis de la Cruz, 1656," p. 3.

22. Toro, *Los Judios en la Nueva España.*

23. Seymour B. Liebman, "Research Problems in Mexican Jewish History," p. 165.

24. William H. Rule, *History of the Inquisition,* vol. 2, p. 275.

25. Ibid., vol. 1, p. 636.

26. Henry C. Lea, *A History of the Inquisition in Spain,* vol. 1, p. 146. In *Los Judeoconversos en España y América,* p. 14. fn. 2, Antonio Domínguez Ortiz writes that in 1380, the Cortes of Soria fined those who called converts "marranos."

27. Yakov Malkiel, "Hispano-Arabic *marrano* and its Hispano-Latin Homophone," *Journal of American Oriental Society* 68 (1948): 175-184.

28. Antonio Domínguez Ortiz, *The Golden Age of Spain,* pp. 102, 216.

29. Yosef Hayim Yerushalmi, *From Spanish Court to Italian Ghetto,* p. 29.

30. Greenleaf, *Mexican Inquisition,* p. 111.

31. See Seymour B. Liebman, "The Great Conspiracy in Peru," p. 176, no. 13.
32. Lea, *A History of the Inquisition in Spain,* vol. 3, p. 283.
33. Domínguez Ortiz, *Los Judeoconversos en España y America,* pp. 18, 28.
34. Ibid., pp. 31, 35, 62.
35. Boleslao Lewin, *Cómo Fue la Inmigración Judía a la Argentina* (Buenos Aires: Editorial Plus Ultra, 1971), pp. 16, 17.
36. O'Brien, *The Inquisition* (New York: Macmillan Pub. Co., 1973), p. 94.
37. Cohen, "The Marranos of Spain," *Jewish Social Studies* 29(1967): 181.
38. Luis Gonzalez Obregon, *Rebeliones Indigenas y Precursores de la Independencia Mexicana,* pp. 214 et seq.
39. Seymour B. Liebman, *The Jews in New Spain,* pp. 272-73.
40. I have discussed the "kiss of peace" in my chapter on the "Sephardim in the New World" in volume 2 of *The Sephardi Heritage* to be published in England in 1975 under the editorship of Dr. Richard D. Barnett.
41. Ernesto Chinchilla Aquilar, *La Inquisición en Guatemala,* p. 185.

Glossary

abjuración—an oath of denial, disavowal, or renunciation; de levi—light suspicion of heresy; de vehementi—strong suspicion of heresy.

audiencia—a hearing by the inquisitors; part of the trial.

auto-da-fé—the ceremony accompanying the pronouncement of judgment by the Inquisition and followed by the execution of sentence by secular authorities if a death sentence were involved.

calificador—an inquisition official who examined the preliminary evidence to determine whether an order of arrest should be issued.

comisario—an agent of the Holy Office who operated in the provinces and rural areas.

coroza—a conical hat worn by penitents in the march to the auto-da-fé.

criollo—a white person born in the New World of white Spanish parents.

crypto-judío—*see* judaizante.

declaración—declaration or deposition made by any witness before the Inquisition.

denunciación—a denunciation made by an individual who was not an official of the Holy Office.

diminuto—an incomplete or dishonest confessor or confession.

dogmatista—a Jew who attempted to bring back to Judaism a person who had been converted to Christianity or who was a descendant of Jews: a religious leader for secret Jews; the word was also used to mean one stubborn in his faith.

Edict of Faith—a public notice giving heretics an opportunity to secure absolution by making a confession within a certain number of days and requesting that all who knew of heretics to inform the inquisition officials or be condemned to anathema.

encomendero—a person who had been granted an estate of land and the inhabiting Indians; also an agent who received and executed orders or commissions or one who held military rank.

familiar—a secular inquisition official devoted primarily to investigations.

fiscal—prosecutor for the Inquisition.

garrote—a cord or iron collar used for strangulation at the stake, a kindness reserved for those who abjured their heresy after being found guilty but before leaving the inquisition cells.

gauchupin—a person born in Spain and residing in the New World.

información—information to justify a charge of accusation.

judaizante—one who observed or professed the Jewish faith; often used as a synonym for Jew.

judío—a Jew.

landrecilla—porging; the removal of the thigh vein and the suet around it from slaughtered animals; a necessary process if the meat is to be considered kosher.

limpieza de sangre—literally, purity of blood. Certificates of limpieza de sangre were issued to those Catholics whose ancestors were all Catholic on both maternal and paternal lines for three previous generations.

Marrano—one who professed Catholicism but secretly practiced Jewish rites.

mestizo (a)—a person of mixed (Indian and white) ancestry.

nuevo cristiano—a New Christian; a convert from Judaism to Catholicism; many nuevo cristianos continued to practice Judaism secretly.

potro—a wooden, bedlike frame with leather thongs instead of mattress, on which Inquisition prisoners were tied while cords were tightened around their ankles, thighs, and arms.

proceso—the judicial records of a trial or hearing.

reconciliado (a)—a heretic, a first offender, who had been brought back into the church; his property was confiscated and he was usually required to wear a sanbenito in public.

relación—an account of an event.

relajado—one who was to be burned at the stake for being convicted as a heretic.

relapso (a)—a person who had reverted to criminal or heretical conduct and was therefore to be turned over to the secular authorities for burning at the stake.

sanbenito—a penitential garment worn over the outer garments for periods of time fixed by the inquisitors.

Selected bibliography

Abbreviations

AGN: Archivo General de la Nación de México
AHN: Archivo Histórico Nacional de Madrid
HAHR: *Hispanica American Historical Review*
PAJHS: *Publications of the American Jewish Historical Society* (now
   American Jewish Historical Society Quarterly)

Archival Material

Madrid. Archivo Historico Nacional de Madrid. Inquisition libros 888,
   1020, 1021, 1023, 1029, 1030, 1032, 1064, 1259, 1328. Inquisition legajos 1601; 1602; 1603; 1623, exp. 2; 1648, exp. 16;
   1731, exp. 36; 1738, exp. 1; 2178.
Mexico City. Archivo General de la Nación de México. Ramo de la
   Inquisición. 1,553 volumes (this number includes the 15-volume
   Riva Palacio Collection) and 15-volume *Indice*.
Philadelphia. University of Pennsylvania. Henry C. Lea Memorial Library. Part of the proceso of Isabel Rodriguez and the entire
   proceso of Manuel Diaz.
Pullman, Washington. Washington State University. Portions of the
   procesos of Aña Nuñez and Simon de Leon.
San Marino, California. Henry E. Huntington Library. Walter Douglas
   Collection, Document 2. *Abecedario*. An original inquisition document consisting of an alphabetical index with data on cases;
   unpaged. Also procesos and parts of procesos.

Tulsa, Oklahoma. Thomas Gilcrease Institute. Register of cases, 1624-1632, with sentences and summaries of about 200 cases. Also procesos and parts of procesos.

Waltham, Massachusetts. American Jewish Historical Society. Typescripts of procesos.

Washington, D.C. Library of Congress. The G. R. G. Conway Archives. Unpublished translation of proceso of Thomas Treviñño de Sobremonte by A. J. Barker.

Published Material

Adler, Cyrus. "The Trial of Jorge de Almeida." PAJHS 4 (1894).

Adler, Elkan N. *Auto de Fé and Jew*. London: Oxford University Press, 1908.

Albanes, Ricardo. *Los judíos a través de los siglos*. Mexico: privately printed, 1939.

Bancroft, Hubert H. *History of Arizona and New Mexico*. Vol. 17.San Francisco: The History Co., 1889.

Bancroft, Hubert H. *A History of Mexico*. 6 vols. San Francisco: A. L. Bancroft & Co., 1883-1888.

Bancroft, Hubert H. *History of the North Mexican States and Texas*. San Francisco: The History Co., 1886.

Baron, Salo W. "Conference Themes." PAJHS 46 (March 1957).

Baron, Salo W. *History and Jewish Historians*. Philadelphia: Jewish Publication Society, 1964.

Beinart, Haim. "The Judaizing Movement in the Order of San Jeronimo in Castile." *Scripto Hierosolymitana* 7 (1961).

Beinart, Haim. "The Records of the Inquisition as a Source of Jewish and Converso History." *Proceedings of the Israel Academy of Sciences and Humanties* 2 (no. 11, 1967):211.

Benítez, Fernando. *Los Primeros Mexicanos*. Mexico: Biblioteca Era, 1965.

Bocanegra, Matias de. *Relación del auto general de la fee . . . celebrado 11 de abril 1649*. Mexico: Santo Oficio, 1649.

Böhm, Gunter. *Nuevos antecedentes para una historia de los judíos en Chile colonial*. Santiago: Editorial Universitaria, 1963.

Boxer, C. R. *Salvador de Sá and the Struggle for Brazil and Angola, 1602-1686*. London: The Athlone Press, 1952. Of special interest for this study, pp. 69-110.

Brenner, Anita. "Cavaliers and Martyrs." *Menorah Journal* 16 (January 1929).

Cantero, Francisco. "Review of the Marranos According to the Hebrew Sources of the 15th and 16th Centuries." *Sefarad* 24 (1964):15.

Carreño, Alberto María. "Luis de Carvajal, el Mozo." *Memorias de la Academia de la Historia de México* 15 (January-March 1956):87-101.

Castañeda, Carlos de. *The Mission Era: The Finding of Texas* Vol. 1. Austin: Von Boeckman-Jones Co.

Chinchilla Aguilar, Ernesto. *La Inquisición en Guatemala.* Guatemala: Editorial del Ministerio de Educación Publica, 1953.

Domínez Ortis, Antonio. *The Golden Age of Spain.* Trans. by James Casey. New York: Basic Books, 1971.

Domínez Ortis, Antonio. *Los Judeoconversos en España y América.* Madrid: Ediciones Istmo, 1971.

Emmanuel, I. S., and Emmanuel, S. A. *History of the Jews in the Netherlands Antilles.* 2 vols.. Cincinnati: American Jewish Archives, 1970.

Encyclopedia Judaica Castellana. 10 vols. Mexico: Encyclopedia Judaica Castellana, 1948.

Estrado y Escobedo, Pedro de. *Relación summaria del auto particular de fe que el tribunal del Santo Oficio ... 16 de abril, 1646.* Mexico: Francisco Robledo, 1646.

Fernández del Castillo, Francisco. *Libros y libros del siglo XVI.* Mexico: Publicaciones del AGN, 1914.

Friede, Juan. "The Catálogo de Pasajeros and Spanish Migration to America to 1550." HAHR 31 (May 1951).

Friedlander, Gunter. *Los Héroes Olvidados.* Santiago: Editorial Nascimiento, 1963.

García, Genaro. *Documentos inéditos o muy raros para la historia de México.* Vols. 5, 28; Mexico: Librería de la Viuda de Ch. Bouret, 1906, 1910.

García Icazbalceta, Joaquín. *Bibliografía mexicana del siglo XVI.* Edited by Agustìn Millares Carlo. Mexico: Fondo de Cultura Económica, 1954.

García de Proodian, Lucia. *Los Judíos en América.* Madrid: Consejo Superior Investigaciones Científicas, 1966.

González Obregon, Luis. *México Viejo.* Mexico: Editorial Patria, 1959.

González Obregon, Luis. *Rebeliones Indígenas y Precursores de la*

Independencia Mexicana. 2nd ed. Mexico: Ediciones Fuente Cultural, 1952.

Greenleaf, Richard E. "Francisco Millan Before the Mexican Inquisition." *The Americas* 21 (1964):184-193.

Greenleaf, Richard E. "Mexican Inquisition Material in the Spanish Archives." *The Americas* 20 (1954):416-420.

Greenleaf, Richard E. *The Mexican Inquisition of the Sixteenth Century.* Albuquerque: University of New Mexico Press, 1969.

Greenleaf, Richard E. *Zumárraga and the Mexican Inquisition.* Washington, D.C.: Academy of American Franciscan History, 1962.

Guijo, Gregoria M. de. *Diario: 1648-1664.* Vol. 1. Mexico: Editorial Porrua, 1952.

Haring, Clarence. *The Spanish Empire in America.* New York: Harcourt, Brace, & World, 1963.

Herculano, Alexandre. *Historia da origem e Estabelecimento da Inquisicâo em Portugal (History of the Origin and Establishment of the Inquisition in Portugal).* 3 vols. Lisbon: Tavares Cardoso and Irmao, 1902.

Herring, Hubert. *A History of Latin America.* 2nd ed. New York: Knopf, 1964.

Hull, Dorothy. "Castaño de Sosa's Expedition to Northern Mexico in 1590." *Old Santa Fe,* Vol. 3, October 1916, No. 12, p. 307.

Ibañez, Muriel Yolanda. *La Inquisición en México durante el siglo XVI.* Mexico: Imprenta Universitaria, 1946.

Jiménez Rueda, Julio. *Herejías y supersticiones en la Nueva España.* Mexico: Imprenta Universitaria, 1946.

Kayserling, M. *Christopher Columbus.* New York: Longmans, Greene & Co., 1894.

Kohut, George A. "Jewish Martyrs of the Inquisition in South America." PAJHS 4 (1894):119.

Konetzke, A. Richard. *La emigración española al Río de la Plata durante el siglo XVI.* Madrid: M. Ballesteros y Berretta, 1951.

Lafuente, Machain R. de. *Los Portugueses en Buenos Aires.* Madrid: C. de la Real Academia, 1931.

Lea, Henry C. *A History of the Inquisition in Spain.* 4 vols. New York: Macmillan, 1907.

Lea, Henry C. *History of the Inquisition in the Spanish Dependencies.* New York: Macmillan, 1922.

Lewis, Boleslao. *La Inquisición en Hispanoamerica: Judíos, Protes-*

tantes y Patriotas. Buenos Aires: Editorial Proyección, 1962.

Lewis, Boleslao. *Mártires y Conquistadores Judíos en la América Hispana.* Buenos Aires: Editorial Candelabro, 1954.

Libro Primero de Votos de la Inquisición de México 1573-1600. Introduction by Edmundo O'Gorman. Mexico: Imprenta Universitaria, 1949.

Liebman, Seymour B. "The Abecedario and a Check-List of Mexican Inquisition Documents at the Henry E. Huntington Library." HAHR 64 (November 1964):554-567.

Liebman, Seymour B. *The Enlightened: The Writings of Luis de Carvajal, el Mozo.* Coral Gables, Fla.: University of Miami Press, 1967. Reprint, Miami: Windward Publishing, Inc., 1973. Paper.

Liebman, Seymour B. "The Great Conspiracy in Mexico." *The Americas* 29 (October 1972):18-31.

Liebman, Seymour B. "The Great Conspiracy in Peru." *The Americas* 28 (October 1971):176.

Liebman, Seymour B. *Guide to Jewish References in the Mexican Colonial Era, 1521-1821.* Philadelphia: University of Pennsylvania Press, 1964.

Liebman, Seymour B. "Hernando Alonso, First Jew on the North American Continent." *Journal of Inter-American Studies* 5 (April 1963):291.

Liebman, Seymour B., Trans. and ed. *Jews and the Inquisition of Mexico; The Great Auto-de Fé of 1649.* Lawrence, Kan.: Coronado Press, 1974.

Liebman, Seymour B. *The Jews in New Spain.* Coral Gables, Fla: University of Miami Press, 1970. Spanish ed. *Los Judíos en México y América Central.* Translated by Cecilia de Frost. Mexico: Siglo XXI Editores S.A., 1971.

Liebman, Seymour B. "Los Judíos en la historia de Mexico." *Cuadernos Americanos* 26 (No. 1, 1967):145.

Liebman, Seymour B. "Research Problems in Mexican Jewish History." *American Jewish Historical Quarterly* 54. (December 1964):165.

Liebman, Seymour B. *Valerosas Criptojudiás en América Colonial.* Trans. by Florinda F. de Goldberg. Buenos Aires: Biblioteca Popular Judaica, 1973.

McClaskey, Josephine Yocum. "Inquisition Papers of Mexico, II, The Trial of Luis de la Cruz, 1656." *Research Studies of the State College of Washington* 15 (March 1947):3.

Martínez de Río, Pablo. *"Alumbrado."* Mexico: Porrua Hnos, 1937.

Medina, José Toribio. *La Inquisición en el Río de la Plata.* Buenos Aires Editorial Huarpa, S.A., 1945.

Medina, José Toribio. *Historia del Tribunal del Santo Oficio de la Inquisición de Cartagena de las Indias.* Santiago: Imprenta Elzeviriana, 1899.

Medina, José Toribio. *Historia del Tribunal del Santo Oficio de la Inquisición en Chile.* Santiago: Fondo Histórico y Bibliográfico J. T. Medina, 1956.

Medina, José Toribio. *Historia del Tribunal del Santo Oficio de la Inquisición de Lima.* 2 vols. Santiago: Fondo Histórico y Bibliográfico J. T. Medina, 1956.

Medina, José Toribio. *Historia del Tribunal del Santo Oficio de la Inquisición en México.* Reprint, with notes by Julio Jiménez Rueda. Mexico: Ediciones Fuente Cultural, 1952.

Mocatta, Frederick David, et al. *The Jews of Spain and Portugal and the Inquisition.* Philadelphia: I. George Dobsevage, 1932.

Monin, José. *Los Judíos en la America Española.* Buenos Aires: Biblioteca Yavne, 1939.

Nehama, Joseph. *Histoire des Isráelites de Salonique.* 5 vols. Salonica: Publications de la Féderation Sephardite Mondiale, 1959.

Novinsky, Anita. "Os Cristaos Novaos Na Colonizacao do Brasil e de Outras Regioes das Americas." *Comentario* (Jul.-Sept. 1963):231, 237.

Nunemaker, J. Horace. "Inquisition Papers of Mexico." Research Studies of the State College of Washington 15 (March 1946):3.

Pallares, Eduardo. *El procedimiento inquisitorial.* Mexico: Imprenta Universitaria, 1951.

Palma, Ricard. *Tradiciones Peruanos completas.* Madrid: Aguilar, 1961.

Perira, Mendez. "Jewish Heretics Executed by the Inquisition." PAJHS 8(1900):9.

Porras Troconis, Gabriel. *Historia de la Cultura en e Nuevo Reino de Granada.* Seville, 1952.

Procesos de Luis de Carvajal, el Mozo. Mexico: Publicaciones del AGN, 1935.

Revah, I. S. "Les Marranes." *Revue des Etudes Juives* 1(3rd series, 1959-60):29-77.

Ricard, Robert. "Pour une étude de judaísme portugais au Mexique pendant la période coloniale." *Revue d'Histoire Moderne* 14(August 1939).

Riva Palacio Vicente. *El Libro Rojo.* Mexico: Diaz de Leon y White Editores, 1867.

Riva Palacio Vicente. *México à través de los Siglos.* 5 vols. Mexico: Publicaciones Herreria [ca. 1885]. Vol. 2 is the most important for this work.

Robles, Antonio de. *Diario de Sucesos Notables 1665-1703.* 3 vols. Mexico: Editorial Porrua, 1946.

Roth, Cecil. "Notes on the Jewish Community of Livorno." *Revue des Etudes Juives* 91(1931):14.

Rueda, Julio Jiménez. *Herejias y Supersticiones en la Nueva España.* Mexico: Imprenta Universitaria, 1946.

Rule, William H. *History of the Inquisition.* 2 vols. New York: Scribner, Welford & Co., 1874.

Toro, Alfonso. *La familia Carvajal.* 2 vols. Mexico: Editorial Patria, 1944.

Toro, Alfonso. *Los Judios en la Nueva España.* Mexico: Publicaciones del AGN, 1932.

"Trial of Gabriel de Granada." Translated by David Fergusson. PAJHS 7(1899).

"Ultimos momentos y conversión de Luis de Carvajal." *Anales del Museo de Nacional de Arquelogía* 3 (1925).

Vallé, Rafael Heliodoro. "Judíos en México." *Revista Chilena de Historia y Geografía* 81(September-December 1936):215-236.

Villegas, Alfonso de. *Flos Sanctorum: Historia general de la vida y hechos Jesus y todos los santos.* Madrid, 1593.

Yerushalmi, Josef Hayim. *From Spanish Court to Italian Ghetto.* New York: Columbia University Press, 1971.

Zavala, Silvio. *Spanish Colonization in America.* Philadelphia: University of Pennsylvania Press, 1943.